THE ANIMAL BOOK

THE ANIMAL BOOK

A visual encyclopedia of life on Earth

LONDON, NEW YORK, MELBOURNE,
MUNICH, AND DELHI

DK LONDON

Senior Editor Daniel Mills
Senior Art Editor Vicky Short
Jacket Designer Mark Cavanagh
Pre-production Producer Lucy Sims
Production Controller Alice Sykes
Managing Editor Paula Regan
Managing Art Editor Owen Peyton Jones
Publisher Sarah Larter
Art Director Phil Ormerod
Associate Publishing Director Liz Wheeler
Publishing Director Jonathan Metcalf

DK DELHI

Senior Editor Alka Ranjan
Senior Art Editor Mahua Sharma
Editors Susmita Dey, Neha Pande
Art Editors Sanjay Chauhan, Rakesh Khundongbam,
Vaibhav Rastogi
Senior DTP Designer Harish Aggarwal
DTP Designer Arvind Kumar
Picture Researcher Ashwin Raju Adimari
Managing Editor Rohan Sinha
Deputy Managing Art Editor Sudakshina Basu
Pre-production Manager Balwant Singh
Production Manager Pankaj Sharma
Picture Research Manager Taiyaba Khatoon

First published in the Great Britain by
Dorling Kindersley Limited
80 Strand, London WC2R ORL
Penguin Group (UK)

2 4 6 8 10 9 7 5 3
007—184809—09/13

A CIP catalogue record for this book is available from
the British Library.

ISBN: 978-1-4093-2349-5

Printed and bound in China by South China Printing Co.

Discover more at **www.dk.com**

AUTHOR

David Burnie is a fellow of the Zoological Society
of London, and has written and contributed to
more than 100 books on the natural world. He was
consultant editor of DK's highly successful *Animal* and
The Natural History Book, and is a former winner
of the Aventis Prize for Science Books.

CONTENTS

Nitrobacter

Hare's ear

Scots pine

Red cushion star

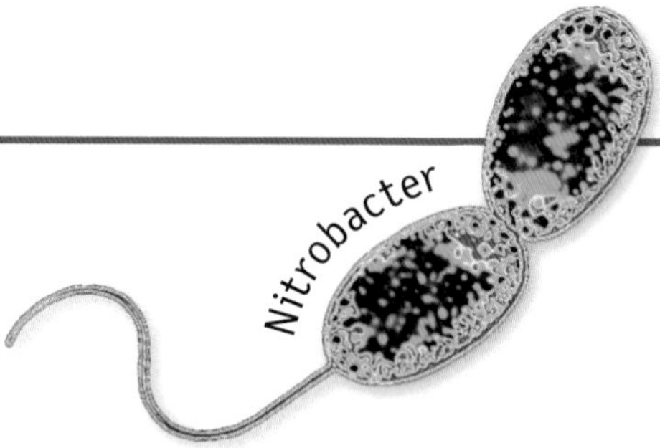

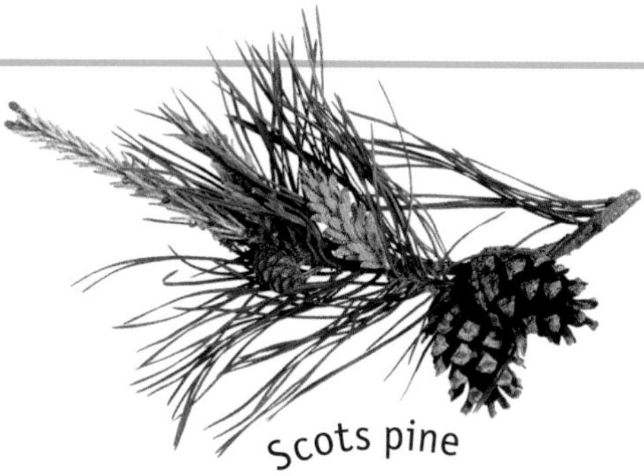

Insects 80

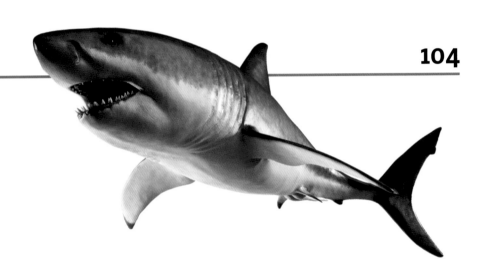

Fish 104

Amphibians 126

Reptiles 138

Birds

Mammals

Index

Enterococcus faecalis

Fly agaric

Flame lily

Foreword

This book is the ultimate guide to all kinds of living things. In it you can find out how different creatures look, how they work, and how they behave, from bacteria to bugs, worms to whales.

If you're already a budding naturalist, you'll know that scientists divide the living world into groups. Each group has special features that set it apart. For example, insects are the only animals with six legs and wings, while mammals are the only animals that produce milk, and the only ones with fur. This book is divided in the same way. In each group you'll find lots of different species, or individual kinds of living things. Tigers, golden eagles, and daisies are all examples of species. So are humans, too.

Life on Earth is incredibly varied, and more species are discovered every year. Researchers have so far identified about 100,000 kinds of fungus, 300,000 kinds of plant, and an amazing 2 million kinds of animal. But even more species are waiting to be found, particularly in remote places such as mountain rainforests and deep seabed mud. The total number of species could be as high as 20 million, with insects topping the list as the most successful animals of all time.

Some species are good at surviving in today's world, but unluckily many are not. They are harmed by hunting, pollution, and deforestation, or by changes in their habitats as wild places are taken over by humans. Some of the world's most vulnerable animals have already become extinct, and many more are in danger of joining them.

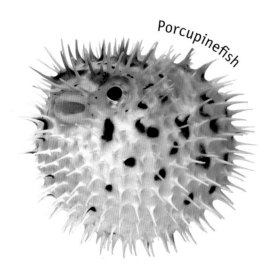

Porcupinefish

Cane toad

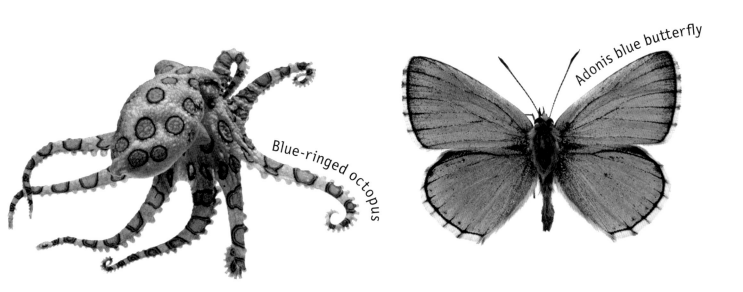

Blue-ringed octopus

Adonis blue butterfly

That's why conservation is more important than ever before. By helping individual animals and protecting their habitats, scientists and volunteers have already brought many species back from the brink of extinction. These success stories include some of the world's favourite animals, such as the giant panda and the humpback whale, and lots of less-known species, from the peregrine falcon and American alligator to the golden lion tamarin. You can find out more about them in this book, and you can help them yourself by joining conservation organizations, such as the World Wildlife Fund (WWF). By getting involved, you can help to ensure life on Earth remains beautiful, varied, and exciting.

David Burnie

Throughout this book you will find scale boxes which show the sizes of living creatures compared to you.

child = 145 cm (57 in) tall

hand = 16 cm (6 in) long

thumb = 3.5 cm (1⅓ in) long

Parson's chameleon

Scarlet ibis

Brown bear

The Tree of Life

Our planet is inhabited by a huge variety of living things. Biologists work out how different organisms are related by studying their DNA. This helps them to divide all life into kingdoms: animals, plants, fungi, and different types of micro-organisms. Within each kingdom are smaller groups, linking together similar kinds of creatures. Living beings which can breed together to produce fertile offspring are said to be of the same species. Most of the labels for the pictures in this book are species names.

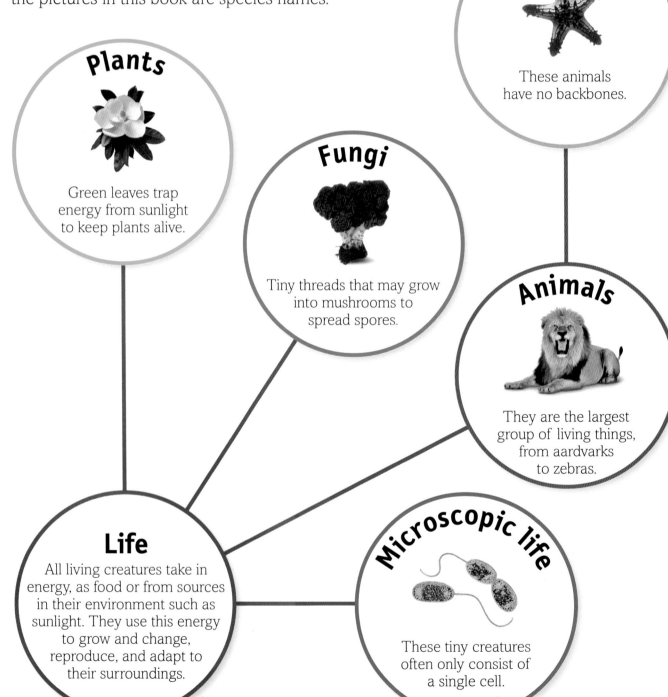

Invertebrates

These animals have no backbones.

Plants

Green leaves trap energy from sunlight to keep plants alive.

Fungi

Tiny threads that may grow into mushrooms to spread spores.

Animals

They are the largest group of living things, from aardvarks to zebras.

Life

All living creatures take in energy, as food or from sources in their environment such as sunlight. They use this energy to grow and change, reproduce, and adapt to their surroundings.

Microscopic life

These tiny creatures often only consist of a single cell.

Insects

Insects are the most successful group of invertebrates.

Birds

Feathers make these vertebrates unique.

Mammals

These warm-blooded, furry vertebrates feed their young on milk.

Reptiles

These cold-blooded vertebrates have scaly skin.

Vertebrates

Animals with backbones are called vertebrates.

Amphibians

These vertebrates live partly in water and partly on land.

Fish

Underwater vertebrates, fish breathe through gills.

Microscopic life

Tiny micro-organisms were the first living things to evolve. They are too small to be seen with the naked eye: the smallest are less than a micrometre long, or one hundredth of the width of a human hair. Nevertheless, they are the most numerous creatures on Earth, and play a vital role in supporting all other life forms.

Cytoplasm ❯ The inside of the cell is made up of a liquid called cytoplasm. Miniature organs, or organelles, float in this liquid. Chemical processes take place in the cytoplasm to keep the organism alive.

Nucleus ❯ This structure contains the cell's DNA, its genetic code. Micro-organisms breed by splitting in half to create two clones, each with a copy of the same DNA.

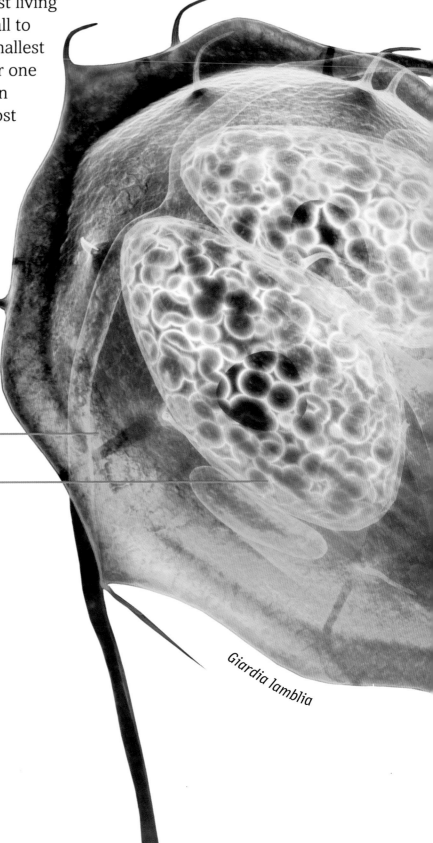

Giardia lamblia

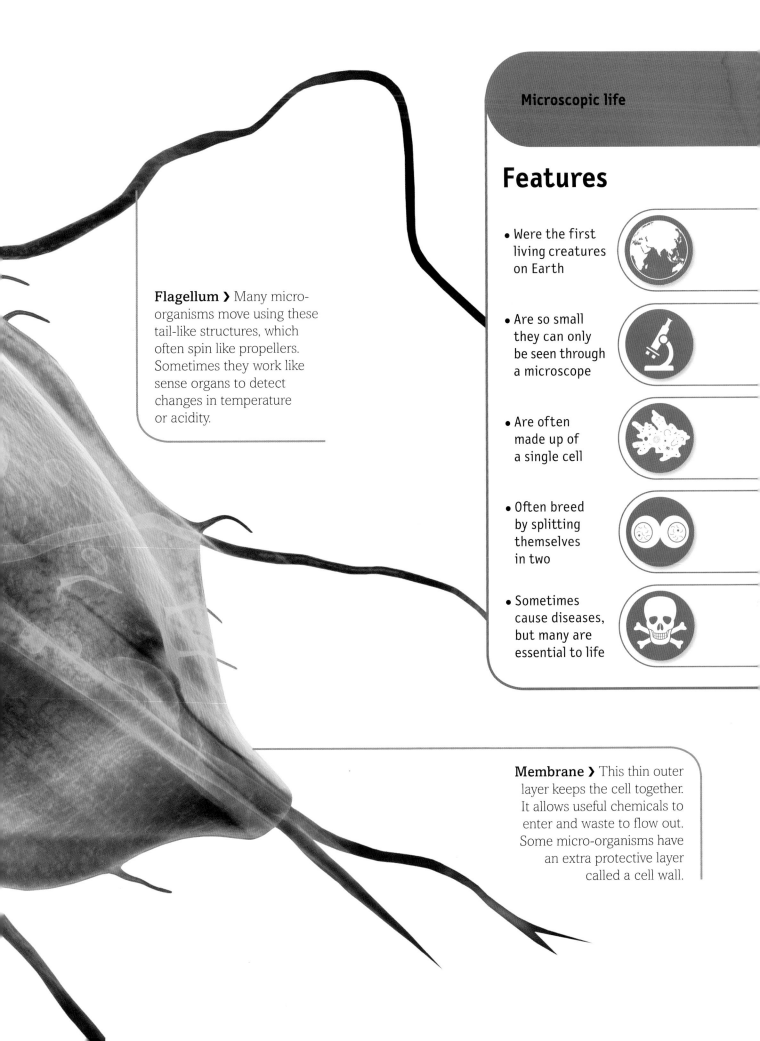

Flagellum ❯ Many micro-organisms move using these tail-like structures, which often spin like propellers. Sometimes they work like sense organs to detect changes in temperature or acidity.

Features

- Were the first living creatures on Earth

- Are so small they can only be seen through a microscope

- Are often made up of a single cell

- Often breed by splitting themselves in two

- Sometimes cause diseases, but many are essential to life

Membrane ❯ This thin outer layer keeps the cell together. It allows useful chemicals to enter and waste to flow out. Some micro-organisms have an extra protective layer called a cell wall.

Bacteria

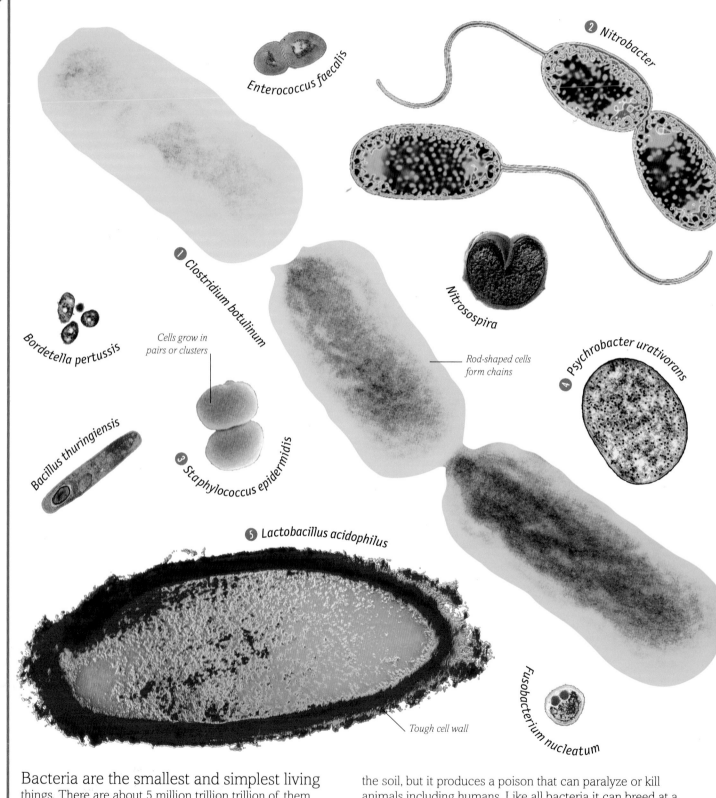

Enterococcus faecalis

② Nitrobacter

① Clostridium botulinum

Nitrosospira

④ Psychrobacter urativorans

Bordetella pertussis

Cells grow in pairs or clusters

Rod-shaped cells form chains

Bacillus thuringiensis

③ Staphylococcus epidermidis

⑤ Lactobacillus acidophilus

Fusobacterium nucleatum

Tough cell wall

Bacteria are the smallest and simplest living things. There are about 5 million trillion trillion of them on Earth, each made of a single cell. They live almost everywhere, from hot springs and seabed ooze to animal intestines and plant roots. Many are essential partners for other living things, but some can cause deadly diseases if they get out of control. **Clostridium botulinum** ❶ normally lives in the soil, but it produces a poison that can paralyze or kill animals including humans. Like all bacteria it can breed at a phenomenal rate by repeatedly dividing in two. **Nitrobacter** ❷ fertilizes soil and water, helping plants and animals to grow. It swims by spinning a long hair, or flagellum, and can move 50 times its own length in a single second. **Staphylococcus epidermidis** ❸ lives on the surface of human skin. Normally

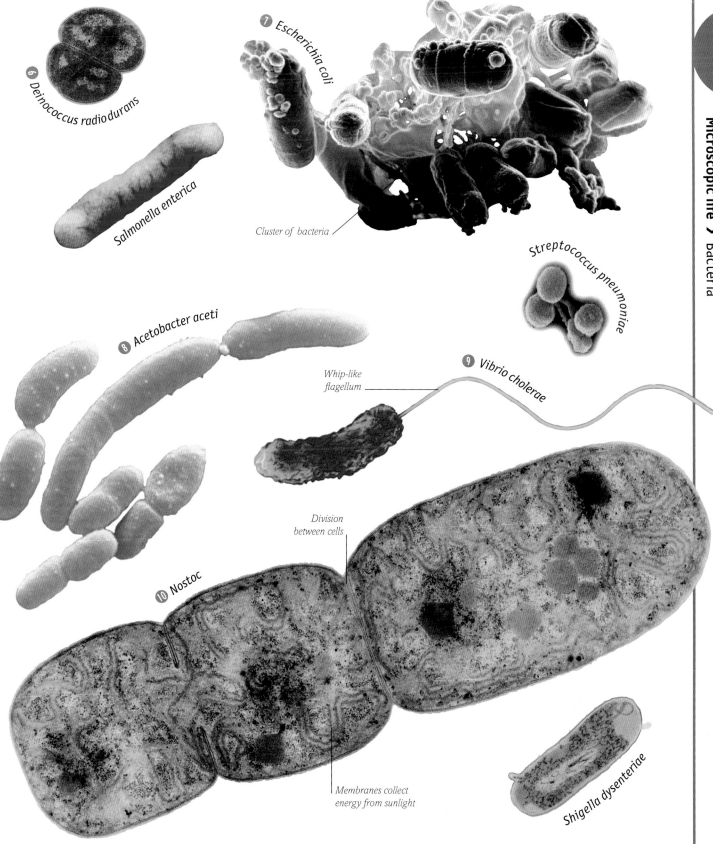

⑥ *Deinococcus radiodurans*

⑦ *Escherichia coli*

Salmonella enterica

Cluster of bacteria

Streptococcus pneumoniae

⑧ *Acetobacter aceti*

Whip-like flagellum

⑨ *Vibrio cholerae*

Division between cells

⑩ *Nostoc*

Membranes collect energy from sunlight

Shigella dysenteriae

it is harmless, but it can cause life-threatening infections if it gets inside the body. ***Psychrobacter urativorans*** ④ contains its own antifreeze, and can live in very cold conditions, while ***Lactobacillus acidophilus*** ⑤ grows well in warm milk and is used for making yogurt. ***Deinococcus radiodurans*** ⑥ is one of the world's toughest bacteria. It can survive intense cold, strong acids, and enough radiation to kill a human

being 1,000 times over. ***Escherichia coli*** ⑦ is one of the most common bacteria in human intestines. Normally it is harmless, but some strains produce food poisoning. ***Acetobacter aceti*** ⑧ is used to make vinegar, but ***Vibrio cholerae*** ⑨ causes cholera if it contaminates water or food. ***Nostoc*** ⑩ grows in damp places. It forms long chains and lives by collecting the energy in sunlight, just like a plant.

Single-celled life

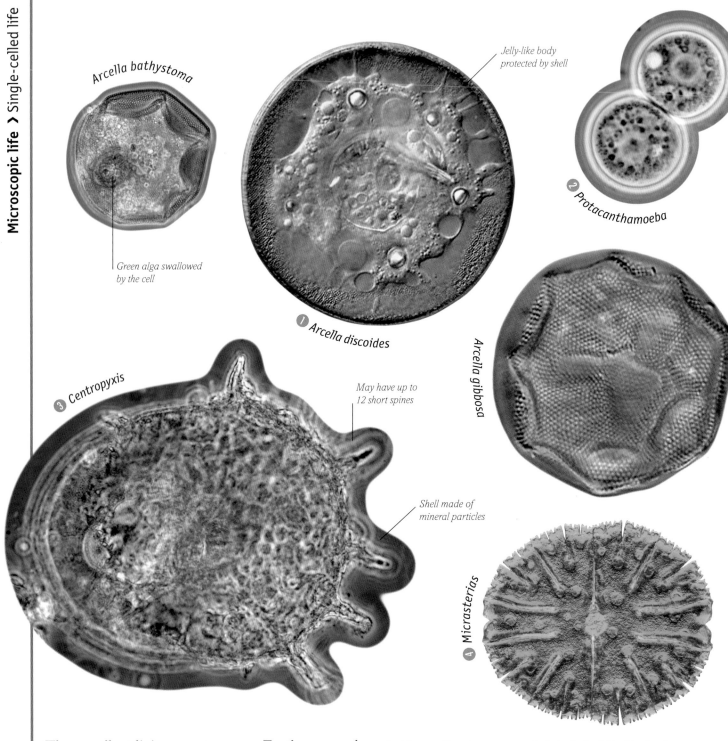

Arcella bathystoma

Jelly-like body protected by shell

Green alga swallowed by the cell

1 Arcella discoides

2 Protacanthamoeba

3 Centropyxis

May have up to 12 short spines

Arcella gibbosa

Shell made of mineral particles

4 Micrasterias

The smallest living creatures on Earth are made up of a single cell. Bacteria are the most numerous, but another group, called protoctists, contains a bewildering variety of life. They are mostly bigger and more complicated than bacteria. Some protoctists are like animals, while others are more like tiny plants. A few are like both at the same time. ***Arcella discoides*** **1** is a protoctist that lives in water, inside a yellow-brown rounded shell. Its jelly-like body reaches out through a hole, trapping any food that drifts by. ***Protacanthamoeba*** **2** also has a shell. Like many single-celled creatures it can reproduce by dividing in two. ***Centropyxis*** **3** lives in lakes and marshes. Its shell is made up of tiny mineral particles stuck together with a special glue, and has short, stubby spines. ***Micrasterias*** **4** is a

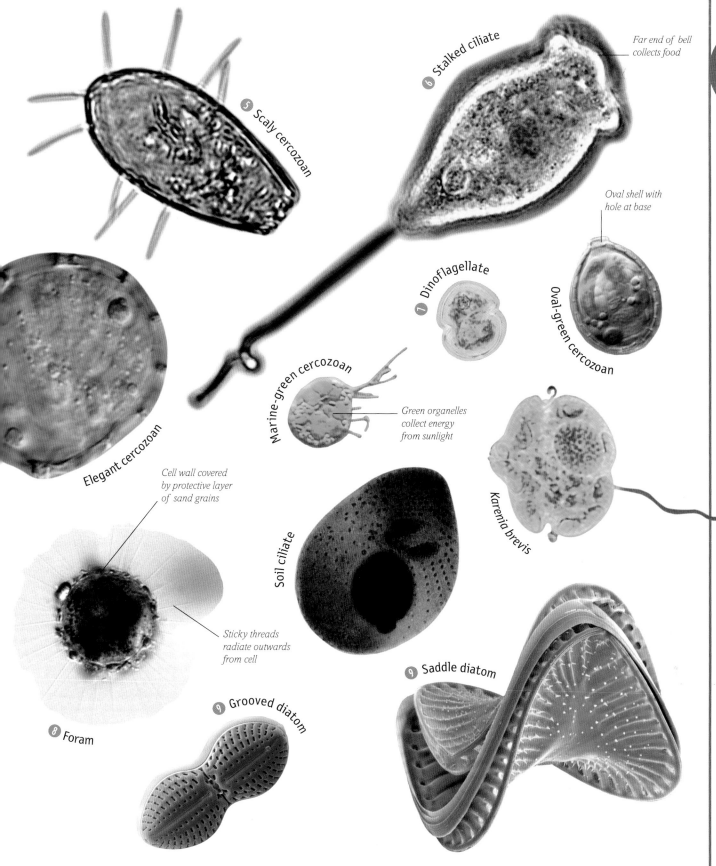

⑤ Scaly cercozoan

⑥ Stalked ciliate

Far end of bell collects food

⑦ Dinoflagellate

Oval shell with hole at base

Oval-green cercozoan

Marine-green cercozoan

Green organelles collect energy from sunlight

Elegant cercozoan

Karenia brevis

Cell wall covered by protective layer of sand grains

Soil ciliate

Sticky threads radiate outwards from cell

⑨ Saddle diatom

⑨ Grooved diatom

⑧ Foram

green alga with a cell made of two matching halves. It lives like a plant by collecting the energy in sunlight, and its presence sometimes turns lakes and ponds bright green. **Scaly cercozoa** ⑤ have oval-shaped shells covered with flat silica plates, while the **stalked ciliate** ⑥ has an inverted bell-shaped body on a slender stalk. If its bell is touched, the stalk coils up like a spring, quickly pulling the body out

of harm's way. **Dinoflagellates** ⑦ live mainly in the sea, and many of them are poisonous. Sometimes they explode in numbers, causing "red tides" that kill millions of fish. **Forams** ⑧ have round cells with a starburst of sticky threads. **Diatoms** ⑨ have silica cells and use sunlight to grow. They are the most important part of plankton, the huge mass of life that drifts in fresh water and the seas.

17

ZOOPLANKTON
Zooplankton are fragile creatures that drift or swim gently through the water. Many species, such as the ones in this picture, are so tiny that they can only be seen through a microscope. Some live as plankton all their lives, while others are the larvae of larger creatures such as fish and crustaceans. Zooplankton are essential to life in the sea and fresh water because so many other animals feed on them.

Size › Range from microscopically small up to several metres long. **Habitat ›** Oceans, seas, lagoons, lakes, rivers, and other water bodies. **Distribution ›** Worldwide **Diet ›** Algae, smaller zooplankton, plant plankton, bacteria, and particles of debris. **Breeding ›** Most produce eggs. Many tiny species live for only a few weeks. In some species, such as *Daphnia*, the females may release eggs every two to three days. **Predators ›** A wide range of water-dwelling animals eat zooplankton, including fish, crustaceans, molluscs, and corals. Larger kinds are food for sea birds and for animals such as seals, sharks, and whales. **Conservation status ›** Vulnerable to warming of the oceans or increased exposure to ultraviolet light from the sun.

Seaweeds

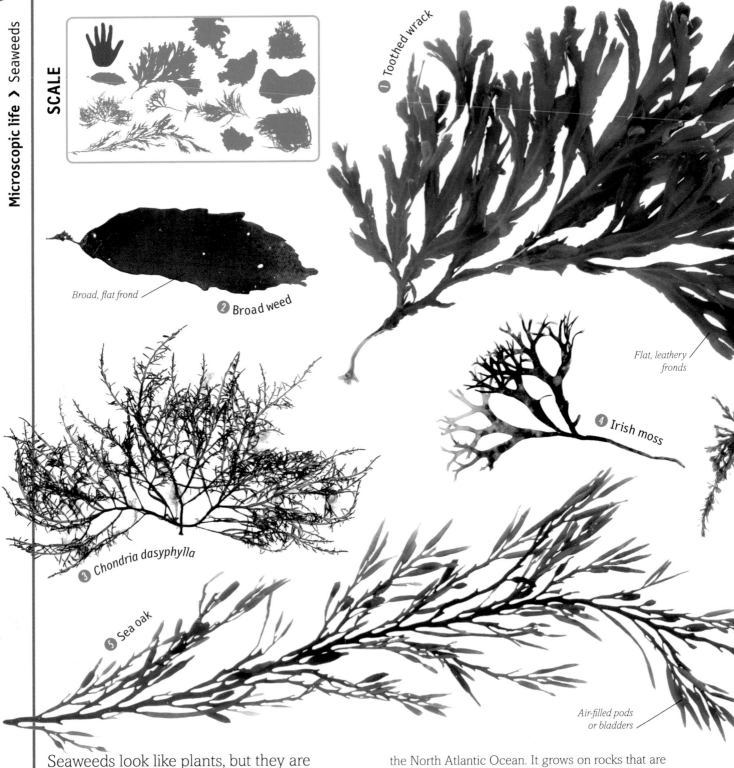

SCALE

① Toothed wrack

Broad, flat frond

② Broad weed

③ Chondria dasyphylla

⑤ Sea oak

Flat, leathery fronds

④ Irish moss

Air-filled pods or bladders

Seaweeds look like plants, but they are actually simple organisms called algae, with fronds that take in nutrients from seawater. Some are tiny, but the biggest are as tall as a five-storey office block. Most seaweeds are firmly attached to rocks, and some are incredibly tough, taking a tremendous battering from the waves. **Toothed wrack** ① is an olive-brown seaweed from the North Atlantic Ocean. It grows on rocks that are uncovered at low tide. Found in temperate areas, **broad weed** ② looks like a big red leaf. *Chondria dasyphylla* ③ lives along shores worldwide. Like most red seaweeds it lives below the low-tide mark and sometimes grows on animal shells. **Irish moss** ④ is another red seaweed, with flat, branching fronds. It contains a substance called

6 Sea lettuce

Thin, translucent fronds

7 Sea beech

Brittle branch

Maerl

8 *Polysiphonia lanosa*

Agardhiella subulata

9 Wireweed

Branching, feather-like fronds

10 Coral weed

carrageenan, which is used to thicken yogurt and ice cream. A large, dark-brown seaweed, **sea oak** 5 has lots of feathery fronds. It often grows in rock pools and has air-filled pods that help it to float. **Sea lettuce** 6 is a green seaweed that grows worldwide on mudflats and sheltered rocks. Its crumply fronds are sometimes collected and used as food. **Sea beech** 7 has paper-thin red fronds, while *Polysiphonia*

lanosa 8 is a red seaweed shaped like mossy tufts. It grows on other seaweeds instead of on rocks. **Wireweed** 9 is a fast-growing brown seaweed that originally comes from Japan. It has accidentally been spread to many other parts of the world. **Coral weed** 10 has a crunchy feel. It grows in rock pools and is reinforced with minerals, making it harder for sea animals to eat.

Mushroom › Some fungi grow structures such as mushrooms above the ground. These develop to spread spores, tiny cells which float off and grow into new fungi.

Fungi

Fungi mostly exist as tangles of microscopic threads called hyphae. Some kinds grow into mushrooms to spread their spores. The threads spread into the organic matter on which they grow, breaking them down into food. By doing this, fungi recycle dead plants and animals, turning them into nutrients that other organisms can re-use.

Cap > The top of this mushroom spreads out to give as much area as possible for spores to grow. The red colour warns hungry animals that it is poisonous.

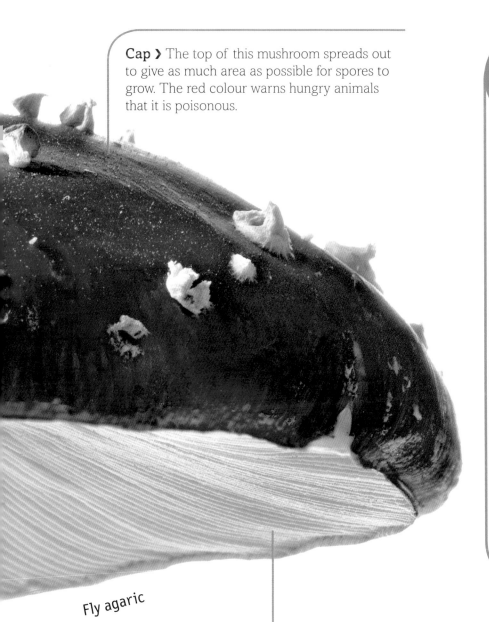

Fly agaric

Features

- Mostly grow as bundles of tiny threads

- Gain energy by breaking down other living things

- Scatter spores, which can grow into new fungi

- Grow structures such as mushrooms to spread spores

Gills > These thin, fragile membranes are where the spores develop. They fill the space under the cap so that they can produce as many spores as possible.

Stem > The stem of the mushroom connects it to the rest of the fungus, which is a network of fine threads buried underground.

Mushrooms

SCALE

Amethyst deceiver

Bright colouring fades with age

1 Violet coral

Petticoat mottlegill

2 Pink waxcap

Fleshy, waxy, pink gills

3 Red cage fungus

Cage bursts from "egg"

Lawyer's wig

Earpick fungus

4 Cultivated mushroom

5 Velvet bolete

6 Fluted bird's nest

Hairy, brown, fluted nests

Jack O'Lantern

7 Sessile earthstar

Most mushrooms grow in damp places, from grassy fields to shady woodlands with lots of fallen leaves. Their purpose is to scatter tiny seed-like spores, so that fungi can spread. Some mushrooms have unusual colours that really stand out. **Violet coral** **1** has brightly coloured coral-like branches, while the **pink waxcap** **2** has a rosy cap on a pale stalk. The unusual **red cage fungus** **3** has

a crimson mesh-like structure, which hatches from a small whitish "egg". The creamy white **cultivated mushroom** **4** is grown around the world for food. Most mushrooms, including the **velvet bolete** **5**, make spores that are blown away in the wind. The **fluted bird's nest** **6** has a different way of spreading. It makes packets of spores inside tiny cups. If a raindrop lands in one of the cups, the packets

⑧ Chanterelle

Oak curtain crust

Silverleaf fungus

Foul-smelling spore mass on cap

Stubble rosegill

Warty scales

⑪ Stinkhorn

Hare's ear

Tall, orange cups

⑩ Fly agaric

Spores grow beneath cap

⑨ Death cap

⑫ Giant puffball

splash out, landing up to 1 m (3 ft) away. The **sessile earthstar ⑦** spreads its spores in a similar way, puffing them out of a papery sac when it is hit by raindrops. While some mushrooms, such as the **chanterelle ⑧**, are good to eat, other types are deadly poisonous. The most dangerous of all mushrooms is the **death cap ⑨**, since it is highly toxic and looks similar to edible kinds. Some fungi are difficult to

mistake because of their size, colour, shape, or smell. The poisonous **fly agaric ⑩** is easy to spot with its bright red-and-white cap. The odour of the smelly **stinkhorn ⑪** carries for long distances. The smell attracts flies, which spread the stinkhorn's spores. The biggest mushroom of all is the **giant puffball ⑫**, which can measure more than 1 m (3 ft) across, and weigh as much as 20 kg (44 lb).

Sac fungi and lichens

Bog beacon

1 Ergot

SCALE

Scaly earthtongue

2 Coral spot

3 Jelly baby

Dust-like fungus attacks mushroom

Fungus growing on grass seeds

Bolete eater

Anemone cup

Spore-producing inner surface

Purple drop

4 Powdery mildew

6 Cramp balls

5 Dead man's fingers

Candlesnuff fungus

Beech woodwart

Fungus forms hard balls

Sac fungi make their spores in tiny containers or sacs, which break open when they are ripe. The sacs are much too small to see, but the fungi that produce them have lots of strange and interesting shapes. Many live on dead wood or rotting plants, but **ergot** ❶ grows on grasses and cereals such as rye and wheat. It produces a powerful poison that can be deadly if it gets into bread. **Coral spot** ❷ attacks

damp wood, while the **jelly baby fungus** ❸ grows in clumps among fallen leaves. Both are harmless, but **powdery mildews** ❹ are a headache for farmers and gardeners because they attack all kinds of living plants. The first signs of trouble are white spots on the leaves, showing where the fungus is at work. **Dead man's fingers** ❺ and **cramp balls** ❻ both feed on dead wood. Unlike most fungi,

Common eyelash

❼ Morel

False morel

Brown, wrinkly cap

Thimble morel

Honeycomb produces spores

❾ Orange peel fungus

❽ Périgord truffle

⓫ Hooded tube-lichen

Fat, blue-grey lobes

Cup faces upwards

⓵⓪ Common wall lichen

⓬ Oakmoss lichen

Cellar cup

they are hard to the touch. The **morel** ❼ looks unappetizing with its sponge-like cap, but is valued for its delicious taste. The **Périgord truffle** ❽ is even more highly prized. It grows underground beneath oak trees, and has to be sniffed out by specially trained pigs or dogs. **Orange peel fungus** ❾ grows on bare ground and has a vivid orange colour that makes it easy to spot. Lichens are living partnerships between fungi and algae or bacteria. They grow very slowly but can live to be hundreds of years old. The **common wall lichen** ⓵⓪ is flat and brightly coloured and grows on bare rock, particularly near the sea, while the **hooded tube-lichen** ⓫ is common on trees, rocks, and walls. **Oakmoss lichen** ⓬ lives on the bark of oak trees. It has a woody smell and is used for making perfumes.

CUP FUNGI
These strange bowls are actually a variety of cup fungus, a group of sac fungi that grow into eye-catching shapes. The cups produce sacs full of spores that are scattered about by wind and rain. In some varieties, these sacs absorb water and swell up until they burst, catapulting the spores out. The biggest cups make an audible pop when this happens, and the spores can sometimes be seen as a faint cloud.

Size ❯ Up to 30 cm (12 in) across **Habitat** ❯ Moist, dead wood in tropical or subtropical forest. **Distribution** ❯ Tropical and subtropical areas worldwide, from the USA, Central and South America, and Africa to Southeast Asia. **Diet** ❯ Dead and rotting wood. Like all fungi, they feed by breaking down organic matter in their environment. This can be useful for getting rid of dead plants and animals, but harmful where the fungus grows through living creatures. **Breeding** ❯ The fungus consists of a network of threads that mostly grow underground. The cup develops only to spread spores, cells a bit like seeds that grow into new colonies of threads. **Number of species** ❯ About 230.

Plants

Plants have the ability to trap energy from sunlight, using it to make food and to grow. By doing this they provide nourishment for themselves and for the animals that feed on them. Plants also absorb carbon dioxide from the atmosphere and release oxygen to replace it, maintaining the balance of gases animals need to survive.

Stargazer lily

Stem › Plant stems can be thin and fragile or thick and woody like tree trunks. They are filled with tiny tubes that carry water from the plant's roots up to the leaves, and food from the leaves back down to the roots.

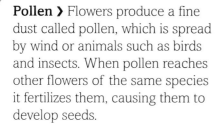

Pollen > Flowers produce a fine dust called pollen, which is spread by wind or animals such as birds and insects. When pollen reaches other flowers of the same species it fertilizes them, causing them to develop seeds.

Flowers > Many types of plants grow flowers to reproduce. They have colourful petals and interesting smells to attract animals, which spread pollen from flower to flower. Some plants offer visitors a meal of sugary nectar.

Features

- Collect energy from sunlight and use it to grow

- Have cells with walls made of microscopic fibres

- Commonly have flowers to produce and fertilize seeds

- Include the longest-living things

- Provide food and oxygen that supports much of life on Earth.

Leaves > The green colouring in leaves is a substance called chlorophyll. Plants use it to trap energy from sunlight by a process called photosynthesis. They use this energy to combine carbon dioxide from the air and water from the soil to form sugars, which the plants use as food.

Liverworts and mosses

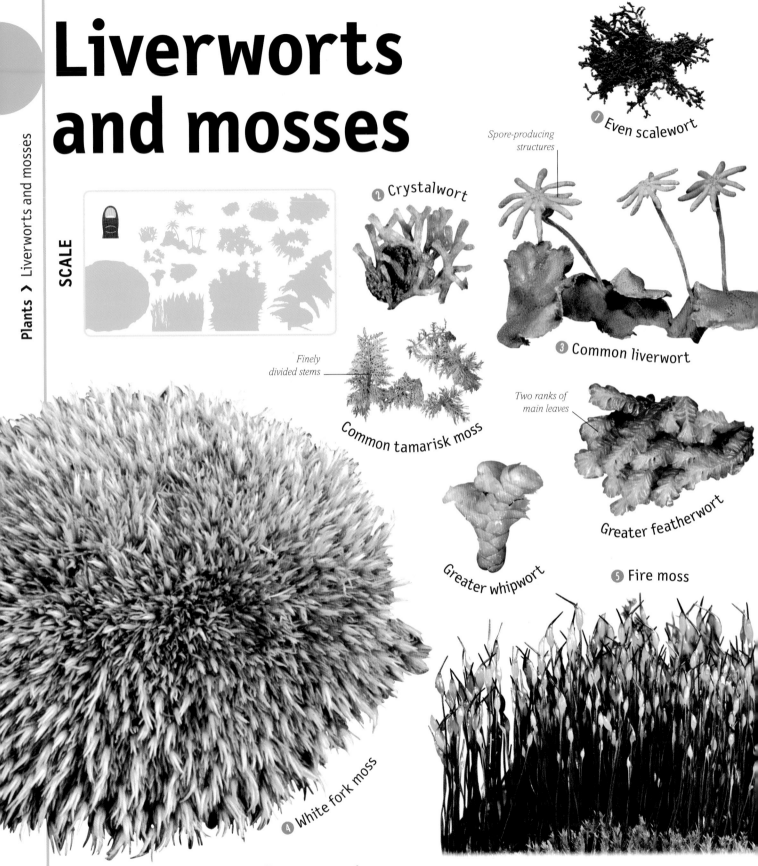

SCALE

① Even scalewort

Spore-producing structures

② Crystalwort

③ Common liverwort

Finely divided stems

Two ranks of main leaves

Common tamarisk moss

Greater featherwort

Greater whipwort

⑤ Fire moss

④ White fork moss

Found mainly in damp places, liverworts and mosses are the world's simplest plants. They don't have roots or flowers, and they spread by making microscopic spores instead of seeds. Some of them could easily sit on a fingernail and even the biggest are only waist-high. Liverworts are often shaped like flat ribbons and keep dividing in two as they grow. Most kinds are green but **even scalewort ①** is often red or

brown. It grows on tree trunks and rocks, usually in the shade. **Crystalwort ②** lives on wet mud or on the surface of ponds. It is sometimes used in aquariums for sheltering newly hatched fish. **Common liverwort ③** is often seen in gardens. In the summer it is covered with growths like tiny palm trees, which make and then scatter its spores. Mosses have thin leaves and wiry stems and often grow in clumps. Many kinds,

32

Cypress-leaved plait moss

Cape thread-moss

Common pocket moss

Rosette of small branches

❻ Swan's-neck thyme moss

❼ Blue-leaved bog moss

❾ Ostrich-plume feather moss

❽ Common hair-cap moss

Narrow, pointed leaves

including the **white fork moss** ❹, turn grey or white if they dry out but become green again within minutes if it rains. **Fire moss** ❺ makes its spores in capsules shaped like matchsticks. It grows on walls and on burned ground. **Swan's-neck thyme moss** ❻ is common in woods, while **blue-leaved bog moss** ❼, or sphagnum, grows in waterlogged places. This moss can hold more than 20 times its own weight in

water and slowly forms peat, a brown, soil-like material, when it dies. **Common hair-cap moss** ❽ is one of the world's tallest mosses, growing in springy tussocks up to 60 cm (24 in) high. Its stems are stiff and unbranched, with narrow painted leaves. **Ostrich-plume feather moss** ❾ gets its name from its stems, which look like tiny feathers or ferns. It lives in forests in the far north of Europe and Canada.

Ferns

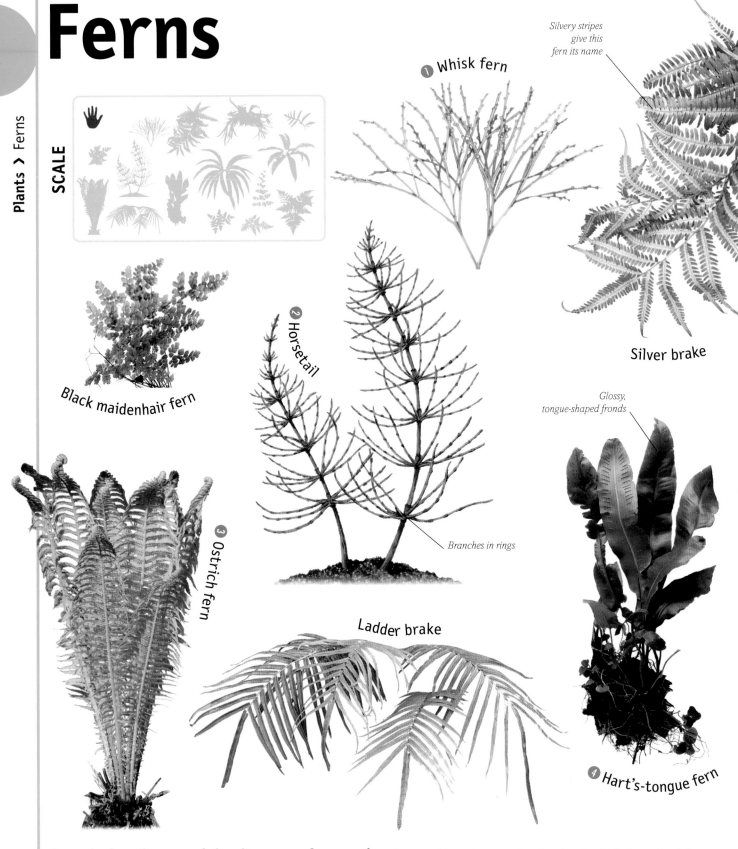

SCALE

① Whisk fern

Silvery stripes give this fern its name

Silver brake

Black maidenhair fern

② Horsetail

Branches in rings

③ Ostrich fern

Ladder brake

Glossy, tongue-shaped fronds

④ Hart's-tongue fern

Long before the age of the dinosaurs, ferns and their relatives were the biggest plants on Earth. Today they still include some tree-like varieties more than 15 m (50 ft) tall, but most ferns grow much closer to the ground. All these plants spread by making tiny spores instead of seeds, and most of them have feathery fronds that unroll as they grow. The **whisk fern** ① is a primitive plant with brush-like stems.

It starts life underground, using fungi to help it get food from the soil. **Horsetails** ② have hollow stems with rings of bright green branches. They contain sharp crystals of silica and were once used for scrubbing pots and pans. The **ostrich fern** ③, found in the Northern Hemisphere, grows near streams and rivers, while the **hart's-tongue fern** ④ grows on shady banks and old walls. **Common staghorn ferns** ⑤

Feathery fronds absorb sunlight

5 Common staghorn fern

Antler-shaped fronds make spores

Toothed, pale green leaflets

Sensitive fern

Umbrella fern

Fronds like umbrella spokes

6 Hard fern

Tough, evergreen fronds

7 Cliff brake

9 Bracken

8 Royal fern

Squirrel's foot fern

live in the forests of the Southern Hemisphere, where they grow on the trunks of trees. Their fronds trap rain and falling leaves, making private compost heaps that help them to grow. **Hard fern** **6** has two types of fronds: feathery ones that catch sunshine, and much narrower ones that spread its spores. Most ferns live in damp places, but **cliff brake** **7** grows in rocky crevices in South Africa, and has wiry black stems that are good at coping with drought. **Royal fern** **8** is an impressive plant with a rosette of spreading fronds. It is sometimes grown in gardens, but **bracken** **9** is a notorious weed. Fast growing and poisonous to animals, it spreads by underground runners, and can form patches more than 500 m (1,640 ft) across. It is found on every continent except Antarctica and on islands far out to sea.

35

Conifers

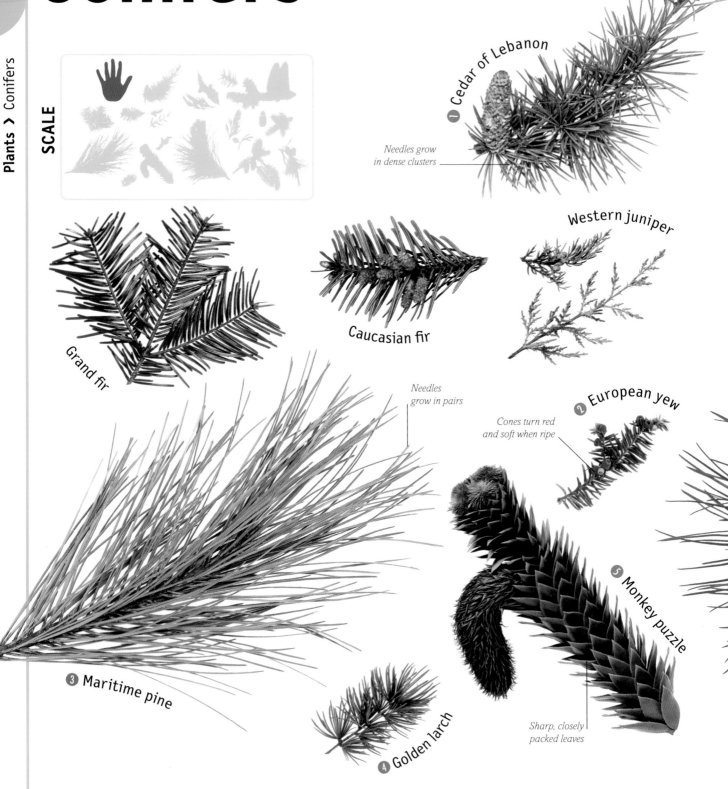

SCALE

Cedar of Lebanon ❶

Needles grow in dense clusters

Grand fir

Caucasian fir

Western juniper

Needles grow in pairs

Cones turn red and soft when ripe

❷ European yew

❸ Maritime pine

❹ Golden larch

❺ Monkey puzzle

Sharp, closely packed leaves

Conifers include the world's tallest, heaviest, and oldest trees. They do not grow flowers, and they make their seeds in cones. Most conifers are evergreen, with tough, waxy leaves that are good at coping with hot summer sunshine as well as freezing winter winds. The **cedar of Lebanon** ❶ comes from the Middle East and is often planted in parks. It has huge branches that spread out like shelves, and short, needle-like leaves. Common in Europe and the Middle East, the **European yew** ❷ has tiny cones that look like bright red berries. They are poisonous to many animals, but birds feed on them, helping the trees to spread. The **maritime pine** ❸ grows wild in southern Europe. It is full of sticky resin, which oozes out if its bark is cut. The **golden larch** ❹ comes from China. It sheds all its leaves

36

California nutmeg

Nut-like seeds

European silver fir **6**

Monterey cypress

Colorado blue spruce

Giant sequoia **7**

Round cones produce seeds

Stone pine

Slender, closely packed needles

Sitka spruce **8**

Scots pine **9**

Cylindrical cones with toothed scales

Cones open to scatter seeds

in late autumn and sprouts new ones in spring. The **monkey puzzle 5** from South America has sharply pointed leaves and an umbrella-like shape whenw it is fully grown. The **European silver fir 6** has upright cones, which disintegrate when they are ripe instead of falling to the ground. **Giant sequoias 7** from California are some of the largest living things on Earth. They can weigh more than 2,000 tonnes

and their fireproof bark is up to 75 cm (30 in) thick. The **sitka spruce 8** comes from North America's west coast but is now grown all over the world as a timber tree. The **Scots pine 9** is one of the world's toughest trees and the most widespread conifer. It grows right across Europe and Russia, including places where winter temperatures hit -60°C (-76°F), far colder than a deep freeze.

37

Flowering plants

① Gorse

Tubular flowers often pollinated by moths

Common jasmine

② Red clover

Flowers protected by thorns

Small flower clusters on long stalks

③ Lilac

Common asphodel

Hydrangea

Flowers grow in rounded clusters

④ Common lavender

⑤ Wild tulip

Flowers come in an incredible variety of shapes. Some are bigger than a washing-up bowl, but the smallest could fit through the eye of a needle with room to spare. Many plants grow flowers to spread their pollen and to scatter their seeds. Like most flowering plants, **gorse ①** attracts insects, which carry its pollen as they wander from plant to plant. It grows its seeds in pods that suddenly snap open when the seeds are ripe. **Red clover ②** is often grown to feed farm animals and to help fertilize the soil. Found on scrubby hill slopes in southeastern Europe, **lilac ③** has strongly scented flowers. An evergreen shrub of dry Mediterranean scrub habitats, **common lavender ④** is full of fragrant oils. **Wild tulips ⑤** have yellow flowers that grow from bulbs. Widespread in Europe, they are close

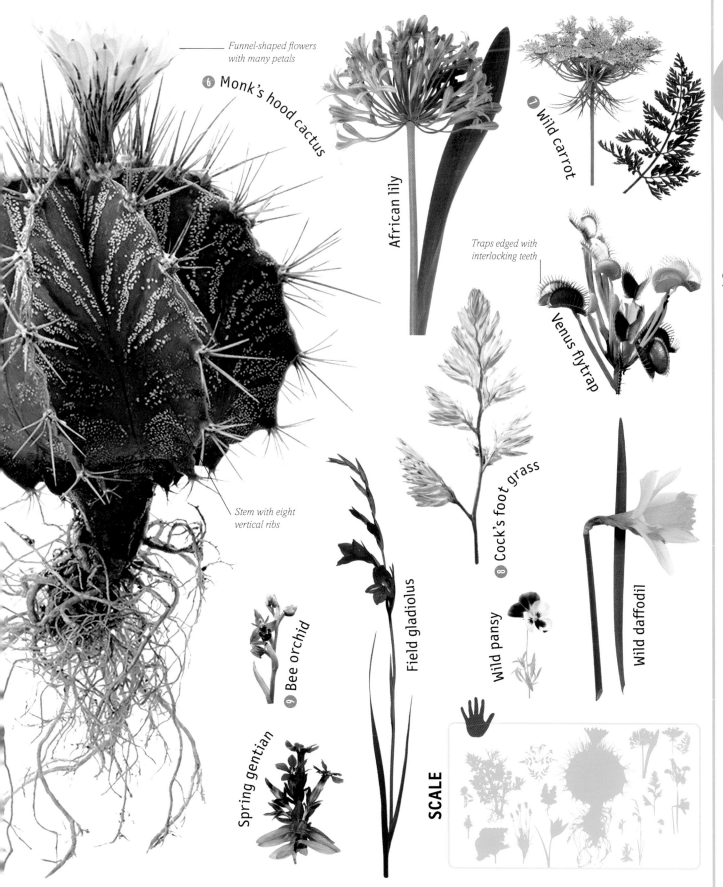

Funnel-shaped flowers with many petals

6 Monk's hood cactus

African lily

7 Wild carrot

Traps edged with interlocking teeth

Venus flytrap

Stem with eight vertical ribs

Cock's foot grass **8**

Field gladiolus

Wild pansy

Wild daffodil

9 Bee orchid

Spring gentian

SCALE

relatives of cultivated tulips, which are grown as garden flowers. The **monk's hood cactus 6** is adapted for life in very dry conditions. It has spines instead of leaves and a juicy water-storing stem. Like most cacti, it has shallow roots, which soak up water during rare periods of rain. **Wild carrot 7** is the ancestor of the carrots that we eat. Grasses are flowering plants, but they use the wind to spread

their pollen, and their flowers are often small. They include wild plants, such as the **cock's foot grass 8**, as well as domestic cereals, such as wheat and rice, which are the world's most important foods. The **bee orchid 9** is a little plant from a giant family. Its flowers mimic female insects, such as bumblebees, and spread pollen by attracting male insects looking for a chance to breed.

39

SCALE

Flowers open at dawn — Morning glory

Fan of four to five flowers

⑩ Apothecary's rose

Strawberry

⑪ Bird-of-paradise plant

Monkshood ⑫

Flowers in tall column

Meadow buttercup

Flowers grow on slender stems

Ring of spines beneath flowerhead

⑬ Milk thistle

⑭ Common poppy

Greater periwinkle

Many flowering plants are grown for their eye-catching blooms. There are more than 100 wild kinds of roses and thousands of cultivated varieties. The **apothecary's rose** ⑩ is one of the oldest. It has been grown in gardens for at least 750 years. The **bird-of-paradise plant** ⑪ from South Africa is also grown for its spectacular flowers. In the wild they are pollinated by

sunbirds, which carry pollen on their feet. Plants are also visited by hungry animals, so some use special defences to survive. **Monkshood** ⑫ is protected by powerful poisons, while **milk thistle** ⑬ has sharp spines that keep hungry animals at bay. The **common poppy** ⑭ is a frequent weed in fields. Its seeds can survive in the soil for many years and they start growing as soon as the ground is ploughed. The

15 Common dandelion

16 Daisy

Top flowers open last

17 Foxglove

Water hawthorn

18 Sacred lotus

Round-headed leek

Royal bluebell

20 White water lily

Gas-filled floats

19 Common water hyacinth

Floating leaves

common dandelion 15 is even more widespread. Its seeds float away on feathery parachutes, and take root on roadsides, in fields, and in lawns. The **daisy** 16 blooms for most of the year. Like the dandelion, its flowers are made up of lots of mini flowers, or florets, packed together in a single flowerhead. **Foxgloves** 17 have tubular flowers that are just the right shape for visiting bumblebees. Flowering plants are also common in fresh water. The **sacred lotus** 18 grows in tropical lakes and has large flowers held above the water, while the **common water hyacinth** 19 has air-filled leaf-stalks that make it float. The **white water lily** 20 has floating flowers that close up in the late afternoon. They hold pollinating insects overnight and release them the next day.

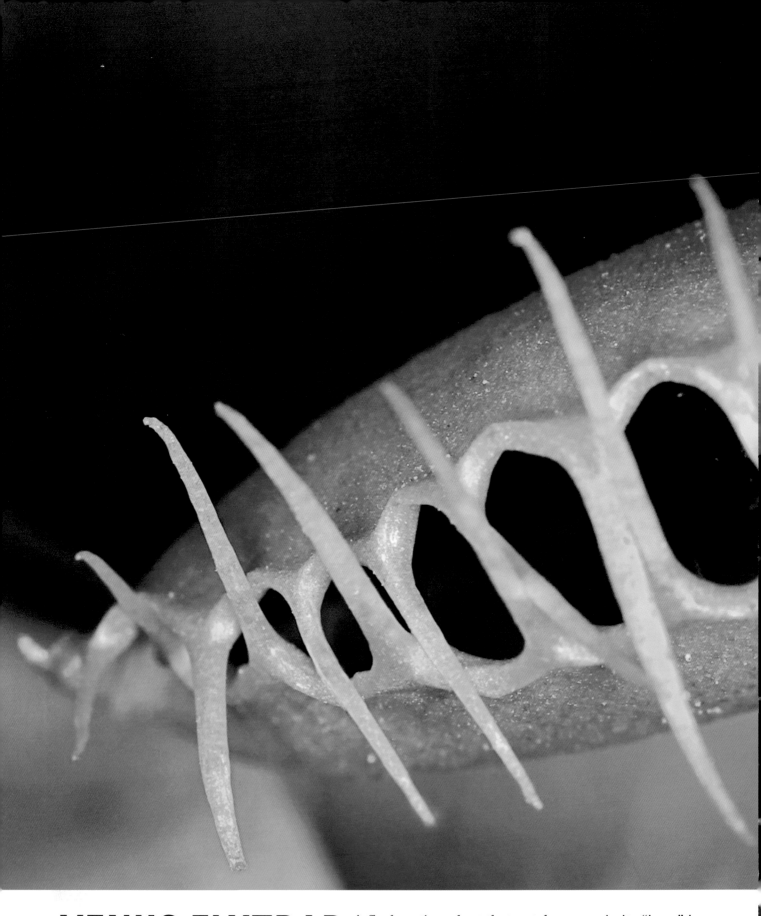

VENUS FLYTRAP
A flesh-eating plant that catches prey in its "jaws" is the stuff of nightmares, but the Venus flytrap is only a threat to flies and spiders. The hinged leaves gape open like a big, red mouth, attracting prey with their bright colour. If an insect or a spider lands on "trigger" hairs on the surface, the leaf snaps shut, trapping the prey inside. The plant then releases juices to digest its food.

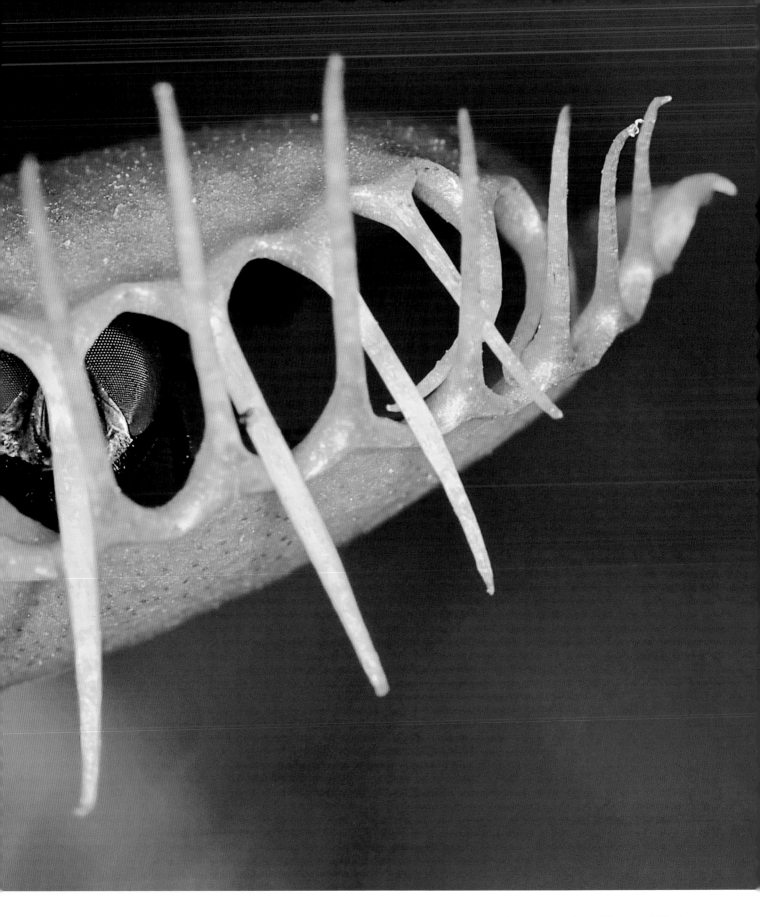

Size › Up to 30 cm (12 in) tall **Habitat ›** Wet, boggy areas of peat or sandy soil. **Distribution ›** Coastal areas of North and South Carolina in the southeastern USA. **Diet ›** Like other plants, the Venus flytrap gets energy from sunlight. It evolved to be carnivorous as it often grows in poor soil and needs the extra nutrients that it can get from insects. **Breeding ›** Bears clusters of white flowers from May to June. The small, black seeds may be dispersed in water or picked up by birds. **Lifespan ›** Up to 30 years if cultivated. **Predators ›** Slugs, birds, rodents, and tiny insects such as aphids and thrips, which suck the plant's juices. **Conservation status ›** At risk due to habitat loss and over-collection for the exotic plant trade.

Broadleaved trees

1 Common fig

Fig contains hundreds of tiny flowers

Paper mulberry

2 Sugar maple

Sandalwood

Yellowhorn

5 Mango tree

Foxglove tree **4**

3 Common ash

6 Cocoa tree

Ribbed, oval fruit

Seeds have papery wings

Unlike conifers, broadleaved trees are flowering plants. There are thousands of different kinds, from mighty giants in wild forests to small, ornamental garden trees. In warm parts of the world, most broadleaved trees are evergreen. Where winters are cold, they often shed their leaves in the autumn and grow a new set in spring. The **common fig 1** is a small broadleaved tree with tiny flowers hidden inside a special bud. When seeds start to develop, the bud ripens into a fig. The **sugar maple 2** tree from North America is famous for its stunning autumn colours. In spring its sweet sticky sap is harvested to make maple syrup. The European **common ash 3** is a fast-growing tree with winged seeds, while the **foxglove tree 4** has beautiful mauve flowers that appear before its leaves. **Mango trees 5** come from

⑦ Ylang-ylang

⑧ Common walnut

White poplar

Leaves have white undersides

Bull bay

⑨ Common pear

Chilean fire bush

⑩ Holly

Berries on female trees

Black gum

⑪ Lemon tree

Strawberry tree

Tubular flame-coloured flowers

SCALE

South Asia. Like many trees, they hide their seeds in sweet, fleshy fruits. Animals that eat the fruit spread the seeds to new areas. The **cocoa tree** ❻ originally comes from Central and South America. Cocoa is made from its seeds, which grow inside fleshy pods. **Ylang-ylang** ❼ from Southeast Asia has richly scented flowers that are used for making perfumes. **Common walnut** ❽ produces valuable timber and nutritious nuts, while the **common pear** ❾ from Europe is the ancestor of pears grown to eat. **Holly** ❿ is a small evergreen tree with very prickly leaves. Holly trees are either male or female. In winter, female ones produce bright red berries, which are eaten by birds. **Lemon trees** ⓫ come from Asia. Their fruit contain lots of citric acid, a chemical that gives them their sharp but mouth-watering taste.

⑫ Common laburnum

⑬ Quinine tree

Flowers in hanging clusters

Red alder

Flowers in catkins

⑭ Silver birch

⑮ Pink silk tree

Leaves are divided into leaflets

Flowers have slender stamens

Broadleaved trees produce many useful substances as well as some that can be harmful. **Common laburnum ⑫** contains a deadly poison, while the **quinine tree ⑬** contains a drug that can be used to treat malaria. It grows in South America, and quinine is extracted from its bark. **Silver birch ⑭** is a hardy tree, living in very cold climates in northern Europe and Asia. Its flowers grow in catkins, which scatter tiny seeds in the wind. The **pink silk tree ⑮** has large, feathery leaves and flowers in upright tufts. It is sometimes called the "sleep tree" because its leaves fold up at dusk and open again at dawn. The **Spanish chestnut ⑯** is a slow-growing tree with edible nuts. These grow inside prickly cases and are often roasted instead of being eaten raw. The **Judas tree ⑰** has rounded,

Turkish hazel

Flowers in upright catkins

17 Judas tree

American beech

18 English oak

Acorns grow in cups

16 Spanish chestnut

19 Pomegranate

Crape myrtle

20 Avocado tree

Bay laurel

SCALE

heart-shaped leaves and beautiful purple-pink flowers that appear in spring. These flowers grow in clusters and often sprout directly from the trunk. The **English oak 18** is a long-lived tree with very hard timber, which was once used to build sailing ships. Like other oaks it has tiny flowers in trailing catkins, and its seeds are acorns, which grow in scale-covered cups. The **pomegranate 19** is a spiny, shrubby tree with large, bright-red flowers. It produces tasty fruit that contain hundreds of seeds. **Avocado trees 20** originally come from Mexico and the West Indies, but they are now grown in warm places across the world. They have small creamy flowers and pear-shaped fruit with a single, very large stone. In the wild, avocados fall off the tree when they are still hard and ripen on the ground.

Invertebrates

The largest group of animals, invertebrates range from sponges and jellyfish to shellfish, crabs, spiders, and insects. They mostly hatch out from eggs. Some start life as larvae, tiny creatures which look very different from their parents. Others hatch as miniature versions of adults, growing bigger as they mature.

Legs > This spider belongs to a group of invertebrates called arthropods, which have jointed legs. Muscles run through the leg joints to enable them to move. As well as spiders, arthropods include centipedes, millipedes, insects, and crustaceans.

Sense organs > The tarantula has complex sense organs, such as these "palps" which feel out its surroundings. Other invertebrates, such as worms and sponges, are much simpler and may not even have brains.

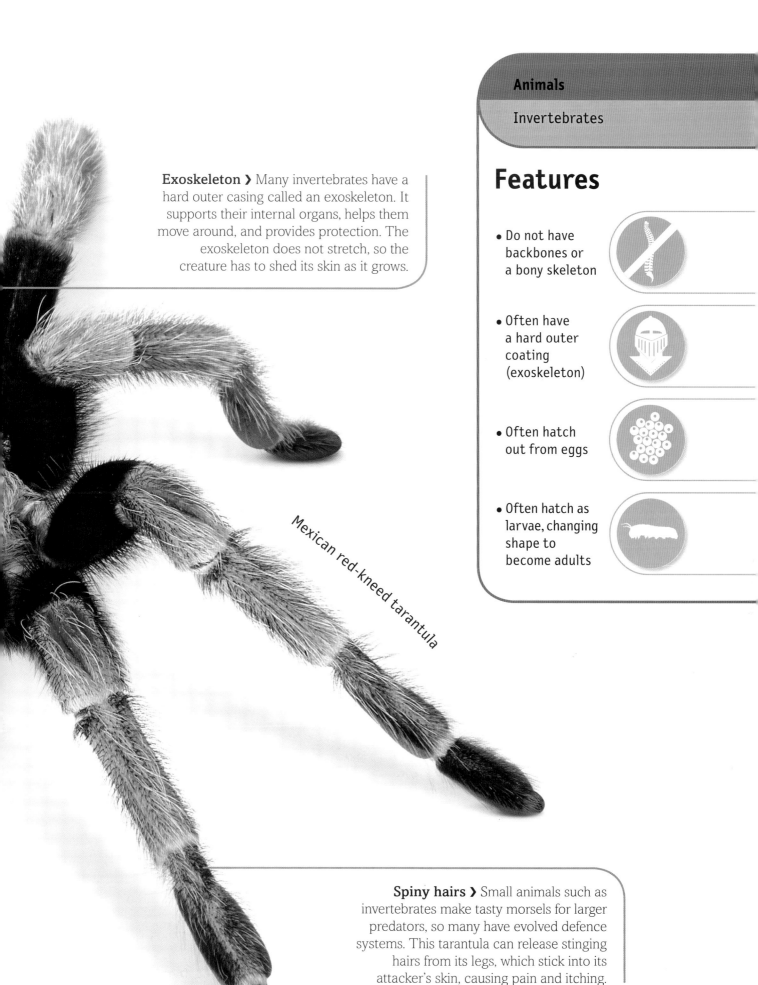

Exoskeleton › Many invertebrates have a hard outer casing called an exoskeleton. It supports their internal organs, helps them move around, and provides protection. The exoskeleton does not stretch, so the creature has to shed its skin as it grows.

Features

- Do not have backbones or a bony skeleton

- Often have a hard outer coating (exoskeleton)

- Often hatch out from eggs

- Often hatch as larvae, changing shape to become adults

Mexican red-kneed tarantula

Spiny hairs › Small animals such as invertebrates make tasty morsels for larger predators, so many have evolved defence systems. This tarantula can release stinging hairs from its legs, which stick into its attacker's skin, causing pain and itching.

Sponges

SCALE

Red tree sponge ❶

Leuconia nivea

Niphates alba

❷ Lemon sponge

Purse sponge

❺ Boring sponge

❹ Yellow finger sponge

❸ Breadcrumb sponge

Water is pumped out through volcano-shaped holes

Clathrina clathrus

Perforated surface

❻ Red purse sponge

Found mainly in the sea, sponges are some of the world's simplest animals. They don't have heads, tails, eyes, or even mouths. Instead of moving about, they pump water through pores in their bodies and filter out tiny particles of food. Sponges don't have bones, but their bodies are often reinforced by mineral crystals and fibres, which give them a crunchy or spongy feel. Some sponges, such as the

red tree sponge ❶, grow upwards like underwater plants. Others, such as the **lemon sponge** ❷, are almost spherical, while some, such as the **breadcrumb sponge** ❸, grow as a crust on rocks. The **yellow finger sponge** ❹ grows in upright columns, peppered with pores. The European **boring sponge** ❺ uses acids to tunnel through shells and solid rock. Growing on shallow reefs in Malaysia and Indonesia, the

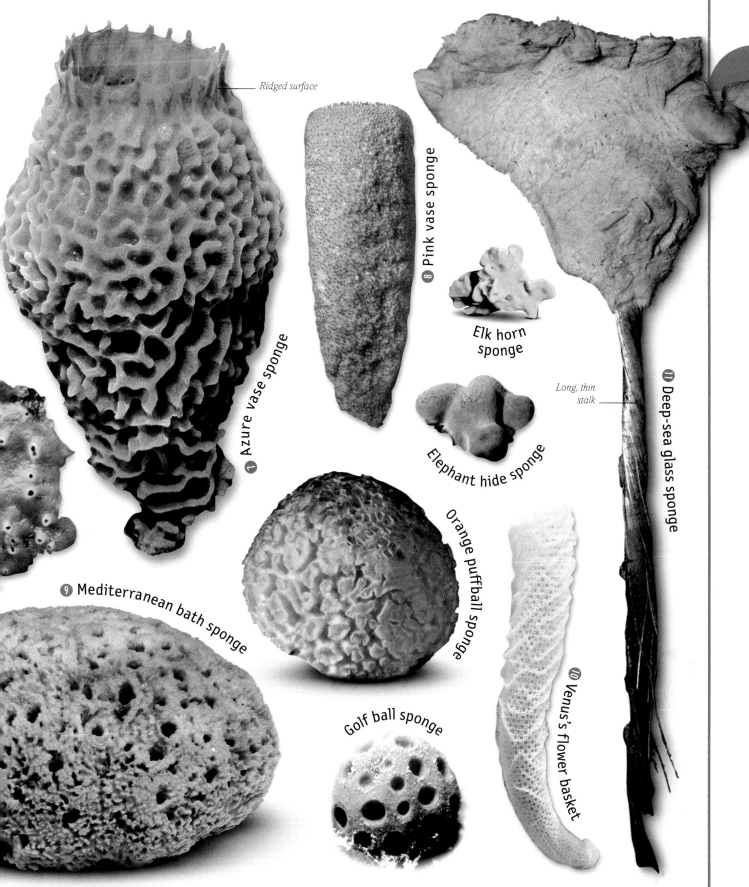

Ridged surface

8 Pink vase sponge

1 Azure vase sponge

Elk horn sponge

Long, thin stalk

11 Deep-sea glass sponge

Elephant hide sponge

9 Mediterranean bath sponge

Orange puffball sponge

Golf ball sponge

10 Venus's flower basket

red purse sponge 6 resembles a miniature balloon. Water flows in through its sides and out through the narrow opening at the top. Vase sponges work in the same way, but are much larger. The **azure vase sponge 7** and **pink vase sponge 8**, both from the Caribbean, can be up to 45 cm (1½ ft) high, but the world's tallest vase sponges grow bigger than a fridge, and are known to live for more than

100 years. The **Mediterranean bath sponge 9** lives on the shallow seabed. Its extra-springy skeleton makes it perfect for washing with, once it has been cleaned. Most sponges grow near the surface of the sea, but **Venus's flower basket 10** lives deep down. Like the **deep-sea glass sponge 11**, it has an intricate skeleton made of silica, which lasts long after the sponge has died.

51

Jellyfish, anemones, and corals

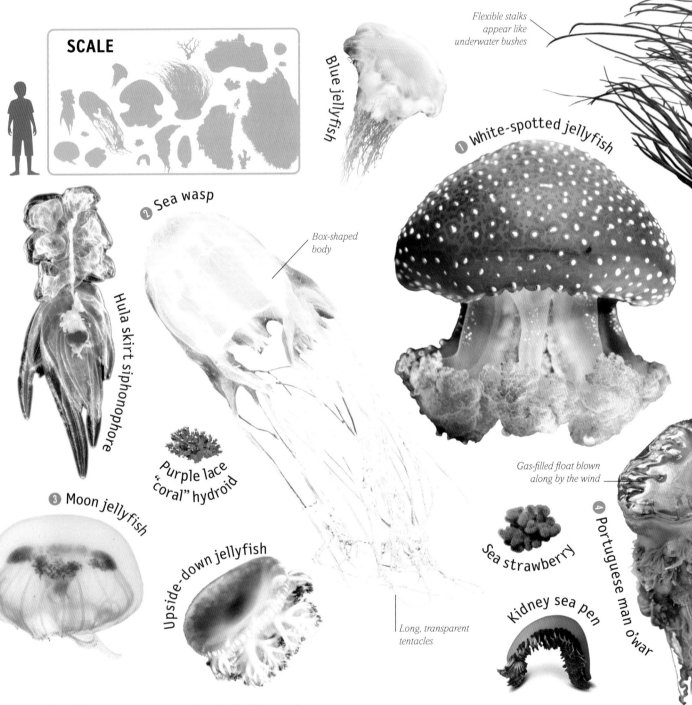

Flexible stalks appear like underwater bushes

SCALE

Blue jellyfish

White-spotted jellyfish 1

Sea wasp 2

Box-shaped body

Hula skirt siphonophore

Purple lace "coral" hydroid

Moon jellyfish 3

Upside-down jellyfish

Long, transparent tentacles

Gas-filled float blown along by the wind

Sea strawberry

Kidney sea pen

Portuguese man o'war 4

Armed with stinging tentacles, jellyfish and their relatives catch and kill prey. All of them are soft-bodied, although many corals protect themselves by building hard cases or tubes. Most kinds, including the **white-spotted jellyfish** 1, have mild venom, but the deadly **sea wasp** 2 from Australia and Southeast Asia can kill humans who brush against its tentacles. The poison acts within seconds, and stings continue to work even when the tentacles are pulled away. The **moon jellyfish** 3 lives close to coasts all over the world. It is quite compact, but the **Portuguese man o'war** 4 has tentacles up to 50 m (164 ft) long, almost the length of four buses. Its powerful venom makes it nearly as dangerous as the sea wasp. The **red coral** 5 has a brightly coloured skeleton, which is sometimes made into

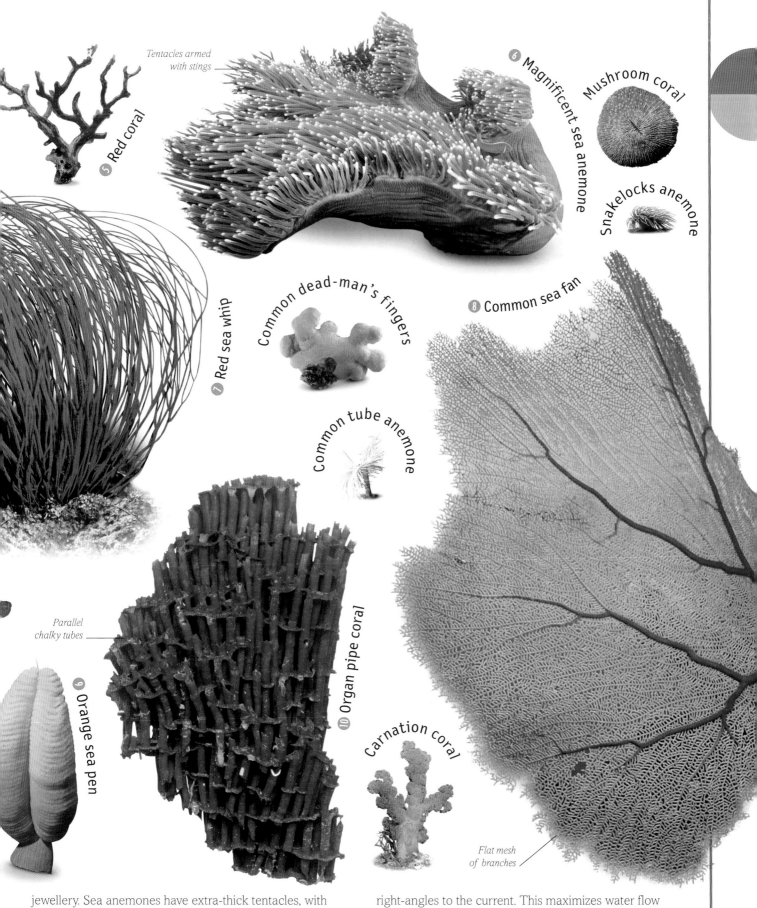

Tentacles armed with stings

⑤ Red coral

⑥ Magnificent sea anemone

Mushroom coral

Snakelocks anemone

⑦ Red sea whip

Common dead-man's fingers

⑧ Common sea fan

Common tube anemone

Parallel chalky tubes

⑩ Organ pipe coral

⑨ Orange sea pen

Carnation coral

Flat mesh of branches

jewellery. Sea anemones have extra-thick tentacles, with stings that work like harpoons. The **magnificent sea anemone** ⑥ is one of the biggest, growing up to 1 m (3 ft) wide. It lives on coral reefs and its tentacles often shelter brightly coloured clownfish, which are immune to its stings. The **red sea whip** ⑦ has thin stalks that bend in the current, while the **common sea fan** ⑧ has large flaps held at right-angles to the current. This maximizes water flow towards the sea fan and allows it to get the most food. The **orange sea pen** ⑨ has two food-collecting lobes and a swollen "root" that anchors it in the seabed. When touched, it vanishes into a burrow in the sand. The **organ pipe coral** ⑩ gets its name from its bright red, pipe-shaped tubes. It is found in shallow waters in the Indian and Pacific Oceans.

PACIFIC SEA NETTLE

With their soft, golden bells and fine, trailing tentacles, these jellyfish look harmless. But they are carnivores. Their tentacles are equipped with millions of tiny barbs which inject poison into anything they touch. The venom paralyzes prey, which is fed into a mouth under the sea nettle's bell. Although it can give humans a painful sting, this jellyfish is rarely dangerous to us.

Size ❯ Bell up to 45 cm (18 in) across; tentacles and arms up to 4.6 m (15 ft) long **Habitat ❯** Surface waters of the Pacific Ocean in autumn and winter, deeper waters in spring and summer. **Distribution ❯** West coast of Canada, the USA, and Mexico. Also found around Japan. **Diet ❯** Small fish, crustaceans, and other jellyfish. **Breeding ❯** Eggs hatch into larvae. These grow into stationary structures called polyps, from which new jellyfish grow. **Lifespan ❯** Up to a year in the wild and up to 18 months in captivity. **Predators ❯** Sea turtles and fish. **Conservation status ❯** The species is not under threat. In fact, in some areas they swarm in large numbers.

Worms

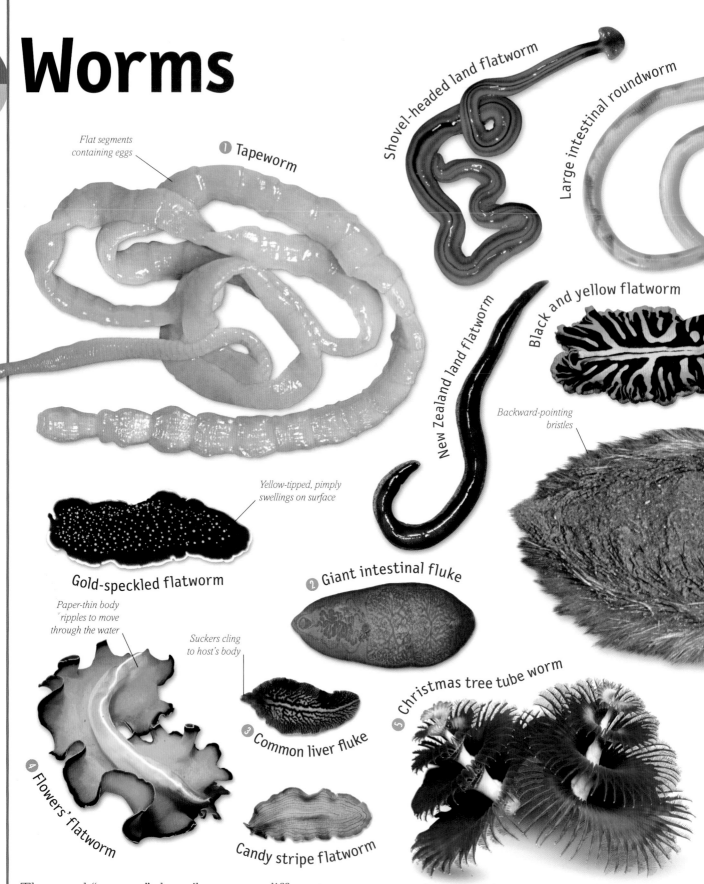

Flat segments containing eggs

1 Tapeworm

Shovel-headed land flatworm

Large intestinal roundworm

Black and yellow flatworm

New Zealand land flatworm

Backward-pointing bristles

Yellow-tipped, pimply swellings on surface

Gold-speckled flatworm

Paper-thin body ripples to move through the water

Suckers cling to host's body

2 Giant intestinal fluke

3 Common liver fluke

5 Christmas tree tube worm

4 Flowers' flatworm

Candy stripe flatworm

The word "worms" describes many different kinds of creatures. Most of them have flat or round bodies with a head and tail. While some are smaller than a full stop, worms also include the world's longest and skinniest animals, stretching further than an Olympic-size swimming pool. Worms usually live in water or wet places, but many are parasites of other creatures. **Tapeworms 1** feed inside the intestines of animals such as cats, pigs, and humans, and can grow to many metres in length. Several leaf-shaped flatworms, such as the **giant intestinal fluke 2** and **liver fluke 3**, also infect people, sometimes causing serious diseases and even death. Fortunately, most other worms are harmless, although their bright colours warn predators that they have a nasty taste. **Flowers' flatworm 4** lives on coral reefs and ripples

SCALE

⑥ Southern African velvet worm

⑦ Caribbean velvet worm

Sea cucumber scale worm

Tiger worm

Food-collecting tentacles

Pacific featherduster worm

⑧ Lugworm

Stream flatworm

Segmented body

⑨ Sea mouse

⑩ Common earthworm

⑪ Fire worm

⑫ King ragworm

Bristly legs

Poisonous bristles used for defence and movement

its body as it swims. The **Christmas tree tube worm** ⑤ stays in the safety of a burrow. It collects food with a spiral tuft of tentacles, which instantly fold up and disappear if a predator comes nearby. **Southern African velvet worms** ⑥ and **Caribbean velvet worms** ⑦ have short, stumpy legs. They creep along the forest floor, and capture their prey by spraying it with sticky threads. **Lugworms** ⑧ live in burrows on beaches and mud-flats. The **sea mouse** ⑨ has a bristly body for digging through sand. Best known of all worms, the **common earthworm** ⑩ helps to make the soil fertile by burrowing through it and eating dead leaves and other waste. The **fire worm** ⑪ has poisonous bristles that help it to crawl over rocks and coral reefs. The **king ragworm** ⑫ eats seaweed and carrion using its two pincer-like teeth.

Molluscs

Pebbles in spiral of shell

1 Sunburst carrier shell

2 Tiger cowrie shell

Dog whelk shell

Shell is covered by skin when cowrie is active

Fool's cap

3 Precious wentletrap shell

Prickly Pacific drupe

Trumpet triton shell **5**

4 Pink conch shell

Tightly coiled spiral

Common northern whelk shell

Banded tulip shell

Poli's necklace shell

Tent olive shell

Slit-shaped opening

Molluscs are amazingly varied animals, ranging from fast-moving squid, to clams, slugs, and snails. Most of them live in water and have shells. Clams and their relatives have two-part shells joined by a hinge. If danger strikes, the shell snaps shut, protecting the animal inside. Snails and their relatives have spiral shells. Like clam shells, they keep growing, so their owners never have to move

house. The **sunburst carrier** **1**, a sea snail, fastens pebbles to its shell, using them as camouflage. The **tiger cowrie** **2** has an egg-shaped shell with a beautiful pattern and glossy sheen. The **precious wentletrap** **3** has a ribbed shell. It preys on anemones and corals, using cutting jaws. Found in tropical oceans, the **pink conch** **4** and **trumpet triton** **5** are two of the largest sea snails. The pink conch grazes on

6 Channelled apple snail

7 Common mussel

Noah's ark

European bittersweet

8 Common pelican's foot shell

Long tentacles

9 Edible oyster shell

Great screw shell

West Indian worm shell

Cat's tongue oyster shell

10 Great scallop shell

Spired shell

Subulate auger shell

Shell covered in spines

seagrass and seaweed, while the triton is a predator, attacking starfish and other slow-moving prey. It hunts at night and paralyzes its victims with poisonous saliva before beginning to feed. Like most apple snails, the **channelled apple snail 6** has gills, and lives in fresh water. The **common mussel 7** lives just below the waterline on rocky shores, using its gills to filter out small particles of food. The **common pelican's foot 8** creeps across mud and sand on the seabed. Its shell has extensions that resemble webbed feet. The **edible oyster 9** and the **great scallop 10** are often harvested to eat. Mussels and oysters glue themselves to rocks using sticky threads. Scallops lie on the seabed. If a predator tries to creep up on them, they swim away by clapping their shells open and shut.

SCALE

Chalky, grit-covered tube

⑪ Philippine watering pot

Giant top shell

⑫ Red abalone shell

⑬ Common limpet

⑭ Black-margined sea slug

⑮ Varicose sea slug

Variable neon sea slug

⑯ Spanish dancer

Common sea angel

Gills for breathing

Red callista

Opalescent sea slug

Some molluscs, such as the **Philippine watering pot** ⑪, do not need to move, because they sieve their food out of the water. But many others, including the **red abalone** ⑫, creep about on a muscle-packed sucker that works like a foot. The red abalone grazes on algae, and its grip is incredibly strong. When threatened, it clamps its shell to the rock and is almost impossible to dislodge. The

common limpet ⑬ is much smaller, but just as tough. It clings to wave-battered rocks and can withstand the fiercest winter storms. Sea slugs, or nudibranchs, have a foot but no shell. They are famous for their brilliant colours. Many kinds, such as the **black-margined sea slug** ⑭, have a tuft of gills on their backs and a pair of tentacles that look like miniature horns. The black-margined sea slug feeds on sponges. So do

Great ramshorn snail

Pacific banana slug 🔟

European black slug 🔞

This species has black or orange skin

West African tellin

Brown garden snail

Silver mouth turban shell

Giant African snail 🔟

Sword razor clam shell

Spotted sea hare

Royal comb venus

Common piddock

Growth rings

🔟 Swan mussel

Soft shell clam

🔟 Fluted giant clam

the **varicose sea slug** 🔟 and the **Spanish dancer** 🔟, a giant sea slug that swims by rippling its body, making it look like a dancer wearing a skirt. Molluscs are also common on land, particularly in damp areas. The **Pacific banana slug** 🔟 and the **European black slug** 🔞 live in cool climates but the **giant African snail** 🔟 is a tropical species that has become a major pest in warm parts of the world because of its large appetite and fast breeding. Back in the water, clams are molluscs with hinged shells. A few, such as the **swan mussel** 🔟, grow in rivers and streams, but most, including the **fluted giant clam** 🔟, live in the sea. Like its big brother the giant clam, it contains microscopic algae that live in its flesh. These algae produce nutrients, which contribute to the clam's food supply.

GIANT CLAM
The giant clam is the world's heaviest shelled animal, and possibly the largest species that has ever lived. It has a huge, thick shell formed of two parts, with a deeply folded edge. The edges of the inner body, or mantle, are often a beautiful iridescent blue-green or gold, and can be seen when the shell opens to feed. It is a myth that a giant clam can catch and swallow people, because a clam will only close, slowly, if it is attacked.

Size > Shell up to 1.5 m (5 ft) long **Weight >** Up to 200 kg (440 lb) **Habitat >** The clams anchor themselves on sand or coral rubble in reefs or in lagoons. **Distribution >** Tropical areas of the Indian and western Pacific Oceans and South China Sea. **Diet >** Giant clams filter plankton out of the sea using their gills. They also get nutrients from plant-like algae called zooxanthellae that live inside their mantle tissues. **Breeding >** Giant clams expel sperm and eggs into the ocean. The eggs develop into larvae called veligers, which swim freely and hunt for food. **Predators >** Sea stars, snails, some fish, and humans. **Conservation status >** Vulnerable due to harvesting for food and the aquarium trade.

Squid, octopuses, and cuttlefish

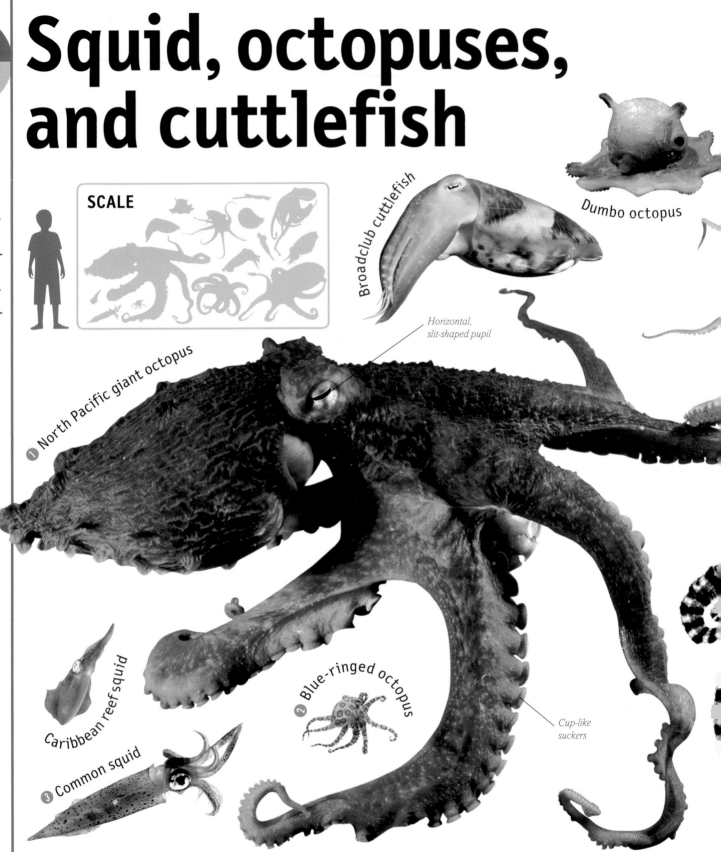

SCALE

Broadclub cuttlefish

Dumbo octopus

① North Pacific giant octopus

Horizontal, slit-shaped pupil

Caribbean reef squid

② Blue-ringed octopus

③ Common squid

Cup-like suckers

Unlike other molluscs, squid and their relatives are fast-moving hunters with keen senses and big brains. Octopuses have eight arms covered in suckers. Squid and cuttlefish also have eight arms, plus two long tentacles which shoot out to catch their prey. Many of these animals can change colour in seconds, helping them to hide. The **North Pacific giant octopus** ① hunts on the seabed. Like many octopuses, it can squirt clouds of black pigment into the water to confuse predators. Fully spread out, its legs can measure over 4 m (13 ft) from tip to tip. Far smaller, but much more dangerous, the **blue-ringed octopus** ② has a highly toxic bite. It can kill humans, although it usually swims away. The **common squid** ③ has a streamlined body with prominent side fins, and lives in the open sea. Like other squid, it zooms

64

Prey-snatching
tentacles

④ Whip-lash squid

Day octopus

⑥ Atlantic octopus

⑤ Chambered nautilus

Bigfin reef squid

⑧ Common cuttlefish

⑦ Australian giant cuttlefish

⑨ Mimic octopus

Long,
muscular arms

Common octopus

backwards by sucking in water and squirting it out in a jet. Jet propulsion is also important for octopuses when they need to make a quick getaway. The **whip-lash squid** ④ hovers in deep water, waiting for prey with its long tentacles extended. The **chambered nautilus** ⑤ has a spiral shell and about 90 tentacles which tightly grip its prey. Mostly found in shallow waters, the **Atlantic octopus** ⑥ spends the daytime in rocky

lairs and hunts after dark. The **Australian giant cuttlefish** ⑦ and **common cuttlefish** ⑧ cruise over the shallow seabed looking for crabs and other prey. The extraordinary **mimic octopus** ⑨ is one of the few octopuses that hunt while the sun is up. As well as changing colour, it can disguise itself to resemble more than a dozen different animals, making it look more dangerous than it really is.

Starfish, urchins, and sea cucumbers

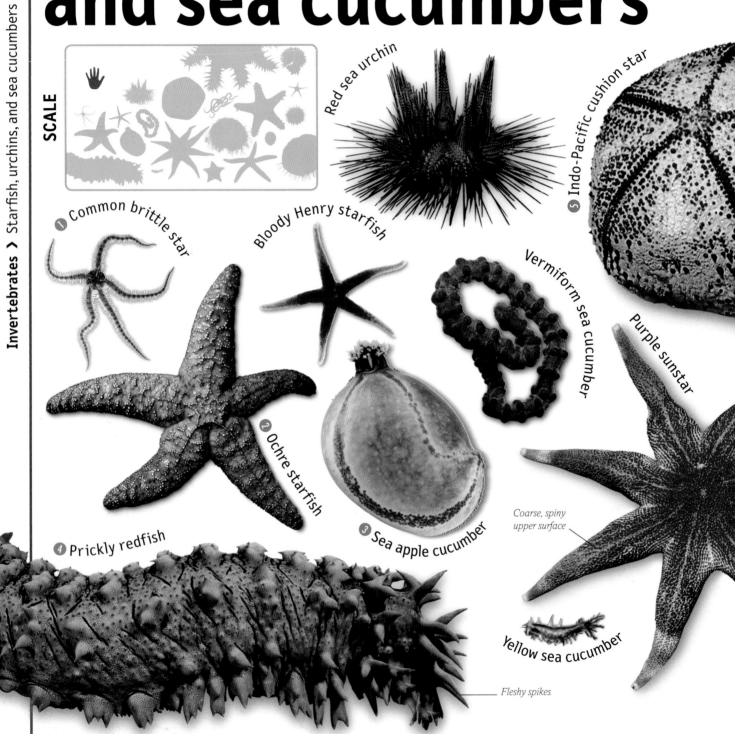

SCALE

Red sea urchin

Indo-Pacific cushion star

① Common brittle star

Bloody Henry starfish

Vermiform sea cucumber

Purple sunstar

② Ochre starfish

③ Sea apple cucumber

Coarse, spiny upper surface

④ Prickly redfish

Yellow sea cucumber

Fleshy spikes

Found only in salt water, starfish and their relatives are unique in many ways. Most of these slow-moving creatures have five arms branching out from the centre of their bodies. They have skeletons or cases made of hard, chalky plates. The **common brittle star** ① moves by snaking its arms, but most animals in this group move around using hundreds of little tubes, which act as feet.

The **ochre starfish** ② feeds on mussels and other molluscs, using the tubes to grip its prey. Sea cucumbers collect food using a ring of tentacles around their mouths. The **sea apple cucumber** ③ is a highly poisonous reef-dweller. It has bright colours warning predators not to attack. Other species, such as the sausage-shaped **prickly redfish** ④, are coloured to match the sand. The **Indo-Pacific cushion star** ⑤ becomes

6 Crown of thorns starfish

Yellow feather star

Rows of red tubercles

Short-spined brittle star

Venomous spines for protection

Red general starfish

Icon starfish

7 Edible sea urchin

8 Purple urchin

Fire urchin

9 Sea potato

Red cushion star

Smooth, spineless surface

10 Blue starfish

Short, venomous spines can deliver painful sting

short-armed as it gets bigger, eventually maturing into a dumpy cushion shape. It often grazes on coral. The notorious **crown of thorns starfish** 6 is a large species with venomous, thorny arms. It can devastate reefs with its voracious appetite for coral. Sea urchins creep over rocks and reefs, scraping up food with their downward-pointing mouths. The **edible sea urchin** 7 has short spines and a rounded

case, while the **purple urchin** 8 has extra-long spines that easily break off. The **sea potato** 9 burrows into seabed mud, and has bristly spines and a streamlined shape. Sea urchins use their spines for self-defence, while sea cucumbers squirt out a mass of sticky threads. The **blue starfish** 10 and its relatives have a different kind of protection: if any of their legs are bitten off, they slowly grow back.

67

Centipedes and millipedes

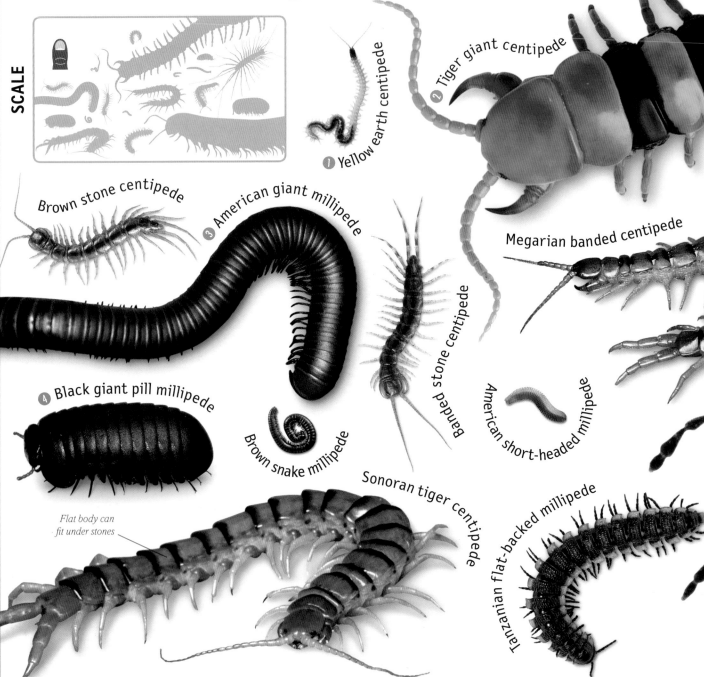

Eastern flat-backed millipede

SCALE

① Yellow earth centipede

② Tiger giant centipede

Brown stone centipede

③ American giant millipede

Megarian banded centipede

Banded stone centipede

American short-headed millipede

④ Black giant pill millipede

Brown snake millipede

Sonoran tiger centipede

Tanzanian flat-backed millipede

Flat body can fit under stones

Centipedes and millipedes belong to a group of animals called arthropods, which have legs with joints and a hard body case. Millipedes are slow-moving vegetarians, but centipedes are agile predators, with keen senses and poisonous fangs. **Yellow earth centipedes** ① hunt underground. With their bendy bodies and short legs, they squeeze between particles of soil. If they are dug

up, they quickly wriggle away. The Indian **tiger giant centipede** ② is one of the biggest, growing up to 25 cm (10 in) long. It can easily kill small rodents and can give humans an extremely painful bite. Centipedes have two legs on each segment of their body, but millipedes have four. The **American giant millipede** ③ can have more than 200 legs. Like other millipedes, it grows extra pairs every time it moults,

68

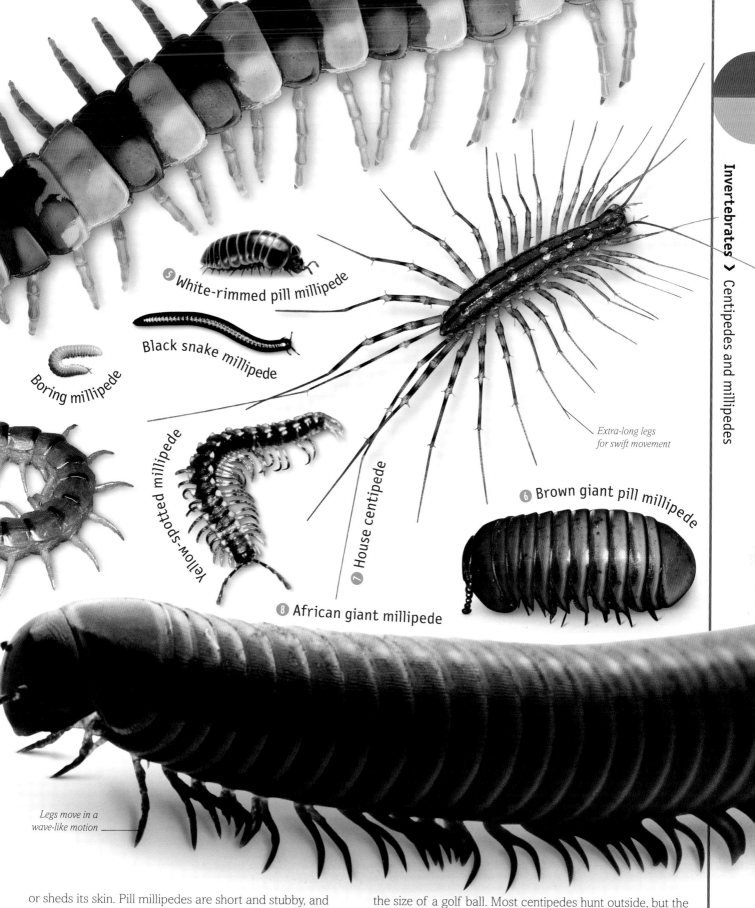

⑤ White-rimmed pill millipede

Black snake millipede

Boring millipede

Yellow-spotted millipede

Extra-long legs for swift movement

⑦ House centipede

⑥ Brown giant pill millipede

⑧ African giant millipede

Legs move in a wave-like motion

or sheds its skin. Pill millipedes are short and stubby, and often have 50 legs or fewer. They get their name because they can tuck in their legs and roll up into a ball. The **black giant pill millipede** ④ comes from Madagascar, while the **white-rimmed pill millipede** ⑤ is found in Europe. The **brown giant pill millipede** ⑥ from the forests of Borneo is one of the biggest pill millipedes. Fully rolled up, it is about

the size of a golf ball. Most centipedes hunt outside, but the **house centipede** ⑦ often comes indoors. With its long legs, it is an amazingly fast sprinter, scuttling up walls and ceilings to catch spiders and other prey. With over 300 legs, the **African giant millipede** ⑧ is one of the largest millipedes. If threatened by predators, it releases a foul-smelling liquid to persuade them it is not nice to eat.

Spiders and relatives

American sun spider

Domestic huntsman spider

❶ Chaco tarantula

Stinging hairs can be fired at enemies

Horned harvestman

❷ Marbled orb weaver

❸ Goldenrod crab spider

❹ Audouin's trapdoor spider

European wolf spider

Say's harvestman

Pear-shaped body and small head

Ladybird spider

Whip spider

Long front legs used as feelers

SCALE

Many people are scared of spiders, but the world would be very different without them. These eight-legged animals are super-efficient hunters. Out of many thousands, scientists have found only one kind that feeds on plants. Close relatives of spiders include sun spiders, whip spiders, and harvestmen, as well as ticks, mites, and scorpions. The **chaco tarantula** ❶ lives in a burrow by day

and comes out to feed after dark. Like all spiders, it kills its prey by injecting venom through a pair of fangs. The **marbled orb weaver** ❷ catches flying insects by spinning wheel-shaped webs, but the **goldenrod crab spider** ❸ sits on top of flowers where it ambushes bees and butterflies. **Audouin's trapdoor spider** ❹ lurks in a silk-lined burrow, equipped with trip-lines and a camouflaged lid. If anything

Legs end in retractable claws

5 Mexican red-kneed tarantula

6 Northern black widow

7 Daddy long-legs spider

European garden spider

Eight small eyes

St. Andrews cross spider

8 Giant house spider

Jumping spider

9 Raft spider

Elegant jumping spider

Brown jumping spider

10 Goliath tarantula

touches a trip-line, the spider flings open the lid and grabs its prey. The **Mexican red-kneed tarantula** 5 is a forest-dwelling spider, and a popular pet. It grows slowly and can live for more than 20 years. The **northern black widow** 6 from North America is far smaller but more dangerous. Females are much bigger than males, and they can give people a fatal bite. The **daddy long-legs spider** 7 often lives indoors, and so does the **giant house spider** 8, a species that spins funnel-shaped webs. **Raft spiders** 9 lie in wait by the edges of ponds and pools where they catch tadpoles and small fish. The enormous **goliath tarantula** 10 from South America eats insects, rodents, frogs, and even bats. It is one of the biggest spiders in the world, with a leg span as big as a dinner plate.

71

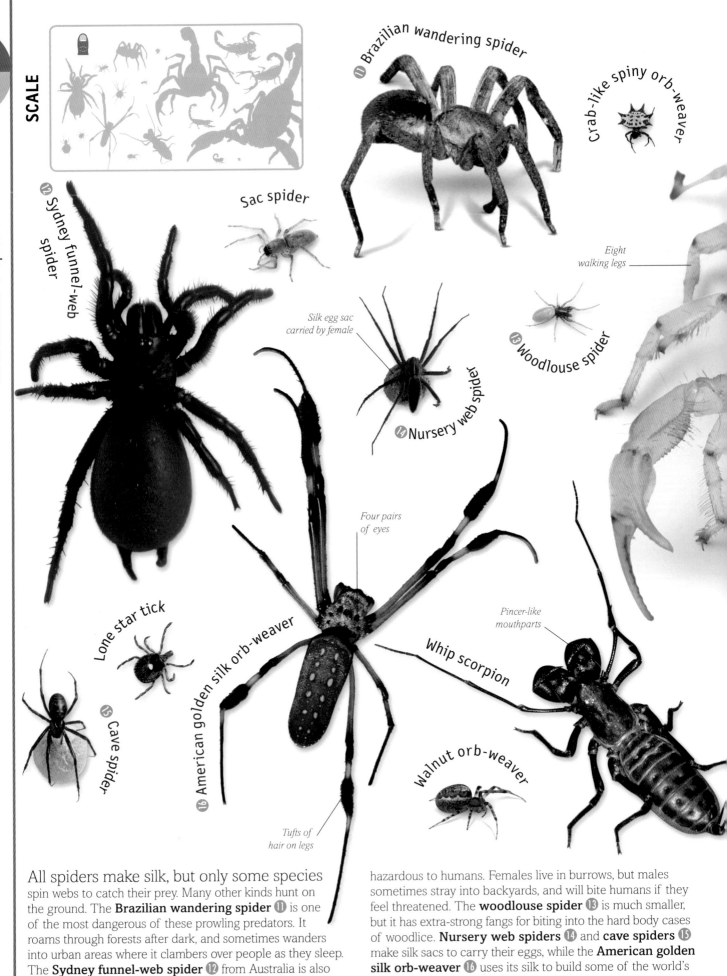

SCALE

⓫ Brazilian wandering spider

Crab-like spiny orb-weaver

Sac spider

⓬ Sydney funnel-web spider

Eight walking legs

Silk egg sac carried by female

⓭ Woodlouse spider

⓮ Nursery web spider

Four pairs of eyes

Pincer-like mouthparts

Lone star tick

Whip scorpion

⓯ Cave spider

⓰ American golden silk orb-weaver

Walnut orb-weaver

Tufts of hair on legs

All spiders make silk, but only some species spin webs to catch their prey. Many other kinds hunt on the ground. The **Brazilian wandering spider** ⓫ is one of the most dangerous of these prowling predators. It roams through forests after dark, and sometimes wanders into urban areas where it clambers over people as they sleep. The **Sydney funnel-web spider** ⓬ from Australia is also

hazardous to humans. Females live in burrows, but males sometimes stray into backyards, and will bite humans if they feel threatened. The **woodlouse spider** ⓭ is much smaller, but it has extra-strong fangs for biting into the hard body cases of woodlice. **Nursery web spiders** ⓮ and **cave spiders** ⓯ make silk sacs to carry their eggs, while the **American golden silk orb-weaver** ⓰ uses its silk to build some of the world's

⑰ Giant desert hairy scorpion

Chilean burrowing scorpion

Sting raised to threaten enemies

Yellow thick-tail scorpion ⑱

⑳ Imperial scorpion

Pincers grip prey

⑲ Gold scorpion

Pincers covered with sensitive hairs

Common European scorpion

Red velvet mite

biggest webs. Shaped like cartwheels, and more than 1 m (3 ft) across, the webs are strong enough to catch hummingbirds and even frogs. Like spiders, scorpions have eight legs, but they also have a pair of pincers and a poisonous sting in their tails. The **giant desert hairy scorpion** ⑰ is the largest kind in North America. Like other scorpions, it uses its pincers to tear apart its prey, while its sting is mainly for self-defence. The

yellow thick-tail scorpion ⑱ is smaller, but its venom is much more powerful. It comes from the Sahara Desert and the Middle East. **Gold scorpions** ⑲ also live in the same part of the world, but the **imperial scorpion** ⑳ is a forest species from tropical Africa. It is one of the biggest scorpions, measuring up to 25 cm (10 in) long. Although it looks menacing, its sting is not much stronger than that of a wasp.

73

SEA SPIDER
Sea spiders belong belong to a group of marine animals called Pantopoda, meaning "all legs". Their legs are so long compared to their tiny bodies that they have to keep some of their internal organs inside them. This strikingly coloured yellow-kneed sea spider comes from coral reefs off the coast of Australia. It is only a few centimetres across, but larger specimens can grow up to 90 cm (35 in) from tip to tip.

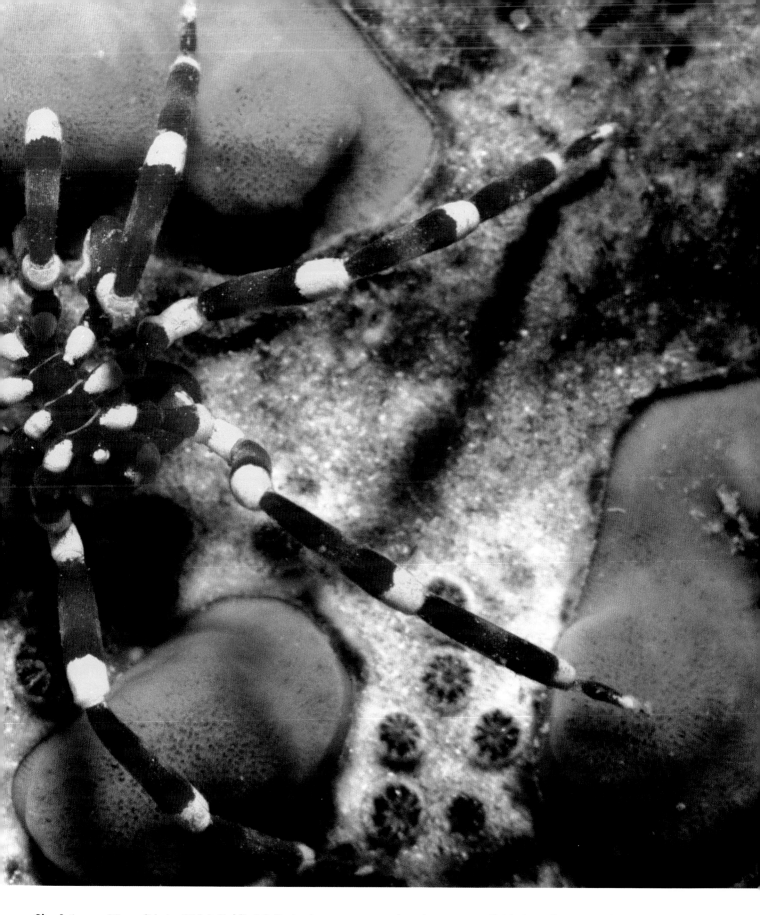

Size ❯ 1 mm–90 cm (¹⁄₂₅ in–35 in) **Habitat ❯** Seabed; smaller species live in shallow water, while larger sea spiders live in the deep waters of the Antarctic Ocean. **Distribution ❯** Seas and oceans worldwide **Diet ❯** Soft-bodied animals such as sea sponges, anemones, and coral polyps. The sea spider uses its sucking mouthpart, or proboscis, to extract fluids from the prey, or breaks off pieces and puts them in its mouth. **Breeding ❯** The eggs hatch into larvae. In most species the larvae float around freely as they grow. In some they live on their father's front legs, while in others the larvae live as parasites in animals such as coral polyps or clams.

Crustaceans

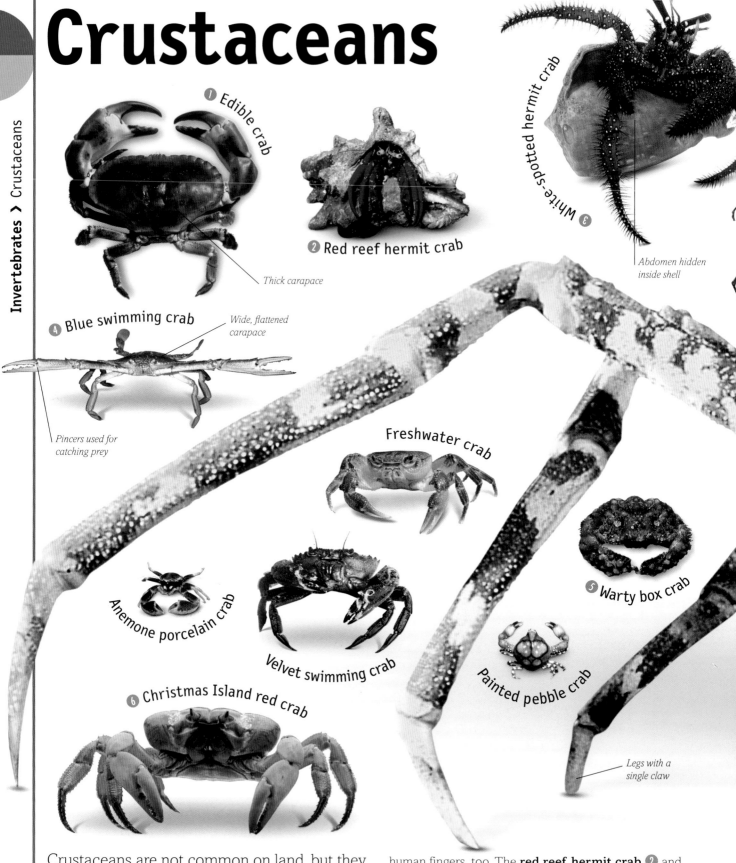

① Edible crab

Thick carapace

② Red reef hermit crab

③ White-spotted hermit crab

Abdomen hidden inside shell

④ Blue swimming crab

Wide, flattened carapace

Pincers used for catching prey

Freshwater crab

Anemone porcelain crab

Velvet swimming crab

⑤ Warty box crab

Painted pebble crab

Legs with a single claw

⑥ Christmas Island red crab

Crustaceans are not common on land, but they flourish in fresh water and the sea. They include lobsters, shrimps, and prawns, and also hundreds of different kinds of crabs. Some crustaceans swim in gigantic swarms, but crabs usually roam the seabed or scuttle over the shore. The **edible crab ①** has an extra-tough shield, or carapace. Its powerful pincers can crack open mollusc shells, and crush human fingers, too. The **red reef hermit crab ②** and **white-spotted hermit crab ③** have small pincers, and live in shells borrowed from other animals. Like other hermit crabs, they change shells as they grow. Each time these crabs move home, they carefully check their new shell to make sure that it is exactly the right fit. **Blue swimming crabs ④** have back legs that work like paddles. These crabs like

76

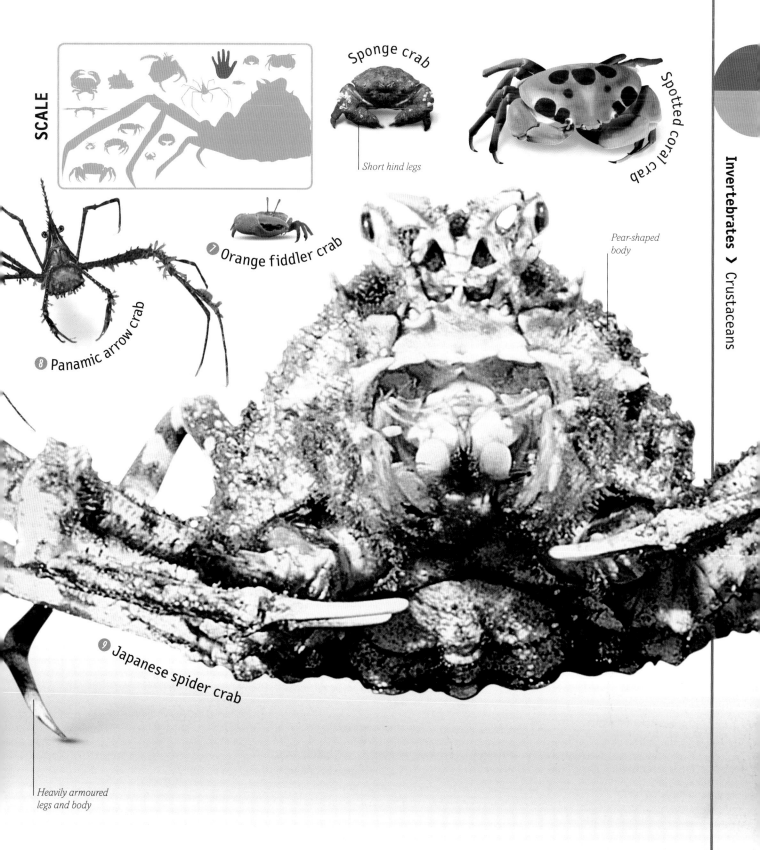

SCALE

Sponge crab

Short hind legs

Spotted coral crab

Pear-shaped body

7 Orange fiddler crab

8 Panamic arrow crab

9 Japanese spider crab

Heavily armoured legs and body

spending time on sandy or muddy coastlines. **Warty box crabs 5** burrow in seabed sand. They shield their faces with their claws, giving them the alternative name, the shame-face crab. **Christmas Island red crabs 6** live in tropical forests, surrounded by the Indian Ocean. During the breeding season, millions of them emerge from the forest and march to the coast, where they mate and lay their eggs.

Orange fiddler crabs 7 make burrows in mangrove swamps. Males have a tiny claw for feeding and a giant one for signalling to females across the mud. The **Panamic arrow crab 8** lives on reefs, while the **Japanese spider crab 9** prowls the seabed. Measuring up to 4 m (13 ft) across, this amazingly leggy animal is the world's biggest crustacean, with a lifespan of up to 100 years.

⑩ Norway lobster

Two pairs of antennae, or feelers

Red, thread-like antennae

⑪ Blue-striped squat lobster

Flexible body ending in a broad tail fan

White-clawed crayfish

Long pincers

⑫ Reef lobster

Aesop shrimp

⑬ Stripe-leg spiny lobster

Black "tiger" stripes

Tiger prawn

Paddles at end of abdomen

⑭ Antarctic krill

⑮ Sculptured slipper lobster

Regal slipper lobster

Giant acorn barnacle

Lobsters, shrimps, and prawns are crustaceans with long bodies and lots of legs. The **Norway lobster** ⑩ lives in a burrow, and feeds at night on live animals and dead remains. **Blue-striped squat lobsters** ⑪ are close relatives of crabs. Like other squat lobsters, they have 10 legs, but the last leg pair is small, and tucked away under their tails. **Reef lobsters** ⑫ are brightly coloured, which makes them popular aquarium pets. The **stripe-leg spiny lobster** ⑬ has extra-long antennae that can make a creaky, clicking sound to scare predators away. If it is cornered, it swims backwards at high speed. **Antarctic krill** ⑭ live in the icy Southern Ocean, in swarms that can stretch for kilometres in every direction. These finger-sized crustaceans are a vital food for penguins, seals, and whales, including the blue whale, which can

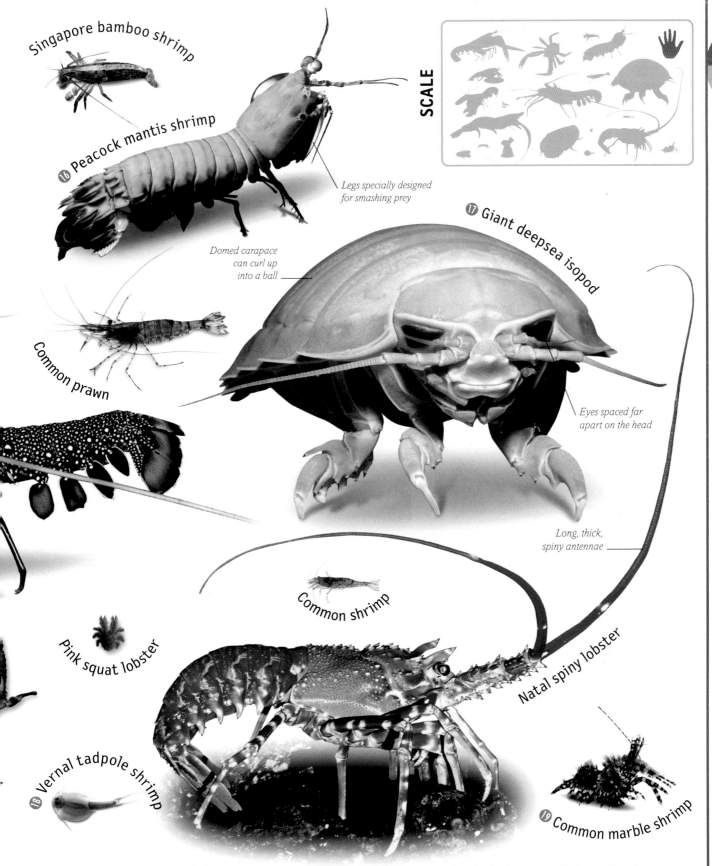

Singapore bamboo shrimp

16 Peacock mantis shrimp

Legs specially designed for smashing prey

Common prawn

Pink squat lobster

Common shrimp

18 Vernal tadpole shrimp

17 Giant deepsea isopod

Domed carapace can curl up into a ball

Eyes spaced far apart on the head

Long, thick, spiny antennae

Natal spiny lobster

19 Common marble shrimp

swallow more than 4 tonnes of krill per day. The **sculptured slipper lobster 15** has a rounded shape, and blends in against seabed sand. The **peacock mantis shrimp 16** is a predator with a knockout punch. Using its front legs, it smashes open snail shells and crabs, and can even shatter the glass of aquariums. The **giant deepsea isopod 17** scavenges food on the sea floor, occasionally feeding on live prey. Since light is extremely faint in deep sea, this isopod has large antennae to help it feel its way around. **Vernal tadpole shrimps 18** from California breed in short-lived freshwater pools. The adult shrimp die when the pools dry up, but their eggs can survive for up to 10 years, hatching when it rains. The **common marble shrimp 19** is brown with green spots during the day, but turns red at night.

79

Insects

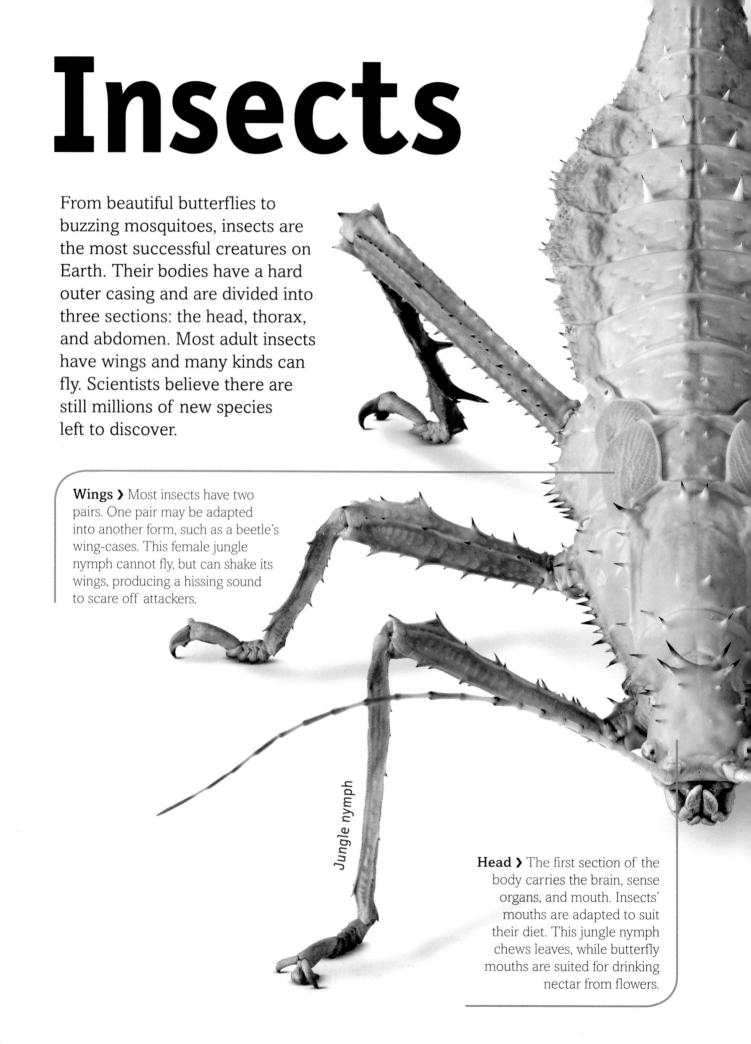

From beautiful butterflies to buzzing mosquitoes, insects are the most successful creatures on Earth. Their bodies have a hard outer casing and are divided into three sections: the head, thorax, and abdomen. Most adult insects have wings and many kinds can fly. Scientists believe there are still millions of new species left to discover.

Wings ❯ Most insects have two pairs. One pair may be adapted into another form, such as a beetle's wing-cases. This female jungle nymph cannot fly, but can shake its wings, producing a hissing sound to scare off attackers.

Jungle nymph

Head ❯ The first section of the body carries the brain, sense organs, and mouth. Insects' mouths are adapted to suit their diet. This jungle nymph chews leaves, while butterfly mouths are suited for drinking nectar from flowers.

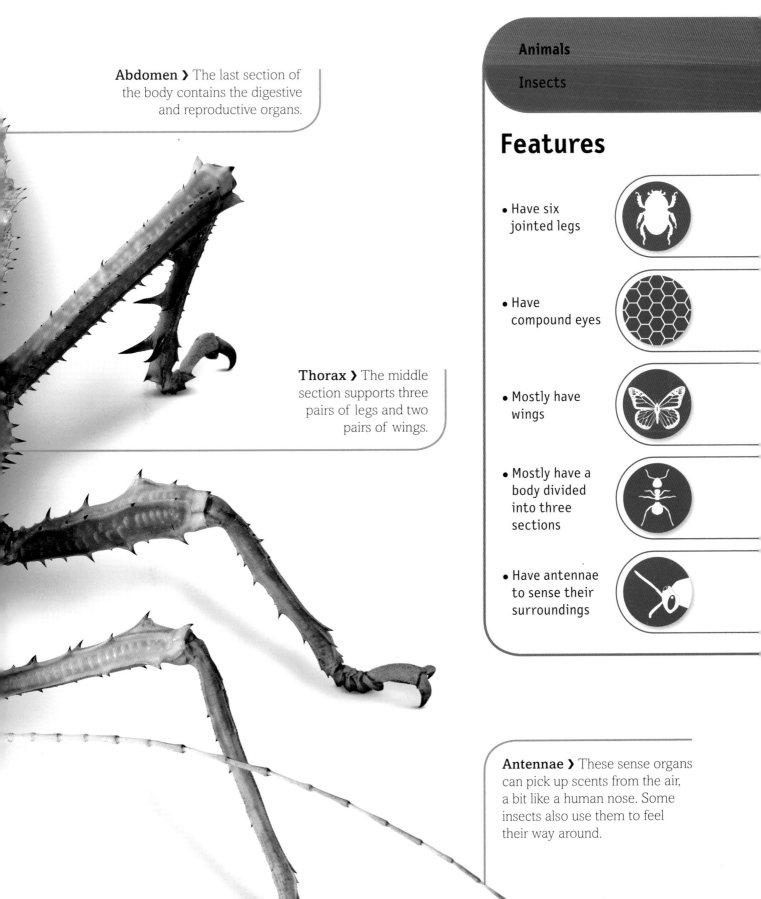

Abdomen › The last section of the body contains the digestive and reproductive organs.

Thorax › The middle section supports three pairs of legs and two pairs of wings.

Animals

Insects

Features

- Have six jointed legs

- Have compound eyes

- Mostly have wings

- Mostly have a body divided into three sections

- Have antennae to sense their surroundings

Antennae › These sense organs can pick up scents from the air, a bit like a human nose. Some insects also use them to feel their way around.

Dragonflies and damselflies

SCALE

1 Common green darner

Tetracanthagyna plagiata

Large wings for speedy flight

2 Southern hawker dragonfly

3 Illinois river cruiser

All four wings almost equal in size

Distinctive stripes on body

Green-eyed dragonfly

Club-shaped end of abdomen

Blue and black markings on male

5 Azure damselfly

4 Flame skimmer

Wingspan is larger than body length

Speeding through the air on transparent wings, dragonflies and damselflies chase insects for food. Dragonflies are robust with rounded heads, whereas damselflies are more slender with broader heads. Both have extra-large eyes for spotting anything that moves and can zoom sideways and even backwards as they close in for a kill. Their young, known as nymphs, are also hunters. They grow up underwater, and use stealth and camouflage to catch their prey. The **common green darner** 1 flies over streams in North America. Its stiff wings stick out sideways when it rests. The **southern hawker dragonfly** 2, from Europe, breeds in small ponds. It hunts away from water, and approaches people that come nearby. The **Illinois river cruiser** 3 patrols rocky streams and rivers, while the **flame skimmer** 4 prefers warm water,

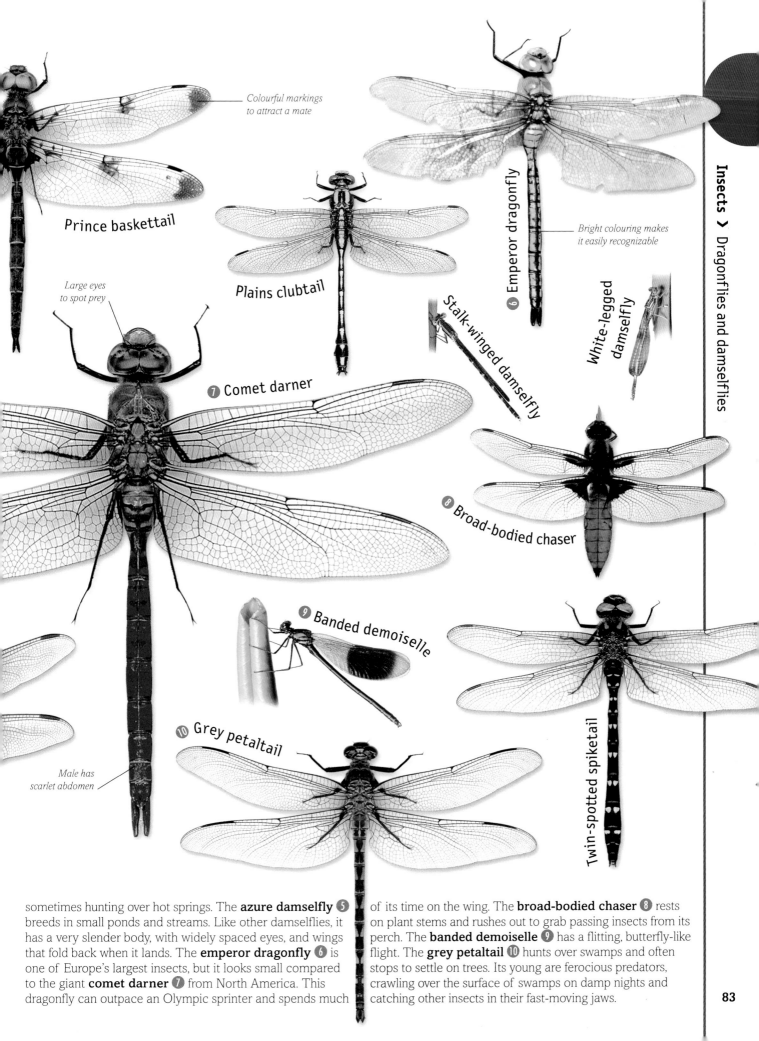

Insects > Dragonflies and damselflies

Colourful markings
to attract a mate

Prince baskettail

Large eyes
to spot prey

Plains clubtail

6 Emperor dragonfly

Bright colouring makes
it easily recognizable

White-legged
damselfly

Stalk-winged damselfly

7 Comet darner

8 Broad-bodied chaser

9 Banded demoiselle

10 Grey petaltail

Twin-spotted spiketail

Male has
scarlet abdomen

sometimes hunting over hot springs. The **azure damselfly** **5** breeds in small ponds and streams. Like other damselflies, it has a very slender body, with widely spaced eyes, and wings that fold back when it lands. The **emperor dragonfly** **6** is one of Europe's largest insects, but it looks small compared to the giant **comet darner** **7** from North America. This dragonfly can outpace an Olympic sprinter and spends much

of its time on the wing. The **broad-bodied chaser** **8** rests on plant stems and rushes out to grab passing insects from its perch. The **banded demoiselle** **9** has a flitting, butterfly-like flight. The **grey petaltail** **10** hunts over swamps and often stops to settle on trees. Its young are ferocious predators, crawling over the surface of swamps on damp nights and catching other insects in their fast-moving jaws.

83

STICK INSECT

Masters of disguise, stick insects sit quietly on tree branches, looking exactly like dead twigs or green shoots so that predators don't notice them. There are thought to be more than 3,000 species across the world, ranging from tiny leaf and twig shapes up to "branches" 55 cm (22 in) long. This stick insect from Madagascar resembles a thorny bramble shoot, a very unappetizing prospect for predators.

Size › 2.5–55 cm (1–22 in) **Weight ›** Up to 65 grams (2¼ oz)
Habitat › Rainforests and jungles. **Distribution ›** Tropical
and subtropical areas of Southeast Asia and Australia, also
Madagascar, South and Central America, and southern USA.
Some species also found in mainland Europe as well as the
British Isles. **Diet ›** Leaves of trees and shrubs and berries.

Breeding › Females lay live eggs on their own or by mating
with males. The eggs hatch into nymphs, which moult several
times as they grow into adults. **Lifespan ›** From a few months
to a few years. **Predators ›** Birds, small reptiles, and rodents.
Defences include camouflage, sharp spines, flashing wings,
hissing, or spraying bad-smelling or burning liquid.

Crickets and grasshoppers

❶ Green milkweed locust

Antennae longer than body

Speckled bush-cricket

Large eyes

❷ Desert locust

Pygmy locust

House cricket

Calliptamus italicus

❸ Foaming grasshopper

Common macrotona grasshopper

With their powerful back legs, crickets and grasshoppers are some of the best jumpers in the insect world. They are also some of the loudest, rubbing their legs or wings to make high-pitched sounds. Many live on their own, but locusts are famous for migrating in enormous swarms. The African **green milkweed locust** ❶ is one of the biggest of these insect travellers, while the **desert** **locust** ❷ holds the record for numbers. Some of its swarms contain more than 30 billion insects, which is four times the number of people on Earth. Most grasshoppers rely on camouflage for protection. The **foaming grasshopper** ❸, however, oozes poisonous froth from behind its head, while its day-glow colours warn that it is dangerous to eat. Adult grasshoppers usually have two pairs of wings, but some

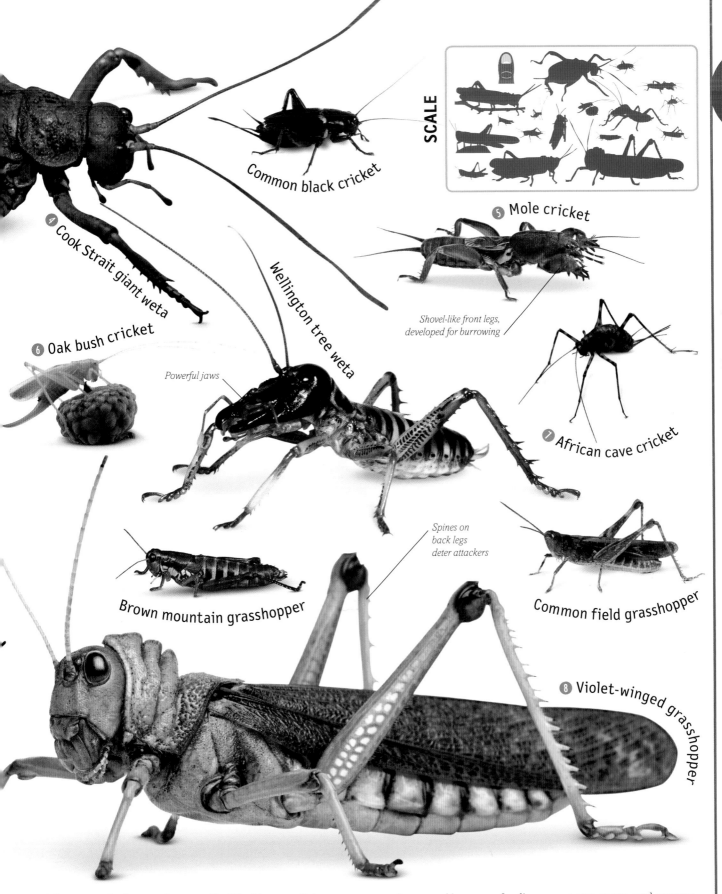

Common black cricket

④ Cook Strait giant weta

⑤ Mole cricket

Shovel-like front legs, developed for burrowing

⑥ Oak bush cricket

Wellington tree weta

Powerful jaws

⑦ African cave cricket

Spines on back legs deter attackers

Brown mountain grasshopper

Common field grasshopper

⑧ Violet-winged grasshopper

crickets are wingless and cannot fly. The biggest of these include wetas from New Zealand. The **Cook Strait giant weta** ④ is almost as large as a mouse. If it is threatened, it raises its spiny back legs over its head, making it look ready for a fight. Most crickets and grasshoppers feed on plants, but some species are predators and scavengers. Some others even feed on their own kind. The **mole cricket** ⑤ spends its life in underground burrows, feeding on worms, roots, and grasses. Like real moles, it has massive front legs that work as shovels. The **oak bush cricket** ⑥ is a hunter, while the **African cave cricket** ⑦ feeds on almost anything, from bat droppings to carrion. The huge **violet-winged grasshopper** ⑧ comes from South America. Measuring up to 12 cm (5 in) long, it is even bigger than some birds.

True bugs and treehoppers

Toad bug

① Thorn bug

Water scorpion

② Wart-headed bug

③ Common green shield bug

Nut-shaped head

⑤ Peanut-headed bug

Water measurer

④ Spittle bug

Common green capsid

Brightly coloured hindwings

Large eye spots to keep away predators

⑥ Bed bug

True bugs are a special group of insects that live in fresh water as well as on land. They have sharp mouthparts for sucking up liquids. Some feed on plant sáp, while others eat blood or fluids from their partly digested prey. Sap-sucking bugs feed in the open, and often use camouflage to hide. The **thorn bug** ❶ has an amazingly realistic spike that looks just like a thorn. Tropical species,

such as the **wart-headed bug** ❷, can be bigger than some butterflies. This bug has brightly coloured hindwings to startle enemies that get too close. The green colour of the **common green shield bug** ❸ helps it to blend in among leaves. Young **spittle bugs** ❹ shelter inside nests of foam, which protect them from hungry birds. The **peanut-headed bug** ❺, another tropical species, has large eye spots on its

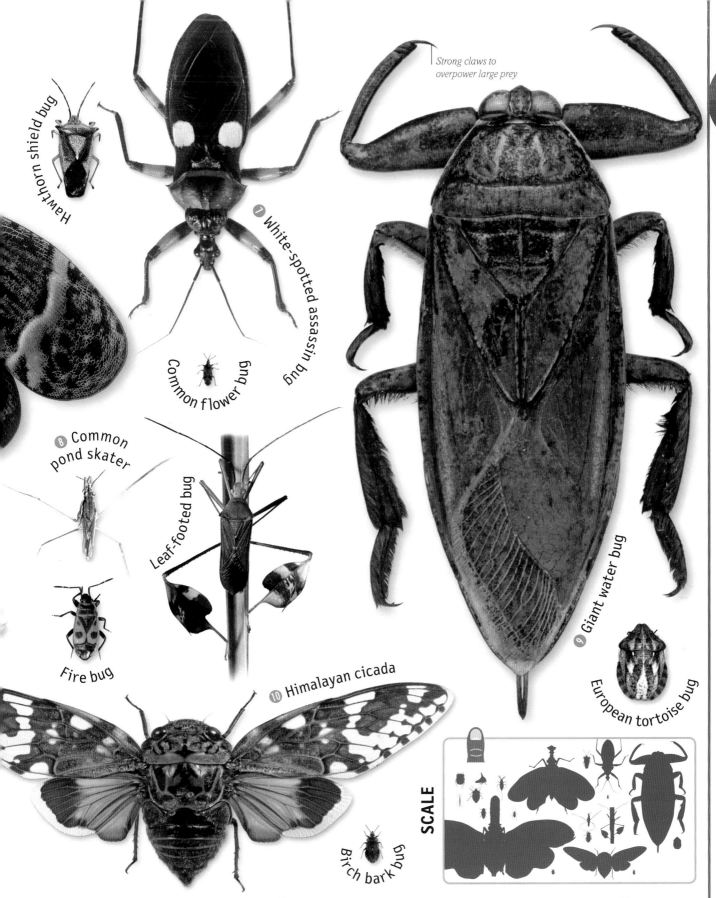

Hawthorn shield bug

❶ White-spotted assassin bug

Common flower bug

Strong claws to overpower large prey

❽ Common pond skater

Leaf-footed bug

Fire bug

❿ Himalayan cicada

❾ Giant water bug

European tortoise bug

Birch bark bug

SCALE

hindwings to confuse predators. The **bed bug** ❻ is a flightless parasite, which emerges after dark to suck human blood. Many predatory bugs ambush their prey. On land they include the **white-spotted assassin bug** ❼ and its many relatives. In fresh water, predatory bugs are even more common. Some, such as the **common pond skater** ❽, live on the water's surface, attacking other insects that crash

land. A strong swimmer, the **giant water bug** ❾ is big enough to prey on frogs and fish. It can even give humans a painful bite. Most bugs are silent, but some make amazingly loud sounds. Male **Himalayan cicadas** ❿ attract females by making a deafening courtship song. Like other cicadas, they sing when they are adult, but the rest of their lives is spent feeding on roots underground.

PRAYING MANTIS
With strange angular features and triangular heads, praying mantises look almost like creatures from another planet. They are instantly recognizable by their long, folded front legs, held up together as if in prayer. These can lash out with astonishing speed to catch hold of live prey. Some species, such as this Thai boxer praying mantis, are brightly coloured, but most blend in with their surroundings.

Size > 1.2–15 cm (½–6 in) **Weight >** up to 10 g (⅓ oz)
Habitat > Rainforests and jungles. **Distribution >** Tropical areas, especially Africa, Southeast Asia, and Australia. Also South and Central America and the southern USA. Some species are also found in Europe, Central Asia, and Japan. **Diet >** Flying insects such as moths, grasshoppers, flies, and other mantises. Females eat males after, or even during, mating. **Breeding >** Females lay hundreds of eggs in an egg case stuck to a plant or buried in the ground. Eggs hatch into nymphs. **Lifespan >** 10–12 months. **Predators >** Large birds, frogs, chameleons, snakes, bats, and monkeys. Mantises protect themselves by camouflage.

Beetles

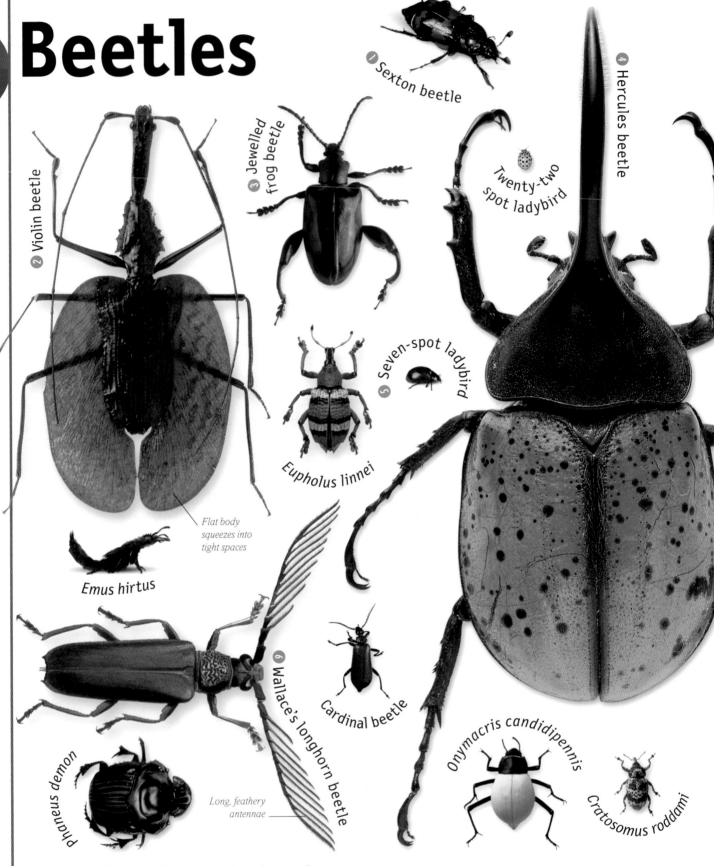

① Sexton beetle

④ Hercules beetle

③ Jewelled frog beetle

② Violin beetle

Twenty-two spot ladybird

⑤ Seven-spot ladybird

Eupholus linnei

Flat body squeezes into tight spaces

Emus hirtus

Dichaeus demon

⑥ Wallace's longhorn beetle

Long, feathery antennae

Cardinal beetle

Onymacris candidipennis

Cratosomus roddami

With around 400,000 species, beetles make up by far the largest group of insects. They start life as larvae, also known as grubs. Adults usually have two pairs of wings. Their front wings, called elytra, are specially hardened and fit over the hindwings like a case. Beetles eat a huge range of different foods. The **sexton beetle** ① buries the dead bodies of small birds and rodents such as mice. The female lays eggs in these remains, so her grubs have their own private food supply. The **violin beetle** ② squeezes its flat body under tree bark, where it feeds on other insects and snails. The grubs of the **jewelled frog beetle** ③ grow up inside plant stems. Beetles vary greatly in size. While the smallest could easily fit on the head of a pin, the biggest kinds, such as the **Hercules beetle** ④, can be more than

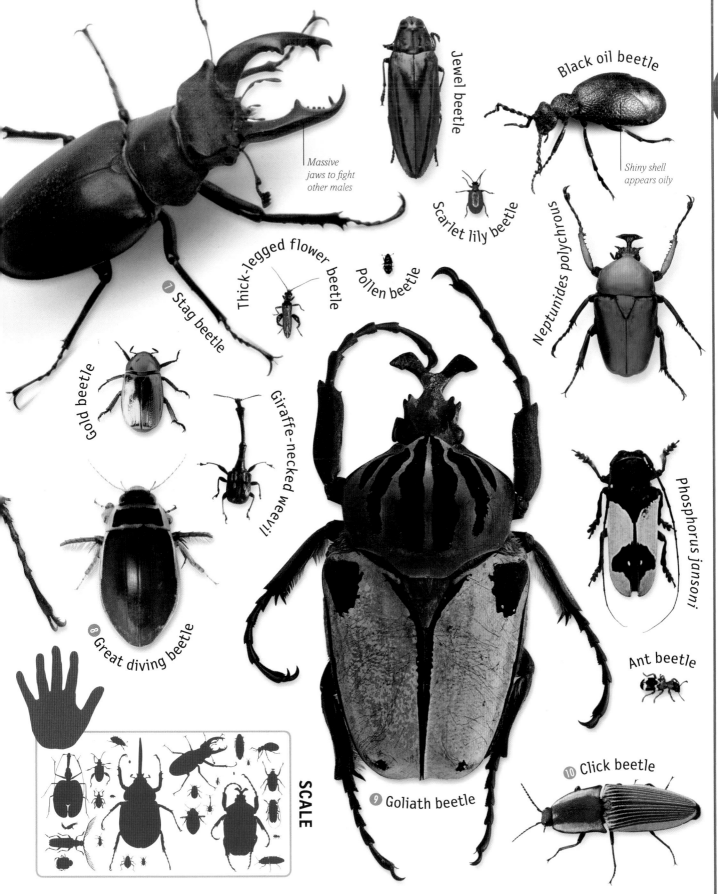

Massive jaws to fight other males

Jewel beetle

Black oil beetle

Shiny shell appears oily

Scarlet lily beetle

Neptunides polychrous

Thick-legged flower beetle

Pollen beetle

1 Stag beetle

Gold beetle

Giraffe-necked weevil

phosphorus jansoni

8 Great diving beetle

Ant beetle

SCALE

10 Click beetle

9 Goliath beetle

15 cm (6 in) long. The **seven-spot ladybird** 5 feeds on aphids, making it a useful ally for farmers and gardeners. **Wallace's longhorn beetle** 6 grubs bore into living trees, while **stag beetle** 7 grubs live in rotting wood. They stay hidden for up to six years, before turning into adults. Adult males fight with their antler-shaped jaws and the winner gets a chance to mate. The **great diving beetle** 8 is found in ponds and streams, where it swims with back legs that work like a pair of oars. It eats tadpoles and even small fish. Measuring up to 10 cm (4 in) long, the **goliath beetle** 9 is the heaviest insect in the world. Its grubs can weigh up to 100 g (3½ oz). Beneath the soil's surface, **click beetle** 10 grubs, known as wireworms, chew their way through roots. They can cause serious damage to crops.

Butterflies and moths

1 Wallich's owl moth

Adonis blue

Garden tiger

Diva moth

Male has feathery antennae

2 Queen cracker

Regent skipper

Snout moth

Australian magpie moth

3 Apollo

Oak eggar

Blue triangle

Blue band on upper side of each wing

Blue tharops

4 Madagascan sunset moth

Six-spot burnet

Coppery dysphania

5 Hercules moth

White plume moth

Cleopatra

Unlike other insects, butterflies and moths are covered with thousands of tiny scales, which create vivid patterns. Butterflies are often brightly coloured, while moths are usually drab. Most moths, including **Wallich's owl moth** 1, fly by night and use their camouflaged markings to hide during the day, but some fly by day and have eye-catching wings. Male **queen cracker** 2 butterflies click

their wings when they fly as a way of marking their territory. **Apollo** 3 butterflies often live in cold climates on mountains, but far more butterflies and moths come from warm parts of the world. Often mistaken for a butterfly, the beautiful **Madagascan sunset moth** 4 is a daytime flyer. The **Hercules moth** 5 is one of the largest species, measuring up to 34 cm (13 in) across. From Papua New Guinea,

Purple emperor

Green dragontail

Hornet moth

Hornet colouring deters predators

Queen Alexandra's birdwing ➏

❼ Monarch butterfly

Guava skipper

Tiger pierid

Clara's satin moth

Small postman

Big greasy butterfly

❽ Indian leaf butterfly

❾ Silk moth

Narrow tail mimics leaf stalk

False eyes frighten attackers

Polyphemus moth

Small copper

❿ American moon moth

Rajah Brooke's birdwing

Duke of Burgundy fritillary

Long hindwing tail

Queen Alexandra's birdwing ➏ is the world's biggest butterfly with a wingspan of up to 31 cm (12 in). It flies high up, and in the past collectors used shotguns to knock it out of the trees. The North American **monarch butterfly** ❼ is the greatest traveller, flying 4,500 km (2,800 miles) from Mexico as far north as Canada to breed. When winter comes, it flies all the way back again to escape the cold. **Indian leaf**

butterflies ❽ are easy to spot with their wings open, but look just like dead leaves with them closed. **Silk moths** ❾ have been bred in captivity for thousands of years. Silk is made by unwinding the cocoons that shelter their caterpillars. The **American moon moth** ❿ lives for less than a week as an adult. Like many other moths, it only eats as a caterpillar. Adults do not have working mouths.

95

⓫ Purple mort bleu

Blue night butterfly

Silver-spotted ghost moth

White admiral

Bent-wing ghost moth

Large emerald

SCALE

⓬ Acacia carpenter moth

⓭ Tiger swallowtail

Drinker moth

Narrow tail on hindwing

Ilia underwing

Cramer's mesene

Cairns birdwing

⓮ Zebra swallowtail

Elephant hawk moth

⓯ Swallowtail

California dog-face

⓰ Scarce swallowtail

Black-veined white

Butterflies and moths live their lives in four stages: egg, caterpillar, pupa, and adult. The caterpillar stage is the main feeding period, and butterflies and moths are often very choosy about their food. The **purple mort bleu** ⓫, from Central and South America, grows up on bamboo leaves, while in Australia caterpillars of the **acacia carpenter moth** ⓬ bore their way into wattle or acacia trees.

The **tiger swallowtail** ⓭ from North America lays its eggs on many kinds of plants, but the **zebra swallowtail** ⓮ always picks out pawpaw trees. The **swallowtail** ⓯ and **scarce swallowtail** ⓰ have caterpillars with inflatable coloured "horns". The horns suddenly appear if the caterpillar is touched, and they have a repulsive smell that helps to keep predators away. The **common morpho** ⓱, from Central

Brown hairstreak

Lappet moth

Buff-tip

⑱ Atlas moth

Metallic blue upperwings

⑰ Common morpho

Transparent "windows" on all four wings

Argent and sable

⑲ Verdant sphinx

Long, oval-shaped forewings

Small white

Orange-barred sulphur

Pine-tree lappet

⑳ Owl butterfly

Spanish festoon

Sonoran blue

㉑ Giant Agrippa

Forewings much longer than hindwings

False eyes on hindwings

Red patches on forewings scare off predators

Schulze's agrias

Orange tip

Giant leopard moth

and South America, has striking, bright blue wings. The butterfly was once collected for use in jewellery because its blue colour does not fade even after it has died. The huge **Atlas moth** ⑱, found in Southeast Asia, has the largest wing area of any butterfly or moth. At over 400 cm² (62 sq in), it is the size of a dinner plate. The **verdant sphinx** ⑲ and its relatives are some of the fastest fliers. Narrow wings and streamlined abdomens help these moths to attain top speeds of more than 35 kph (22 mph). The **owl butterfly** ⑳ gets its name from the huge eyespots on its hindwings. They give it a scary "face", making birds think twice before risking an attack. The **giant Agrippa** ㉑ has the biggest wingspan of any insect. The largest giant Agrippa moth on record measured 36 cm (14 in) from tip to tip.

97

SLUG MOTH CATERPILLAR
Butterflies and moths begin life as wingless larvae called caterpillars. Some of these are hard to spot but others, such as this slug moth caterpillar from Papua New Guinea, are brightly coloured and bizarrely shaped. You might expect such a colourful creature to develop into an equally striking adult, but fully developed slug moths are often dull in colour.

Size ❯ Variable, but small **Habitat ❯** Lowland forest, swamps, and mangroves. **Distribution ❯** Tropical, subtropical, and some temperate areas, including the eastern USA, sub-Saharan Africa, South and Southeast Asia, and Australasia. **Diet ❯** In many species adults have no mouthparts. They do all their eating as caterpillars, devouring the leaves of plants such as figs. Some species are seen as pests as they eat crops. **Breeding ❯** Caterpillars retreat into hard, round cocoons, from which they emerge as adult moths. Adults mate and lay eggs that will hatch into new caterpillars. **Predators ❯** Parasitic flies and wasps. Pest species may be killed by humans. **Number of species ❯** About 1,000 slug moth species.

Flies

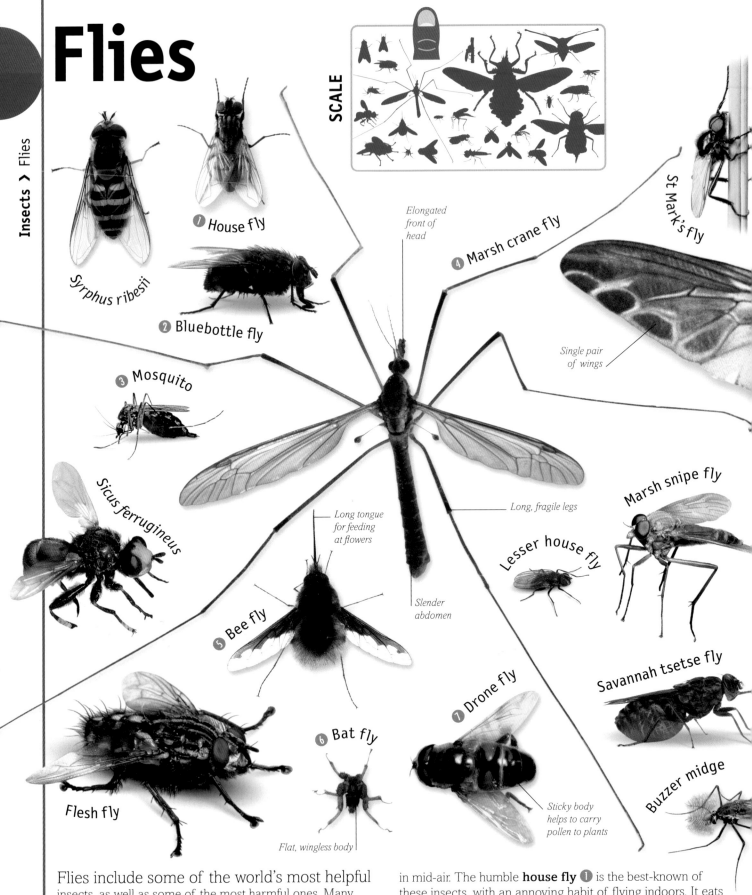

SCALE

① House fly

Syrphus ribesii

② Bluebottle fly

③ Mosquito

Sicus ferrugineus

Elongated front of head

④ Marsh crane fly

St Mark's fly

Single pair of wings

Long tongue for feeding at flowers

Marsh snipe fly

Lesser house fly

Long, fragile legs

Slender abdomen

⑤ Bee fly

⑥ Bat fly

⑦ Drone fly

Savannah tsetse fly

Sticky body helps to carry pollen to plants

Flesh fly

Flat, wingless body

Buzzer midge

Flies include some of the world's most helpful insects, as well as some of the most harmful ones. Many of them have bristly bodies, and most have just one pair of wings. In place of the rear wings, they have a pair of tiny knobs. These work like an aircraft's gyroscopes, keeping the fly stable in the air so it can perform extreme aerobatics. These include landing upside down and hovering steadily in mid-air. The humble **house fly** ① is the best-known of these insects, with an annoying habit of flying indoors. It eats anything sweet and spreads germs as it feeds. The **bluebottle fly** ② lays its eggs on meat and carrion, which its maggots burrow into, eating as they go. **Mosquitoes** ③ have sharp mouthparts and drink blood by piercing the skin of other animals. In some parts of the world they carry parasites

Long, flexible snout for stabbing and sucking prey

Giant blue robber fly ❽

❾ Stalk-eyed fly

Cabbage root fly

❿ Banded brown horsefly

Forest fly

Legs with strong claws

Moth fly

Platyura marginata

⓫ Timber fly

Dark cloud on wing

Leucozona leucorum

Marmalade hoverfly

Dumpy abdomen

that can cause malaria and other killer diseases. The **marsh crane fly** ❹ has extra-long legs that break off if it is touched. **Bee flies** ❺ do a useful job by pollinating flowers. The **bat fly** ❻ has no wings. It does not need them because it spends its adult life in the fur of bats. **Drone flies** ❼ are very good at mimicking honey bees. Like bee flies, they are effective pollinators. The awesome-looking **giant blue robber fly** ❽ from Australia grabs other insects on the wing, and flies with a distinctive buzzing sound. Male **stalk-eyed flies** ❾ have bizarre heads with eyes set far apart. In the breeding season, males stand head to head, and the one with the widest eyes wins. The **banded brown horsefly** ❿ bites horses, and sometimes humans, too, but **timber flies** ⓫ are harmless and do not feed at all as adults.

101

Bees, wasps, and ants

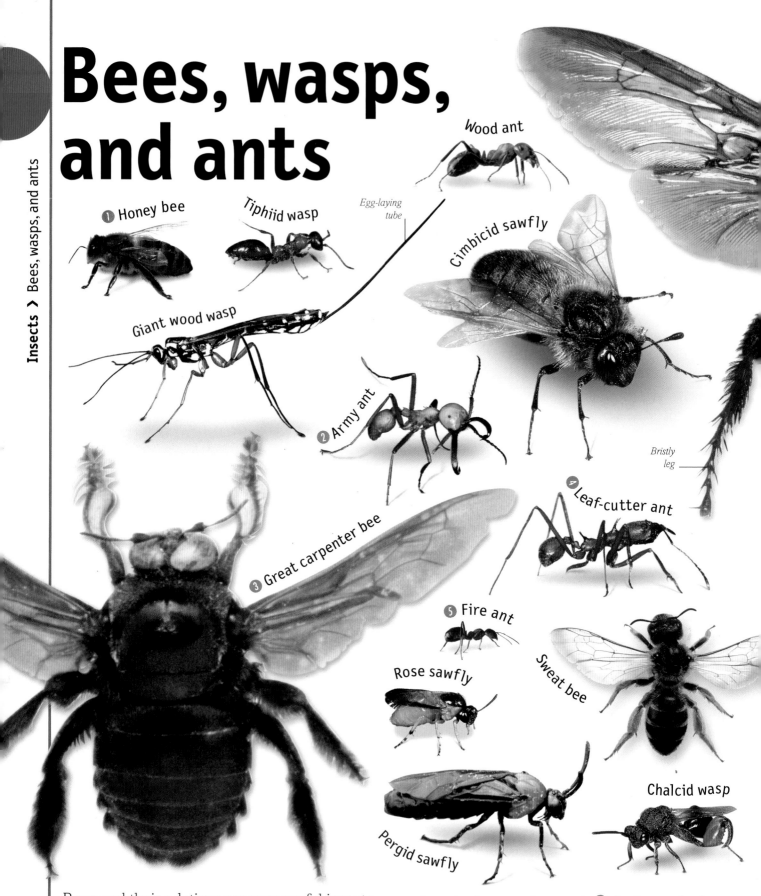

Wood ant

1 Honey bee

Tiphiid wasp

Egg-laying tube

Cimbicid sawfly

Giant wood wasp

2 Army ant

Bristly leg

4 Leaf-cutter ant

3 Great carpenter bee

5 Fire ant

Rose sawfly

Sweat bee

Chalcid wasp

Pergid sawfly

Bees and their relatives are very useful insects. Although many of them pack a painful sting, they help farmers by pollinating crops and killing pests. Apart from sawflies, they all have slender waists and most have two pairs of transparent wings. **Honey bees** 1 live in nests containing thousands of workers ruled by a single queen. The queen lays the eggs, while the worker bees build the nest, collect food, and care for the young. **Army ants** 2 also live together but do not make a permanent home. Instead, millions of them rush across the rainforest floor, grabbing small animals with their powerful jaws. The **great carpenter bee** 3 feeds on nectar from flowers, and lays its eggs in tunnels in dead wood. Like other bees, it uses its sting only if attacked. **Leaf-cutter ants** 4 make giant nests underground, and feed on a special

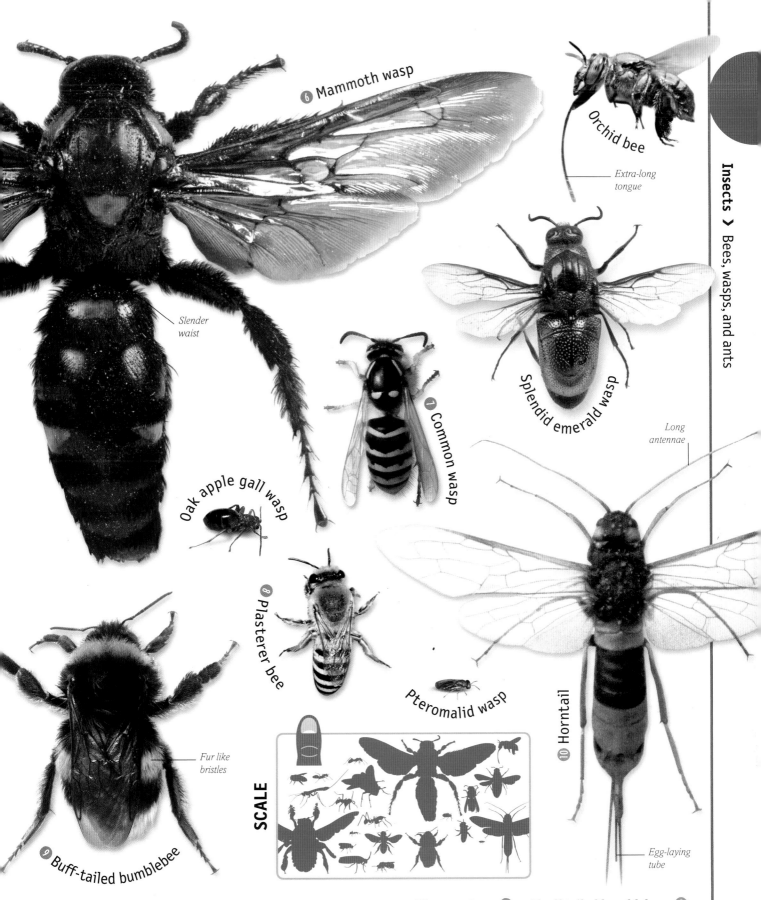

6 Mammoth wasp

Slender waist

Orchid bee

Extra-long tongue

Splendid emerald wasp

Long antennae

7 Common wasp

Oak apple gall wasp

8 Plasterer bee

Pteromalid wasp

10 Horntail

Egg-laying tube

Fur like bristles

9 Buff-tailed bumblebee

SCALE

fungus which they grow on chewed-up leaves. These ants are harmless, but some others are not. Tropical **fire ants** 5 have a vicious sting that feels worse than a burn. The **mammoth wasp** 6 is a predator. It paralyzes the grubs of scarab beetles and lays eggs on their bodies, so its young have a private food supply. **Common wasps** 7 make papery nests, and help to get rid of pests by hunting insects to feed their young. **Plasterer bees** 8 and **buff-tailed bumblebees** 9 nest in the ground. Plasterer bees waterproof the walls of their nests with a fluid from their bodies. Bumblebees have furry insulation which lets them fly in the cold days of early spring. They are good crop pollinators. The **horntail** 10 looks dangerous, but cannot sting. Females lay their eggs in pine trees, and their grubs feed by chewing through wood.

103

Fish

Fish were the first vertebrates to evolve. They live underwater and their streamlined bodies are adapted for speedy swimming. They breathe by absorbing oxygen from the water through their gills. Fish have a special extra sense, using organs along their sides to detect vibrations in the water.

Tail › Most fish use their tails to power themselves through the water. This lionfish can use its tail to stay steady in the water, so it can hang motionless, ready to ambush passing prey.

Fins ❯ Fish fins consist of bony spines linked by membranes. The fish uses them to steer its body through the water. In some species they are adapted for other purposes such as burrowing into mud or sand to hide. This lionfish can inject venom through spines in some of its fins.

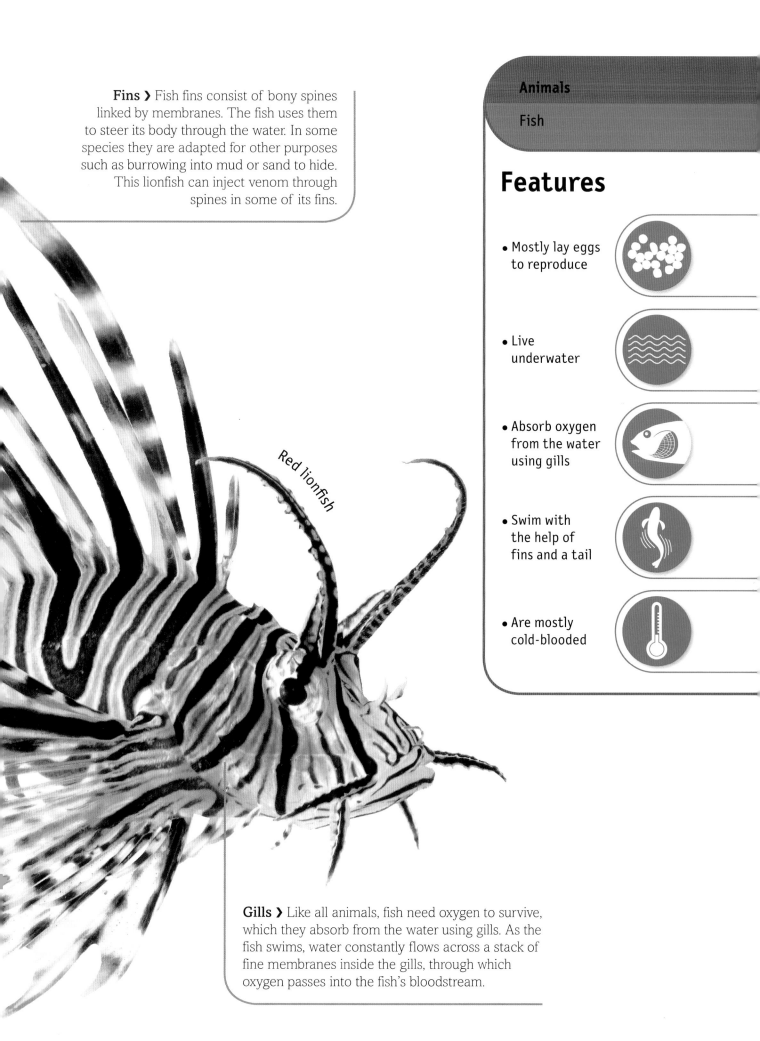

Red lionfish

Features

- Mostly lay eggs to reproduce

- Live underwater

- Absorb oxygen from the water using gills

- Swim with the help of fins and a tail

- Are mostly cold-blooded

Gills ❯ Like all animals, fish need oxygen to survive, which they absorb from the water using gills. As the fish swims, water constantly flows across a stack of fine membranes inside the gills, through which oxygen passes into the fish's bloodstream.

Sharks, rays, and skates

SCALE

① Frilled shark

Undulate ray

② Bluntnose sixgill shark

③ Spotted ratfish

④ Elephant fish chimaera

Blue skate

Parallel gill slits

Tail fin almost half of body length

⑤ Zebra shark

⑥ Common stingray

⑦ Spotted eagle ray

Thornback ray

Blue-spotted ribbontail ray

Haller's round ray

⑧ Giant manta ray

Flap funnels plankton into mouth

Razor-sharp teeth and powerful jaws make sharks the most fearsome hunters in the seas. Like skates and rays, they have skeletons made of cartilage or gristle. **Frilled sharks ①** and **bluntnose sixgill sharks ②** live in deep water, but many other sharks live near the surface, in open water or close to the shore. Most sharks have a streamlined body and several rows of sharp teeth, which are constantly replaced throughout their lives. Their relatives chimaeras, a group of blunt-headed fish, have teeth that last the whole of their lives. The **spotted ratfish ③** and **elephant fish chimaera ④** use their flat teeth for crushing molluscs and crabs. Some sharks have to swim non-stop to breathe, but **zebra sharks ⑤** spend the day resting on the seabed, waking up to hunt after dark. Skates and rays have wing-like front fins

⑨ Smalltooth sawfish

Nurse shark

Snout can sense prey buried in seabed

⑩ Longnose sawshark

Sensory barbels used to detect vibrations

Wing-like front fins

Sand devil

Brownish grey colour acts as camouflage on the ocean floor

Marbled electric ray

Epaulette catshark

and mouths on their undersides. Some kinds, including the **common stingray** ⑥, have a venomous spine in their tails. Accidentally treading on these fish can be very dangerous. In some cases, a single jab from a spine can kill a person. Rays swim by beating their front fins like a bird's wings. The **spotted eagle ray** ⑦ feeds on seabed animals, while the **giant manta ray** ⑧ scoops up plankton as it "flies" through the open sea.

Measuring up to 9 m (30 ft) across, this colossal but harmless fish is the largest ray in the world, with an exceptionally big brain. The **smalltooth sawfish** ⑨ is a rare and unusual ray with a toothed snout like a saw. It uses this to dig up animals in the seabed and to slash at other fish that come nearby. The **longnose sawshark** ⑩ looks similar, but is much smaller, with two barbels, or feelers, attached to its snout.

107

⑪ Shortfin mako

⑫ Great white shark

Piked dogfish

Large, saw-like teeth for ripping apart prey

Blacknose shark

Kitefin shark

Large dorsal fin

Starry smooth-hound

⑬ Blue shark

⑮ Smooth hammerhead

Sharply pointed snout

SCALE

⑭ Small-spotted catshark

Pectoral fins act as stabilizers

Some of the world's biggest sharks roam the open seas. The **shortfin mako** ⑪ is one of the fastest of these tireless hunters. In short bursts, it can swim at more than 70 kph (43 mph). Makos feed mainly on fast-swimming fish and squid, but the **great white shark** ⑫ has a taste for seals, dolphins, and occasionally humans, too. Growing up to 7 m (24 ft) in length, and weighing as much as 2 tonnes, this gigantic and much-feared predator typically attacks from below, and sometimes bursts out of the water as it slams into its prey. The beautifully streamlined **blue shark** ⑬ travels thousands of kilometres a year, between the places where it feeds and the places where it breeds. Like most large sharks it gives birth to live young. **Small-spotted catsharks** ⑭ and their relatives lay eggs with leathery cases. Called

⑯ Port Jackson shark

Highly flexible tail used to stun prey

⑰ Horn shark

⑱ Thresher shark

Light and dark shading hides shark from above and below

Sharpnose sevengill shark

Tail with two equal-sized blades

⑲ Blacktip reef shark

⑳ Whitetip reef shark

㉑ Bull shark

"mermaid's purses", they can take over a year to hatch. The **smooth hammerhead** ⑮ belongs to a family of sharks with strange T-shaped heads. Its eyes are at each end of the head, enabling it to see all around as it swims. **Port Jackson sharks** ⑯ and **horn sharks** ⑰ live on the seabed. They have downward-facing mouths and flat back teeth, which crunch up molluscs and other hard-bodied animals. The **thresher shark** ⑱ is an open-water predator. Its extra-long tail works like a whip, stunning other fish and making them easy to catch. **Blacktip reef sharks** ⑲ and **whitetip reef sharks** ⑳ rarely harm humans, but the **bull shark** ㉑ is a notorious man-eater, with a habit of swimming up rivers and cruising close to the shore. Despite its size, up to 3.4 m (11 ft) long, it can hunt in water just 1 m (3 ft) deep.

WHALE SHARK
By far the largest fish in the world, the whale shark has a huge mouth that stretches almost as wide as its whole body, armed with up to 300 rows of tiny teeth. However, despite its fearsome appearance, this gentle giant feeds on plankton. In fact, it is often followed by shoals of smaller fish that keep the shark clean by eating bacteria and debris from its mouth.

Size ❯ 7–12 m (23–40 ft). Some may grow even larger.
Weight ❯ Up to 18½ tonnes **Habitat ❯** Tropical and warm
temperate seas. They migrate thousands of kilometres
every year. **Distribution ❯** Pacific, South Atlantic, and Indian
Oceans. **Diet ❯** Plankton, small fish, and crustaceans. Whale
sharks feed by taking in water then pushing it through their
gills to filter out the food. **Breeding ❯** The female carries
up to 300 embryos and gives birth to live young. **Lifespan ❯**
Unknown but thought to be up to 150 years. **Predators ❯**
Adults have no enemies except humans. Other sharks,
sailfish, and killer whales may attack the young.
Conservation status ❯ Vulnerable due to hunting.

Saltwater fish

① Spotted boxfish

White-spotted puffer

Warty frogfish

Body swollen with water

② Long-spine porcupinefish

Spiny front fins can grip seaweed

③ Clown triggerfish

④ Sargassumfish

Large mouth has blunt teeth adapted for crushing prey

⑤ Zebra moray

Spotted garden eel

Tail burrows into sand as anchor

Saltwater fish come in a mind-boggling variety of shapes, sizes, and colours, and scientists discover many new kinds every year. Rays and sharks have rubbery (cartilaginous) skeletons, but most saltwater fish have bony skeletons and are covered in scales. The **spotted boxfish's** ① scales fit together like armour plating, while the **long-spine porcupinefish** ② has scales with sharp spines. If it feels threatened, this fish swallows lots of water and turns into a prickly ball. The **clown triggerfish** ③ lives in the Indian and Pacific Oceans and jams itself in coral reefs if danger comes its way. It feeds by crunching up sea urchins and other hard-shelled animals. The **sargassumfish** ④ lives in floating seaweed around the world. Even in broad daylight, its incredible camouflage makes it almost impossible to see. The **zebra moray** ⑤

112

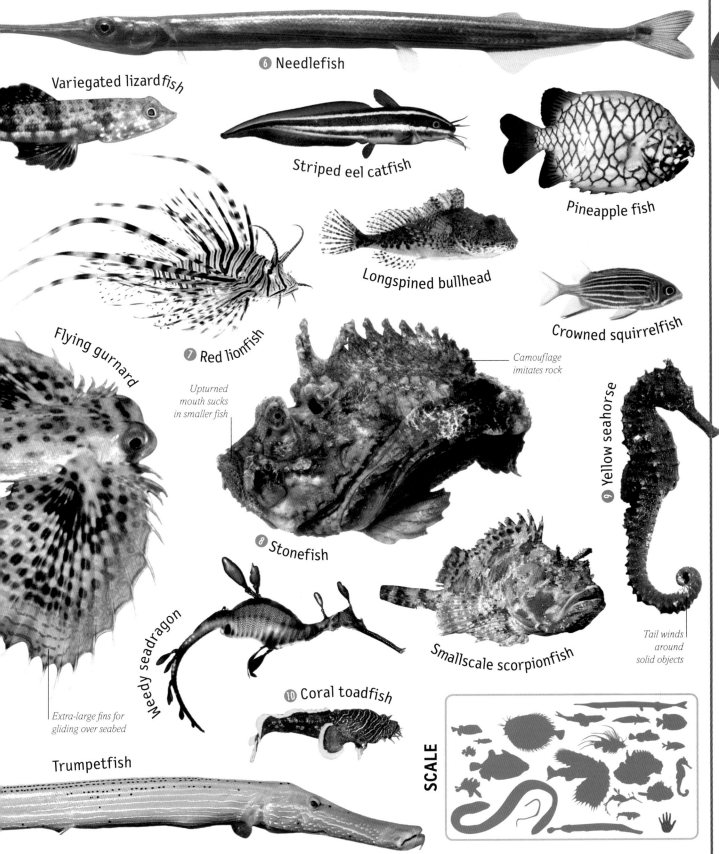

⑥ Needlefish

Variegated lizardfish

Striped eel catfish

Pineapple fish

Flying gurnard

⑦ Red lionfish

Longspined bullhead

Crowned squirrelfish

Camouflage imitates rock

Upturned mouth sucks in smaller fish

⑨ Yellow seahorse

⑧ Stonefish

Tail winds around solid objects

Weedy seadragon

Smallscale scorpionfish

Extra-large fins for gliding over seabed

⑩ Coral toadfish

Trumpetfish

SCALE

comes out to feed at night. To firmly grip its prey, it has a second set of jaws in its throat, which can spring forward into its mouth. **Needlefish** ⑥ live near the surface of the sea. Large specimens have been known to spear people by jumping on to boats. The **red lionfish's** ⑦ striped colours warn predators that this fish is venomous. It defends itself by spreading out its poison-tipped fins. The **stonefish** ⑧

can give humans a lethal jab with its venomous spines. The **yellow seahorse** ⑨ swims with its body upright. Like other seahorses it is one of the world's slowest fish, with a maximum speed of just a few metres an hour. Male **coral toadfish** ⑩ make strange grunting or whistling sounds to attract females. After the females have laid their eggs, the males guard them until the young fish hatch and swim away.

SCALE

⑪ Emperor angelfish

⑫ Banded archerfish

Royal angelfish

Royal gramma

Long dorsal fin raised like a sail

Ochre-striped cardinalfish

Brown meagre

Butterfly blenny

⑬ Blue-spotted seabream

⑭ Powder-blue surgeonfish

Longnose hawkfish

⑮ Clown anemonefish

Slender body fits in burrow

Red mullet

Fleshy barbels help detect buried prey

More fish live on coasts and coral reefs than anywhere else in the seas. The **emperor angelfish** ⑪ and its relatives are some of the most colourful reef-dwellers with vivid markings that change as they mature. **Banded archerfish** ⑫ live in estuaries in Southeast Asia. They look for insects on overhanging branches and knock them off by squirting a jet of water from their mouths. The **blue-spotted**

seabream ⑬ eats animals on the seabed, while the beautiful **powder-blue surgeonfish** ⑭ feeds mainly on algae and underwater plants. Surgeonfish look harmless, but when attacked they fight back using two sharp blades on either side of their tails. The **clown anemonefish** ⑮ hides in the tentacles of sea anemones. Unlike other fish, it is not harmed by their stings. **Common bluestripe snappers** ⑯

Harlequin sweetlips

16 Common bluestripe snapper

Bold pattern camouflages eyes

17 Harlequin tuskfish

Bluefish

18 Mediterranean parrotfish

19 Atlantic mudskipper

Foxface rabbitfish

Red bandfish

20 Albacore tuna

live on coral reefs. They move in fast-swimming shoals by day, dispersing at night to feed. **Harlequin tuskfish** **17** flip stones over with their teeth to get at small animals hiding underneath. The **Mediterranean parrotfish** **18** crunches up food with its beak-shaped mouth. Like many other parrotfish it starts out life as female, but may change into a male as it grows older. **Atlantic mudskippers** **19** live in

mangrove swamps where they climb up roots or hop across the mud. Their front fins work like stubby legs, and they can survive out of the water by breathing air through their skin. The **albacore tuna** **20** belongs to a family of high-speed swimmers with muscle-packed bodies and long, razor-like fins. Unlike most fish, tunas are warm-blooded, and can hurtle through water at up to 80 kph (50 mph).

SCALE

㉑ Shore rockling

Snake-like body

Three fins on back

Slippery body without scales

Gunnel

㉓ Turbot

Upper side camouflaged against seabed

㉒ Atlantic mackerel

㉔ Lesser weeverfish

Small sandeel

Sea fish thrive in cold water because it is often full of food. **Shore rocklings** ㉑ search for shrimps and crabs in rock pools using sensitive whiskers or barbels. **Atlantic mackerels** ㉒ live in the open sea. Like tunas they have muscle-packed bodies and a streamlined shape for speeding through the water. They have to keep swimming, as they rely on the flow of water to breathe. **Turbot** ㉓ and other flatfish live on the seabed. Very young flatfish look like other fish. As they grow up, one eye moves around their heads until, as adults, they swim on one side with both eyes facing up. The **lesser weeverfish** ㉔ also lives on the bottom, with its body half-buried near the shore. This venomous fish has spines on its back, which it raises to defend itself against predators. It can even give humans a painful sting. **Sockeye salmon** ㉕ spend

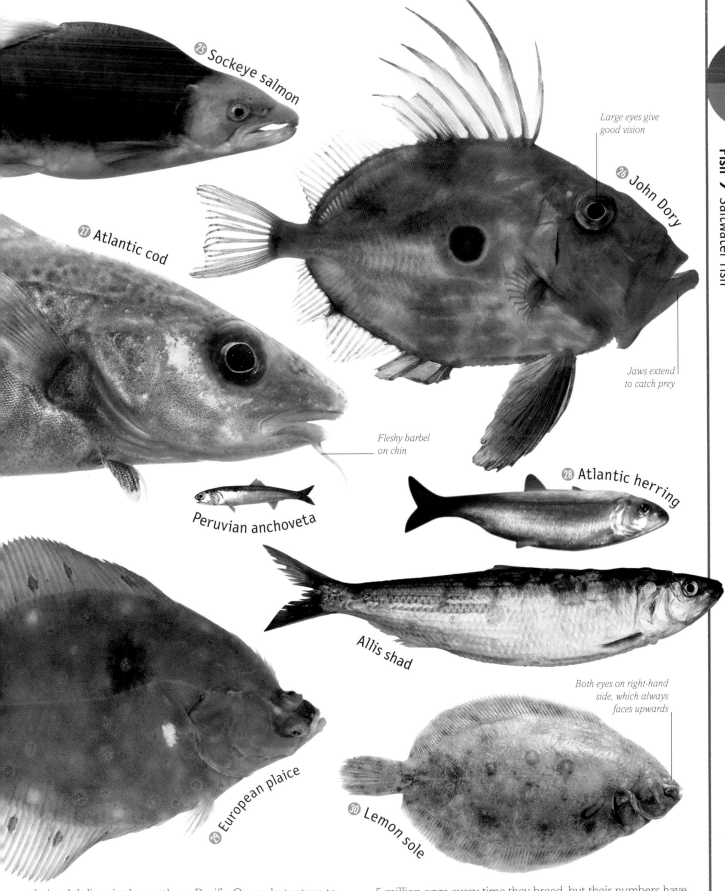

25 Sockeye salmon

Large eyes give
good vision

26 John Dory

27 Atlantic cod

Jaws extend
to catch prey

Fleshy barbel
on chin

28 Atlantic herring

Peruvian anchoveta

Allis shad

Both eyes on right-hand
side, which always
faces upwards

29 European plaice

30 Lemon sole

their adult lives in the northern Pacific Ocean but return to fresh water to breed. In some rivers, thousands of sockeyes fight their way upstream, creating a feast for fish-eating eagles and bears. The **John Dory** 26 looks big when seen from the side, but it is good at sneaking up on other fish because its body is as thin as a human hand. The **Atlantic cod** 27 and **Atlantic herring** 28 are often fished for food. Cod can produce

5 million eggs every time they breed, but their numbers have plummeted due to overfishing. Herrings are some of the most common fish in seas. A single shoal can contain more than a billion members, attracting predators such as seals, whales, and larger fish. The **European plaice** 29 and **lemon sole** 30 are two flatfish that are highly prized as food. Both of them often hide on the seabed by covering themselves with sand.

117

BLACK-STRIPED SALEMA

These tropical fish are found in waters around the Galápagos Islands. They form huge schools of hundreds or thousands. When a predator approaches, the school bunches into a tight cluster known as a bait ball. By swarming together, splitting, and changing direction in a flash, these fish try to confuse predators, making it difficult for them to attack.

Size ❯ Up to 30 cm (12 in) long **Habitat ❯** Reefs and rocky areas in shallow waters. They gather in large shoals during the day, but disperse at night. **Distribution ❯** Eastern Pacific Ocean, only around the Galapagos Islands. **Diet ❯** Plankton and fish larvae **Breeding ❯** The female releases eggs that float freely in the ocean. These eggs hatch into tiny larvae without scales or fins, which slowly develop into young fish. **Predators ❯** Dolphins, seals, penguins, and sharks. **Conservation status ❯** Vulnerable due to changes in its environment. Recently, a weather system called El Niño has disrupted the oceans around the Galapagos, increasing water temperatures, which may affect fish like these.

Deep-sea fish

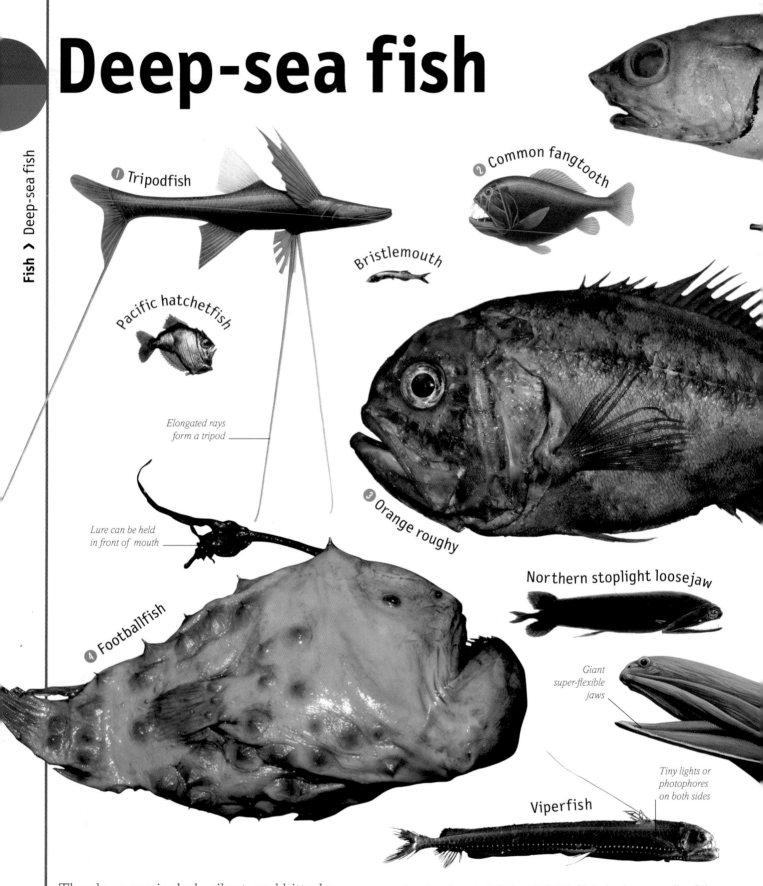

① Tripodfish

② Common fangtooth

Bristlemouth

Pacific hatchetfish

Elongated rays form a tripod

③ Orange roughy

Lure can be held in front of mouth

④ Footballfish

Northern stoplight loosejaw

Giant super-flexible jaws

Tiny lights or photophores on both sides

Viperfish

The deep sea is dark, silent, and bitterly cold. The fish that live here have evolved strange shapes to survive. Food is hard to find, so deep-sea fish cannot waste any chance to catch a meal. The **tripodfish** ① perches above the seabed, propped up by three long rays that stick out from its fins. It faces into the current and catches small animals that drift by. The **common fangtooth** ② lives at depths of up to 5,000 m (16,400 ft). It feeds on smaller fish, grabbing them with its needle-like fangs and swallowing them whole. The **orange roughy** ③ gathers over ocean ridges and underwater mountains. It grows very slowly and can live to be 150 years old. **Footballfish** ④ attract their prey using luminous lures that dangle in front of their mouths. If other fish come near to investigate, they are

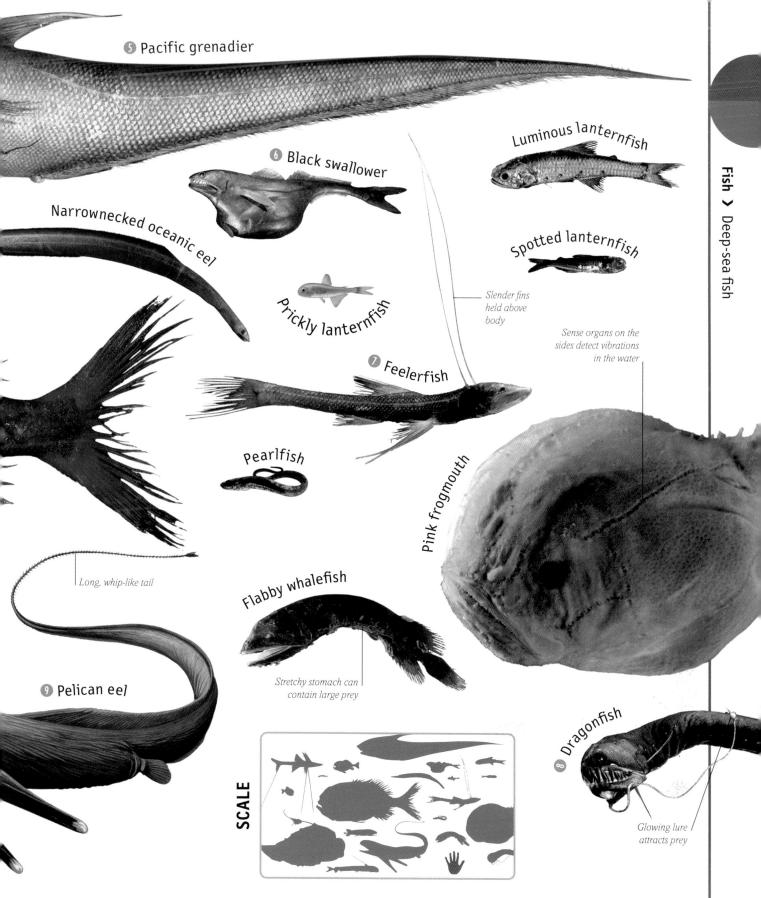

⑤ Pacific grenadier

⑥ Black swallower

Luminous lanternfish

Narrownecked oceanic eel

Spotted lanternfish

Slender fins held above body

Prickly lanternfish

Sense organs on the sides detect vibrations in the water

⑦ Feelerfish

Pearlfish

Pink frogmouth

Long, whip-like tail

Flabby whalefish

Stretchy stomach can contain large prey

⑨ Pelican eel

SCALE

⑧ Dragonfish

Glowing lure attracts prey

instantly sucked inside. Female footballfish really are as big as footballs, but the males are tiny and often fasten themselves to the females as parasites. The **Pacific grenadier ⑤** cruises over the ocean floor, gently rippling its long, rat-like tail, while the **black swallower ⑥** has a super-stretchy stomach and can gulp down prey larger than itself. **Feelerfish ⑦** stay close to the ocean floor. Their front

fins are thin and whiskery and work like antennae to sense food. The **dragonfish ⑧** is a ferocious predator. Like many deep-sea fish, it has special organs called photophores which glow in the dark, to attract prey or signal to mates. The **pelican eel ⑨** has enormous jaws but tiny teeth. It uses its mouth like a scoop to catch its prey. Like the black swallower, it has an expandable stomach to deal with over-sized meals.

121

Freshwater fish

① Goldfish

Green sunfish

Clown loach

Extra-large decorative scales

② Koi carp

③ Glass catfish

Tench

Brown bullhead

④ Tiger shovelnose catfish

⑤ Chain pickerel

Sensitive barbels to probe for food

Giant whiptail catfish

Fish live in a huge variety of freshwater habitats, from lakes and rivers to streams and ponds. They can be found in hot springs where the water temperature is a steamy 40°C (104°F), and in chilly caves hundreds of metres underground. The smallest fish, even the fully grown ones, are not much bigger than a grain of rice, while the biggest are as long as a family car. Some freshwater fish,

including the **goldfish** ① and **koi carp** ②, have been raised in captivity for hundreds of years. There are many varieties of both these fish, and the rarest koi carp can be worth more than $1 million. Catfish are common freshwater fish, particularly where the water is murky or the current is slow. The **glass catfish** ③ from Southeast Asia has a transparent body. The South American **tiger shovelnose catfish** ④ has

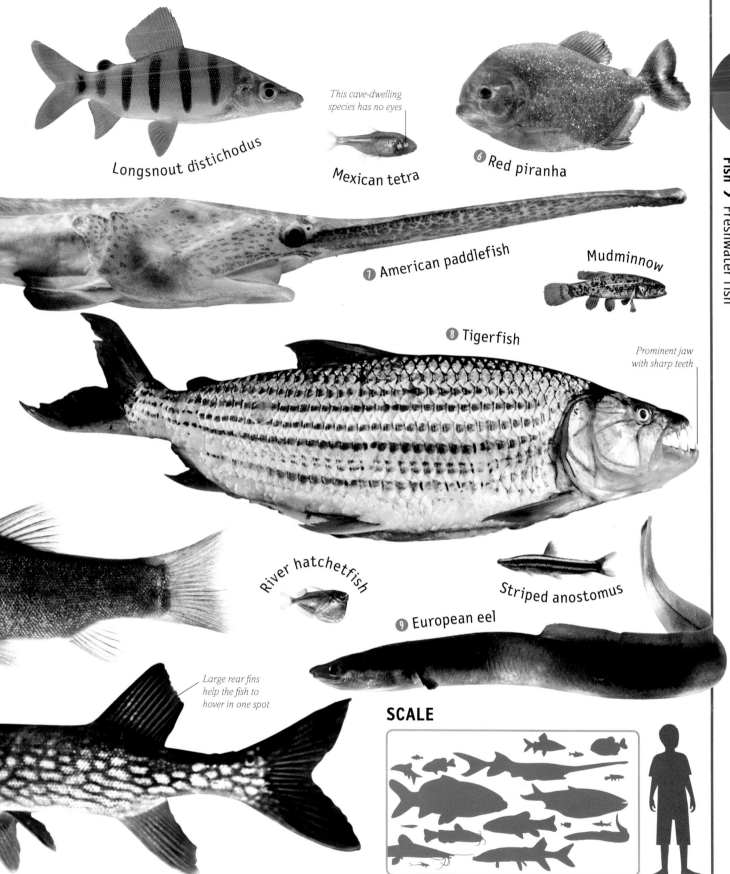

Longsnout distichodus

This cave-dwelling species has no eyes

Mexican tetra

6 Red piranha

7 American paddlefish

Mudminnow

8 Tigerfish

Prominent jaw with sharp teeth

River hatchetfish

Striped anostomus

9 European eel

Large rear fins help the fish to hover in one spot

SCALE

long barbels that probe the riverbed for food. The **chain pickerel 5** is an ambush hunter. It lurks in the shallows and lunges at other fish with a powerful flick of its tail. The **red piranha 6** from South America usually eats fish, worms, and crustaceans, but a large group of red piranhas can attack big mammals, stripping away chunks of flesh with their razor-sharp teeth. The **American paddlefish 7** looks ferocious, but it feeds only on tiny animals filtered out by its gills. **Tigerfish 8** are fierce predators from Africa's rivers. They are famous for putting up a tremendous fight if hooked. The **European eel 9** is a long-distance migrant. It spawns in the Sargasso Sea, in the North Atlantic Ocean, and its tiny young travel all the way back to Europe's rivers, an epic journey of up to 6,000 km (3,700 miles).

SCALE

Long lower jaw used to probe for food

⑩ Elephantnose fish

Chipokae

Clown knifefish

⑪ Electric eel

Mouth can gulp air in stagnant water

⑫ Foureyed fish

Slippery skin without scales

Burbot

Large mouth with strong jaws

Spotted ctenopoma

⑬ Siamese fighting fish

Thin, rounded tail

Zebrafish

⑭ Arctic char

Many freshwater fish have special skills that help them to survive. The **elephantnose fish** ⑩ from tropical Africa lives in murky rivers. It finds its way by giving off weak electric signals and probes for food using its long lower jaw. The **electric eel** ⑪ from South America uses electricity to find and kill prey. It can give a jolt of up to 650 volts, enough to knock a person off their feet. The

foureyed fish ⑫ has eyes that are divided into two, letting it see clearly above and below the waterline. **Siamese fighting fish** ⑬ are small but famously aggressive. When two males clash, they sometimes fight to the death. Far away from the tropics, the **Arctic char** ⑭ lives in icy rivers and cold lakes. It is one of the world's most northerly freshwater fish, surviving as close as 800 km (500 miles) from the North

⑮ European perch

⑯ Nile tilapia

⑰ African lungfish

Blade-shaped tail

⑱ Rainbow trout

*Thread-like
front fins*

⑲ Longnose gar

Pole. The **European perch** ⑮ is a patient predator, lying in wait for its prey. It lays eggs in long ribbons and fastens them to underwater plants. A distant relative of the European perch, the African **Nile tilapia** ⑯ breeds in a very different way. The female scoops up her eggs, up to 2,000 at a time, and holds them in her mouth until they hatch and her young swim away. **African lungfish** ⑰ live in lakes and swamps

that can dry out for months at a time. They seal themselves up in cocoons of mud and survive by breathing air. The **rainbow trout** ⑱ originally came from North America but has been introduced into lakes and rivers in many other parts of the world for food and sport. Another American fish, the **longnose gar** ⑲ bursts out of hiding to stab other fish with its needle-sharp teeth.

Amphibians

Amphibians spend part of their lives in the water and part on land. Some kinds undergo metamorphosis, like many invertebrates, starting out as water-based tadpoles with gills and evolving into air-breathing adults. They need fresh water to survive, and many species are threatened with extinction due to pollution, disease, and destruction of their habitat.

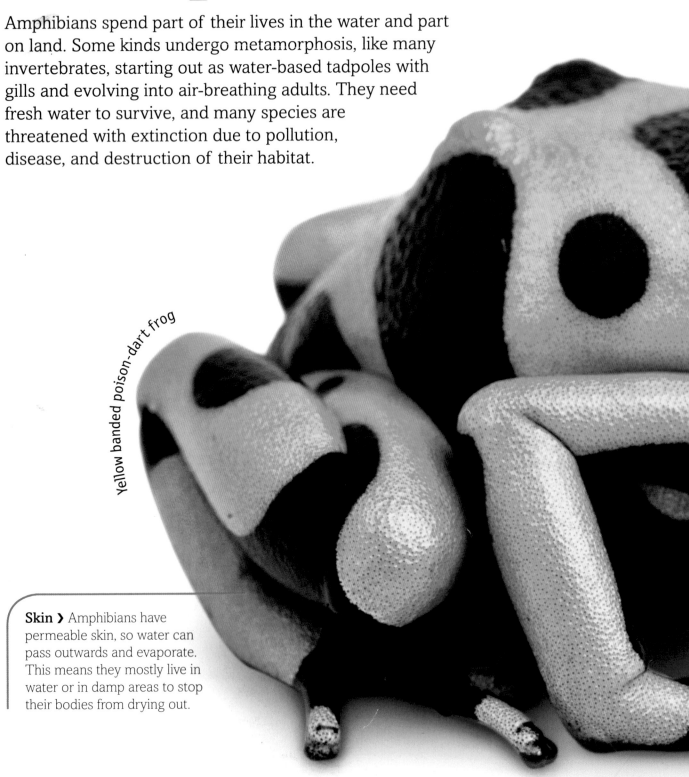

Yellow banded poison-dart frog

Skin › Amphibians have permeable skin, so water can pass outwards and evaporate. This means they mostly live in water or in damp areas to stop their bodies from drying out.

Poison glands › Many species of amphibian secrete a poisonous slime from glands in their skin. This helps to keep them moist as well as to deter predators. Some amphibians simply taste nasty, while others, like this yellow banded poison-dart frog, can be deadly to some predators.

Features

- Usually lay eggs to reproduce

- Have moist skin, and may die if they dry out

- Often spend much of their lives in water

- Some hatch as tadpoles, and change shape to become adults

- Are cold-blooded

Legs › Some amphibians only have legs as adults. These kinds hatch out from eggs as tadpoles, tiny swimming creatures with tails. As the tadpoles mature, legs grow out of their bodies and their tails shrink and disappear.

Frogs and toads

Tongue flips out
to catch prey

A grub makes
a tasty morsel

① Lemur frog

② Giant broad-headed treefrog

③ Australian green treefrog

Loose skin soaks
up water for use
in dry conditions

Fringe-limbed treefrog

Suckers on
all toes

Yucatan casque-headed treefrog

④ Amazon milk frog

Orange-legged leaf frog

⑤ Paradoxical frog

SCALE

⑥ Solomon Islands horned frog

Frogs and toads look very different to other amphibians, with their stubby bodies and long back legs. Frogs are usually sleek and slippery, but most toads have dry, warty skin. Nearly all of these animals start life as tadpoles, changing shape as they grow up. The **lemur frog** ① from Central America hunts insects by night and hides under leaves during the day. Like other treefrogs, it is an expert climber with slender, sucker-tipped toes. The **giant broad-headed treefrog** ② lives in South American forests. It clings to tree trunks and branches, while the **Australian green treefrog** ③ sometimes climbs into houses, where it makes itself at home in water tanks and kitchen sinks. The **Amazon milk frog** ④ lays its eggs in rain-filled tree-holes. It lives high in the treetops and hardly ever comes to the

⑦ European common toad

⑧ Golden mantella

Elegant Madagascan frog

Guyanan stubfoot toad

Eyes with slit-shaped pupils detect small, moving prey

⑨ Malayan tree toad

⑩ Cane toad

Raucous toad

Warts on male's skin develop dark, sharp spines in the breeding season

Natterjack toad

ground. The South American **paradoxical frog** ⑤ spends its life in lakes and pools. It gets its name from its monster tadpoles, which are up to four times the adult's length. The **Solomon Islands horned frog** ⑥ has a pointed snout and horn-like projections above its eyes, camouflaging it perfectly among fallen leaves. The **European common toad** ⑦ hunts all kinds of small animals, including beetles, snails, and slugs.

The rare **golden mantella** ⑧ frog from Madagascar is brilliantly coloured, warning predators that it has poison-covered skin. The **Malayan tree toad** ⑨ is one of the few true toads that lives off the ground. The enormous **cane toad** ⑩ gulps down mice and even snakes. Originally from Central America, this ravenous predator has become a major pest in Australia and other parts of the world.

Common parsley frog

Brazil-nut poison-dart frog

⑪ European common frog

⑬ Granular poison-dart frog

Yellow-banded poison-dart frog

⑫ Golden poison-dart frog

Dyeing poison-dart frog

Circular eardrums behind eyes

Three-striped poison-dart frog

⑭ Edible frog

⑯ American bullfrog

⑮ Wood frog

SCALE

Tungara frog

Toads usually move by crawling, but frogs often hop and jump. In emergencies, the **European common frog** ⑪ can leap more than seven times its own length, equivalent to a human athlete clearing a school bus without a run-up. In Central and South America, tiny poison-dart frogs climb up trees or hop over the rainforest floor. Their bright colours are a warning to predators to stay away. The **golden poison-dart frog** ⑫ is the deadliest, with enough poison to kill two African elephants, while the **granular poison-dart frog** ⑬ is one of the smallest, and could easily fit inside a matchbox. In the past, native Americans used these frogs to make poison hunting darts, which is how they got their names. In the breeding season, frogs and toads often make loud calls. Male **edible frogs** ⑭

⑰ Asian horned frog

⑱ Indian bullfrog

Bolifamba reed frog

Giant stump-toed frog

Common skittering frog

⑲ Painted toad

Rajamally wart frog

Couch's spadefoot

Sticky, bright red skin to ward off predators

⑳ Tomato frog

Foulassi banana frog

㉑ Tinker reed frog

and **wood frogs** ⑮ sound like quacking ducks, while the male **American bullfrog** ⑯ sounds more like a mooing cow. This massive frog swallows almost anything it can cram into its mouth, including smaller frogs, young turtles, and small water birds. The "horns" and the brown colour of the **Asian horned frog** ⑰ help it blend in among fallen leaves. The **Indian bullfrog** ⑱ leaps into water if it is disturbed.

It usually climbs out after a few minutes, but can stay underwater for several hours. **Painted toads** ⑲ and **tomato frogs** ⑳ live on land and come out to feed at night. Their skin is covered with a glue-like substance, which helps to protect them from attack. **Tinker reed frogs** ㉑ from Africa lay their eggs on waterside plants. Their tadpoles wriggle down into the water after hatching.

131

22 Mexican burrowing toad

Spotted-thighed poison-dart frog

SCALE

23 Horned marsupial frog

Oriental fire-bellied toad

painted frog

Eggs wrapped around male's hind legs

25 Fleischmann's glass frog

24 Midwife toad

26 Ornate horned frog

Mouth as wide as head

Big-headed rain frog

Mascarene ridged frog

Frogs and toads have lots of different shapes, and varied lifestyles that help them to survive. If threatened, the **Mexican burrowing toad** 22 can blow itself up to resemble a small balloon. It lives underground and feeds on ants, coming to the surface only when it breeds. The **horned marsupial frog** 23 has a strange way of breeding that lets it stay high up in trees. The female carries her eggs in a pouch on her back. Instead of producing tadpoles, they hatch directly into baby frogs. The **midwife toad** 24 is so called because the male carries the female's eggs. When the eggs are ready to hatch, he takes them to water so that the tadpoles can swim away. **Fleischmann's glass frog** 25 lives in trees. On its underside, its tiny beating heart can be seen through its transparent skin. The **ornate horned frog** 26 is a sit-and-

African foam-nest treefrog

Darwin's frog

Webbed feet work like parachutes

Coromandel New Zealand frog

㉗ Desert rain frog

Mossy frog

Southern whipping frog

㉘ Wallace's flying frog

African treefrog

West Cameroon forest treefrog

Puerto Rican coqui

Brown-striped marsh frog

㉙ Fraser's clawed frog

Limon robber frog

㉚ African bullfrog

㉛ Common spadefoot toad

wait hunter from the grasslands of Argentina. Camouflaged by its green and brown markings, it lurks in muddy ground and grabs anything edible that comes nearby. The **desert rain frog** ㉗ lives and breeds among Namibian sand dunes, hiding beneath the surface during the day. **Wallace's flying frog** ㉘ glides through the forests of Southeast Asia on its webbed feet. **Fraser's clawed frog** ㉙ from Africa stays in water all its life. It has a flat body, sensitive fingers, and upward-facing eyes. The **African bullfrog** ㉚ lives in grassland and savanna. Big and aggressive, it sometimes eats its own kind. It spends the dry season underground. Males of this species defend their eggs fiercely until they hatch. The **common spadefoot toad** ㉛ digs burrows with its back legs, and spends half the year hidden away.

TREE FROGS
There are more than 900 known species of tree frogs, most of which live high up in the branches of tropical rainforests. These red-eyed tree frogs are easy to recognize, thanks to their startling colouring. Their bright eyes are thought to surprise predators and discourage them from attacking. However, during the day they often keep their eyes shut, relying on their green skin to camouflage them among forest leaves.

Size › Up to 7 cm (2¾ in) **Habitat ›** Trees and shrubs near water in warm, tropical forests and jungles. **Distribution ›** Central America **Diet ›** Insects such as crickets, flies, and moths, also worms and spiders. **Breeding ›** Females lay a batch of 50 eggs on a leaf over water. This process is repeated several times. The eggs hatch after about five days and tadpoles fall into the water. **Lifespan ›** Up to five years. **Predators ›** Many climbing and flying birds, reptiles, and mammals, including snakes and monkeys. Fish may prey on tadpoles. **Conservation status ›** Numbers of some species are declining where their forest habitats are being cut down.

Salamanders and newts

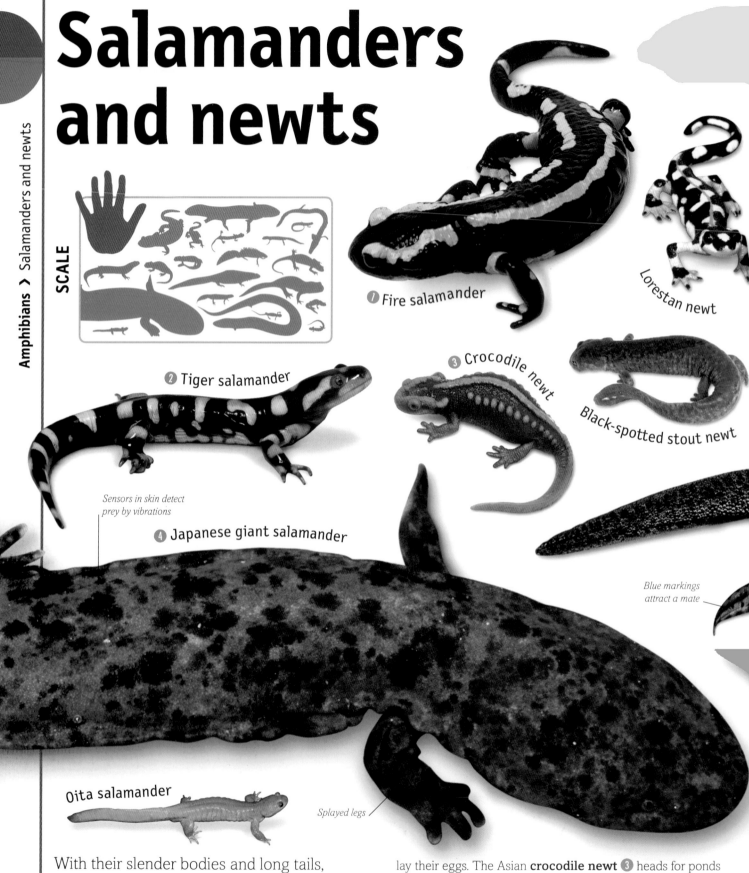

SCALE

① Fire salamander

Lorestan newt

② Tiger salamander

③ Crocodile newt

Black-spotted stout newt

Sensors in skin detect prey by vibrations

④ Japanese giant salamander

Blue markings attract a mate

Oita salamander

Splayed legs

With their slender bodies and long tails, salamanders and newts look very different from frogs and toads. Many are well camouflaged, but others, including the **fire salamander** ① and **tiger salamander** ②, have bright warning colours. This shows other animals that they are poisonous and best left alone. Some species spend all their lives on land, but most return to water to mate and lay their eggs. The Asian **crocodile newt** ③ heads for ponds at the beginning of the monsoon, while the **Japanese giant salamander** ④ is fully aquatic and never leaves its watery home. Measuring up to 1.5 m (5 ft) long, this huge, wrinkly-skinned amphibian feeds on fish and freshwater insects, and hunts after dark. Young salamanders and newts breathe using feathery gills. Some salamander species, such as the

⑤ Axolotl

Feathery gills

Three-lined salamander

⑥ Olm

Sardinian brook salamander

Italian cave salamander

⑦ Great crested newt

⑧ California newt

Sharp-ribbed salamander

Bones can poke through sides for defence

California giant salamander

Alpine newt

⑨ Ensatina salamander

Spectacled salamander

⑩ Three-toed amphiuma

Four-toed salamander

axolotl ⑤ and olm ⑥, keep their gills throughout their lives. If the axolotl loses a body part, it can regrow the entire part within months. The olm lives in dark, flooded caves. Extremely slender and totally blind, it finds its food by smell and touch. **Great crested newts** ⑦ breed in ponds, and have elaborate courtship displays. The male grows his impressive crest in spring and uses it to attract females waiting to lay their eggs.

On land, salamanders and newts live in damp woodlands and rocky places, and hunt mainly after dark. During the summer, many species, such as the **California newt** ⑧ and **Ensatina salamander** ⑨, keep moist by hiding under rotting logs. The **three-toed amphiuma** ⑩ buries itself in mud, and makes a waterproof cocoon. This slimy, snake-like amphibian has tiny legs but a powerful bite.

Reptiles

Millions of years ago reptiles ruled the Earth in the form of dinosaurs. Modern reptiles are mostly smaller, although they still include fearsome predators such as the Komodo dragon, giant snakes, and ferocious crocodiles, which can attack and kill human beings. However, they also include gentle vegetarians, such as giant tortoises and the green sea turtle.

Cold-blooded › Unlike birds and mammals, reptiles cannot keep their bodies warm by burning food. Instead they rely on sources of heat in their environment to keep warm.

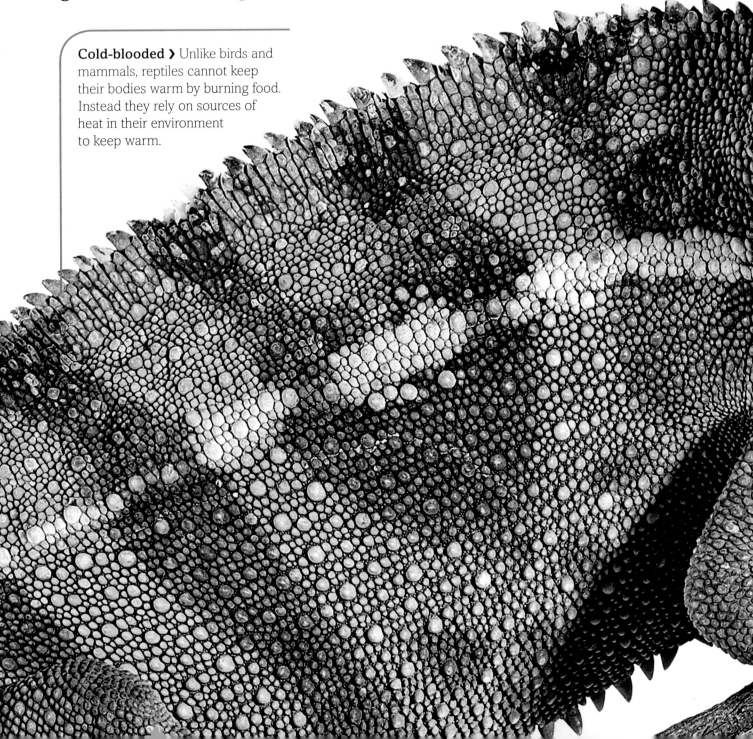

Scaly skin › As well as skin, reptiles have an outer layer of protective armour. Lizards and snakes are covered in scales. Turtles, tortoises, crocodiles, and alligators have scutes, horny layers of skin backed by bony plates.

Panther chameleon

Features

- Mostly lay eggs to reproduce

- Have dry, scaly skins

- Are mostly meat-eaters

- Mostly live in warmer climates

- Are cold-blooded

Lungs › Reptiles have lungs and must breathe air to survive. Even turtles that live under water, usually return to the surface to breathe.

Legs › Most reptiles have four legs. Some groups, such as snakes, have no legs at all. They move by pushing against the ground with their flexible bodies.

Turtles and tortoises

Blanding's turtle

Golden coin turtle

① Yellow-marginated box turtle

② Red-bellied turtle

Hawksbill sea turtle

Jaws can cut fish in two

④ Leatherback sea turtle

③ Carolina box turtle

Red-eared slider

Rubbery shell

Saltwater terrapin

⑤ Common snapping turtle

Hooked beak delivers a powerful bite

140

With their domed shells and beak-like mouths, turtles and tortoises are easy to recognize. The **yellow-marginated box turtle** ① has a hinge on the underside of its shell. If danger strikes, it quickly pulls in its head and legs, and shuts itself away. The American **red-bellied turtle** ② likes sunning itself near the shore, while the **Carolina box turtle** ③ escapes the heat by retreating into cover or by burying itself in mud. Turtles and tortoises come in many sizes. The smallest ones are not much bigger than a baseball, but the record-breaking **leatherback sea turtle** ④ can weigh as much as a small car. It is one of the greatest travellers in the animal world, swimming vast distances with its large flippers. Sea turtles live mainly in tropical oceans, but freshwater turtles live in rivers and lakes, where they eat

Big-headed turtle

Chinese soft-shelled turtle **6**

1 Painted turtle

European pond turtle

Matamata

False map turtle

Common snake-necked turtle

Asian leaf turtle

8 Alligator snapping turtle

Mississippi mud turtle

Common musk turtle

Ornate box turtle

9 Loggerhead sea turtle

Paddle-like limb

SCALE

Yellow slider

plants or animal prey. The **common snapping turtle 5**, from North America, is one of the world's biggest freshwater turtles. It lurks in the mud at the bottom of rivers and lakes. The **Chinese soft-shelled turtle 6** has a nose like a snorkel, and spends most of its time in the water. Turtles and tortoises breed by laying eggs. Freshwater kinds, such as the **painted turtle 7**, lay theirs in holes not far from the water's edge. The

female **alligator snapping turtle 8** leaves the water in spring to lay eggs, whereas the male spends most of his time at the bottom of rivers or lakes. Sea turtles, including the **loggerhead 9**, dig nests in sandy beaches. After hatching, the young turtles dig their way to the surface and then scuttle towards the sea. It is a dangerous time, and many are caught by predators before they reach the water's edge.

141

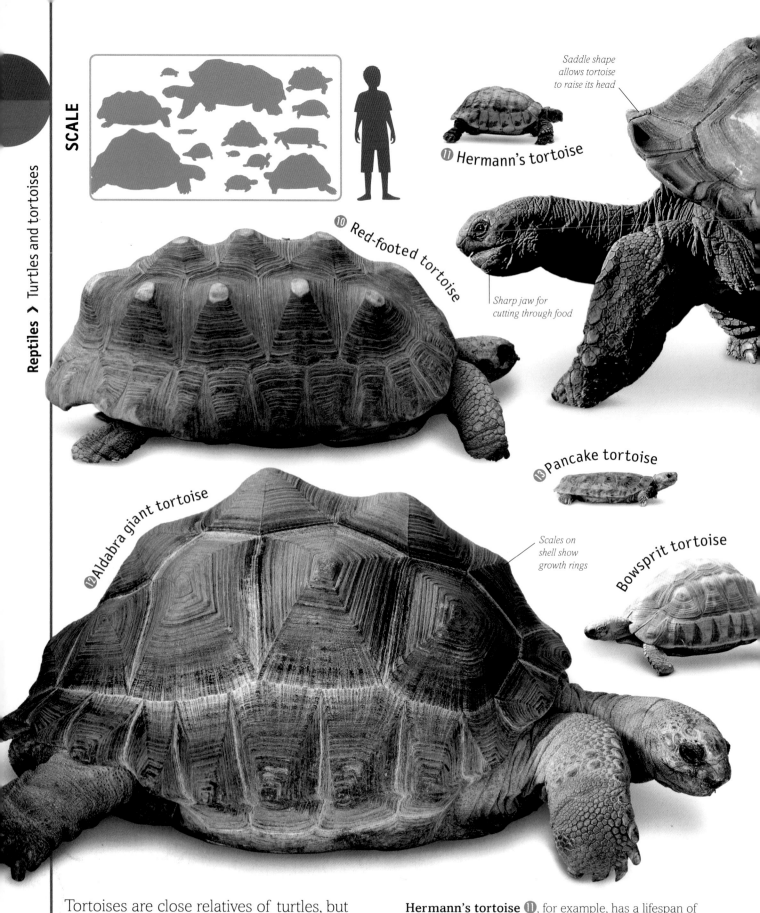

SCALE

Saddle shape allows tortoise to raise its head

⑪ Hermann's tortoise

Sharp jaw for cutting through food

⑩ Red-footed tortoise

⑫ Aldabra giant tortoise

⑬ Pancake tortoise

Scales on shell show growth rings

Bowsprit tortoise

Tortoises are close relatives of turtles, but they have stronger legs and spend all their lives on land. Like turtles, tortoises breed by laying eggs. Most of them are vegetarian, although some, including the South American **red-footed tortoise** ⑩, also eat small animals and dead remains. Tortoises are famous for being slow, but to make up for this, they can be amazingly long-lived. The

Hermann's tortoise ⑪, for example, has a lifespan of 50 years, while the **Aldabra giant tortoise** ⑫ from coral islands in the Indian Ocean can survive for more than two centuries. One recently died in captivity at the astonishing age of 255. Most tortoises have high shells, which predators find hard to break. The African **pancake tortoise** ⑬ is almost flat, which allows it to hide in rocky cracks to avoid

⑭ Galápagos tortoise

⑮ Radiated tortoise

Shell with vertical streaks

Elongated tortoise

⑯ Indian starred tortoise

Knobbly shell

Serrated hinge-back tortoise

Wood turtle

⑰ Spur-thighed tortoise

Leopard tortoise

⑱ Desert tortoise

predators. It has the tiniest families, as it lays just one egg at a time, although it usually breeds several times each year. **Galápagos tortoises** ⑭ live on islands in the Pacific Ocean. They are as large as the Aldabra giant tortoise, and often have shells with a saddle-shaped front. This lets them stretch their necks high up to munch prickly cacti, their primary food. **Radiated tortoises** ⑮, from Madagascar,

have shells with raised knobs, but the lumpiest shell belongs to the **Indian starred tortoise** ⑯, which has star-like markings that hide it in dry grass. The **spur-thighed tortoise** ⑰ from Europe and North Africa has bony projections on its hind legs. It lays up to 20 eggs at a time, while the **desert tortoise** ⑱, found in small burrows in the deserts of North America, lays as few as four eggs.

143

Lizards

SCALE

① Emerald skink

Slender toes for climbing trees

Green anole

Cape girdled lizard

Shiny, beadlike scales

② Gila monster

Desert horned lizard

③ Asian water monitor

④ Madagascar day gecko

Toes with sharp claws for climbing

There are more than 4,000 lizard species in the world, more than all other reptiles put together. Most of them hunt small animals, and most lay eggs, although some give birth to live young. The **emerald skink** ① preys on insects. It spends most of its time on tree trunks, while the heavy-bodied **Gila monster** ② stays on the ground. Found in North American deserts, the Gila monster is one of the few lizards with a poisonous bite. Fortunately, it is a slow mover, so attacks on people are very rare. The fierce **Asian water monitor** ③ grows up to 2 m (6½ ft) long. A good swimmer, it hunts all sorts of animals, from fish and frogs to crabs. The **Madagascar day gecko** ④ is mostly found on trees and belongs to a family of lizards famous for their "sticky" toes. Like other geckos, it can cling to almost

5 Frilled lizard

Frill opens like
an umbrella

6 Sandfish skink

Knight anole

Strong back legs
built for speed

Long, flattened tail
used in swimming

7 Green basilisk

Large psammodromus

Spiky crest

8 Marine iguana

Rough-scaled plated lizard

Viviparous lizard

Wonder gecko

any surface, and can even hunt upside down. When faced with danger, many lizards shed their tails. This distracts their enemies while they run away. The Australian **frilled lizard 5** has a different technique to protect itself. It stands its ground and opens up its frill, making it look much more threatening than it really is. The North African **sandfish skink 6** dives for safety, disappearing into the desert sand by "swimming" through it. The **green basilisk 7** from Central America has the most impressive escape trick of all. Standing on its back legs, it runs over the surface of lakes and streams, before swimming away from the predator. Found in the Galapagos Islands, the **marine iguana 8** is the only lizard that feeds in the sea. It uses its blunt jaws to tear seaweed from underwater rocks.

145

9 Common leopard gecko

10 Slow worm

Solomon Islands skink

11 Common scaly foot

Berber skink

Mediterranean gecko

12 Green iguana

Italian wall lizard

Moorish gecko

13 Parson's chameleon

Tail can wrap around branches

Colorado desert fringe-toed lizard

SCALE

Fringe-toed lizard

Geckos are widespread in warm parts of the world, where there are plenty of insects for them to hunt. One of the most popular reptile pets, the **common leopard gecko 9** from South Asia is easy to look after. This small gecko has an amazingly loud call for an animal just 20 cm (8 in) long. The **slow worm 10**, from Europe, has no legs at all while the **common scaly foot 11**, from Australia,

looks like a snake with tiny leg flaps, Both these lizards hunt insects and spiders, finding their prey on the ground. The Central American **green iguana 12** is a much bigger reptile, with a spiky crest. Although it looks dangerous, it feeds mainly on plants and often climbs high up trees. Chameleons are even better climbers and hardly ever come to the ground. **Parson's chameleon 13** from Madagascar

Western banded gecko

14 Tokay gecko

Yellow-spotted night lizard

Green-striped tree dragon

15 African fat-tailed gecko

Body fat in tail used as a food reserve

16 Jackson's chameleon

17 Red tegu

is the largest chameleon. It creeps along branches using its feet and its tail and catches insects by shooting out its unbelievably long, sticky tongue. Like other chameleons, its eyes swivel in all directions, and it can change colour to match its background or to show its mood. The **tokay gecko 14** gets its name from its harsh "to-kay" call. This large gecko from Southeast Asia lives in houses and often

hunts indoors. **African fat-tailed geckos 15** live in deserts. Unlike other geckos, they do not have sticky toes, and rarely climb. **Jackson's chameleon 16** lives in East Africa. The males of this species are identified by the three horns on their snouts. The **red tegu 17** is one of the biggest lizards in South America. A predator and a scavenger, it sometimes steals chickens from farms.

147

KOMODO DRAGON
Like a creature out of a horror film, the Komodo dragon lurches over the ground in search of carrion and live prey. The world's largest lizard, it has a poisonous bite, and can smell food more than 5 km (3 miles) away by flicking out its forked tongue. It can swallow small prey whole and knock down bigger animals with a swipe of its powerful tail, killing them with a bite to the throat.

Size › Up to 3.1 m (10 ft) long **Weight ›** Males up to 90 kg (198 lb); females weigh about half as much. **Habitat ›** Tropical forest and scrub. Adults live on the ground, but young dragons are more agile and live in trees to stay safe. **Distribution ›** Indonesian islands of Komodo, Rinca, Padar, and western Flores. **Diet ›** All kinds of carrion and live prey, including wild pigs, water buffalo, snakes, and lizards. **Lifespan ›** About 30 years **Top speed ›** 20 kph (12 mph), but only in short bursts. **Predators ›** Adults have no natural enemies. Young dragons may be eaten by snakes, birds of prey, and even other dragons. **Conservation status ›** Komodo dragons are threatened by hunting and by forest and scrub clearance.

Snakes

SCALE

Prairie rattlesnake

① Gaboon viper

Malayan pitviper

Asp viper

④ Boa constrictor

② Mole viper

Red spitting cobra

Red colour darkens with age

③ Desert death adder

Sunbeam snake

Wide scales on underside

Ceylonese pipesnake

East African sand boa

⑤ King cobra

Neck widens into "hood" to scare off predators

Rainbow boa

⑥ Monocled cobra

With their sleek, shiny bodies and needle-sharp fangs, snakes often trigger panic and fear. Most kinds are harmless to humans, but venomous ones kill more than 20,000 people a year. All snakes are legless, and nearly all eat live prey. Their amazingly flexible jaws and stomachs let them swallow animals much wider than themselves. The African **Gaboon viper** ① waits to ambush its prey with record-breaking fangs up to 5 cm (2 in) long. In a single bite, it can inject enough venom to kill a baboon or an antelope. The African **mole viper** ② catches small animals underground, while the extremely venomous **desert death adder** ③ from Australia attracts food by using the thin, worm-like tip of its tail as a lure. The **boa constrictor** ④ from Central America is non-venomous and kills by muscle power alone. Like other

Western diamond-backed rattlesnake ➐

"Rattle" made of dry skin

Desert horned viper

Dusty colour provides camouflage

➑ Green anaconda

Central American coral snake

➒ Eurasian blindsnake

Rosy boa

➓ yellow-lipped seakrait

constrictors, it coils around its prey, tightening its grip while the victim slowly suffocates. Boas feed mainly on mammals and birds, but the Asian **king cobra** ➎ is an expert at eating other snakes. At 5 m (16 ft) long, it is the biggest venomous snake on Earth. The **monocled cobra** ➏ expands its neck into a "hood" when threatened, while the North American **western diamond-backed rattlesnake** ➐ makes a rattling sound with

its tail to warn off enemies. The mighty **green anaconda** ➑ is one of the world's longest and heaviest snakes, weighing more than 100 kg (220 lb). At the other extreme, the **Eurasian blindsnake** ➒ is often less than 30 cm (12 in) long. It feeds on ants, spiders, and centipedes. Most snakes are good swimmers. The **yellow-lipped seakrait** ➓ spends its life in tropical seas, coming to land only when it is time to breed.

151

⑪ Blood python

Long-nosed snake

⑬ Banded flying snake

⑫ Green tree python

⑭ Burmese python

Balkan racer

Heat sensors in front of eyes to detect prey

California mountain kingsnake ⑮

Smooth snake

Some snakes give birth to live young, but most breed by laying eggs. Female **blood pythons** ⑪ from Southeast Asia coil around their eggs to keep them warm. The mother stays with her eggs for up to three months, and does not eat until her young have hatched. The **green tree python** ⑫ from Australasia is a superb climber, but the Asian **banded flying snake** ⑬ is even better at moving about in trees. It jumps from tree to tree, gliding up to 100 m (330 ft) by stretching out its body and flattening its underside. The **Burmese python** ⑭ is one of the longest snakes in the world, measuring up to 7 m (23 ft) from head to tail. Like all pythons and rattlesnakes, it has heat sensors on its head, letting it "see" warm-blooded prey even when it is completely dark. The brightly patterned **California**

Spotted python

Pointed snout
adapted for
burrowing

16 Pine snake

17 Grass snake

*Distinctive yellow
collar*

Giant Malagasy hognose snake

Brown treesnake

Ruthven's kingsnake

18 False water cobra

*Broad black
streak behind eyes*

Red-tailed green ratsnake

19 Garter snake

*Tail used as an
anchor while climbing*

SCALE

mountain kingsnake **15** looks venomous, but its colours
are a trick and it is actually non-poisonous. Other snakes
use different kinds of self-defence. The **pine snake** **16** from
North America squirts out horrible-smelling fluid when
threatened, while the European **grass snake** **17** turns upside
down with its tongue hanging out and pretends to be dead.
The South American **false water cobra** **18** has a dangerous

bite, and warns away enemies in the same way as a
true cobra by widening its neck. In places with cold
winters, snakes hide away and hibernate. Most hide on
their own, but North American **garter snakes** **19** gather
together in hundreds in underground dens. They come
to the surface in spring and squirm in tangled masses as
they fight for the chance to mate.

153

AFRICAN BUSH VIPER
This small but deadly snake hunts mostly at night. Although it eats small animals, its venom can cause serious illness or even death in humans. However, this hasn't stopped people from keeping it as a pet. This snake is sometimes called the variable viper because it exists in a variety of colours, including green, yellow, red, and orange, and because it may change colour as it matures.

Size ❯ Males average 65 cm (26 in) in length; females average 71 cm (28 in) **Habitat ❯** Bushes and shrubs in tropical forests and other densely vegetated areas. **Distribution ❯** West and Central Africa **Diet ❯** Small nocturnal mammals such as rodents and shrews, small birds, frogs, and reptiles. **Breeding ❯** Mating occurs in the rainy season. Females give birth to up to nine live young, abandoning them immediately afterwards. The young are venomous and able to hunt for themselves from birth. **Lifespan ❯** 10–20 years in the wild. Captive vipers may live longer. **Predators ❯** Adult African bush vipers have few if any predators. They may eat the young of their own species.

Crocodiles and alligators

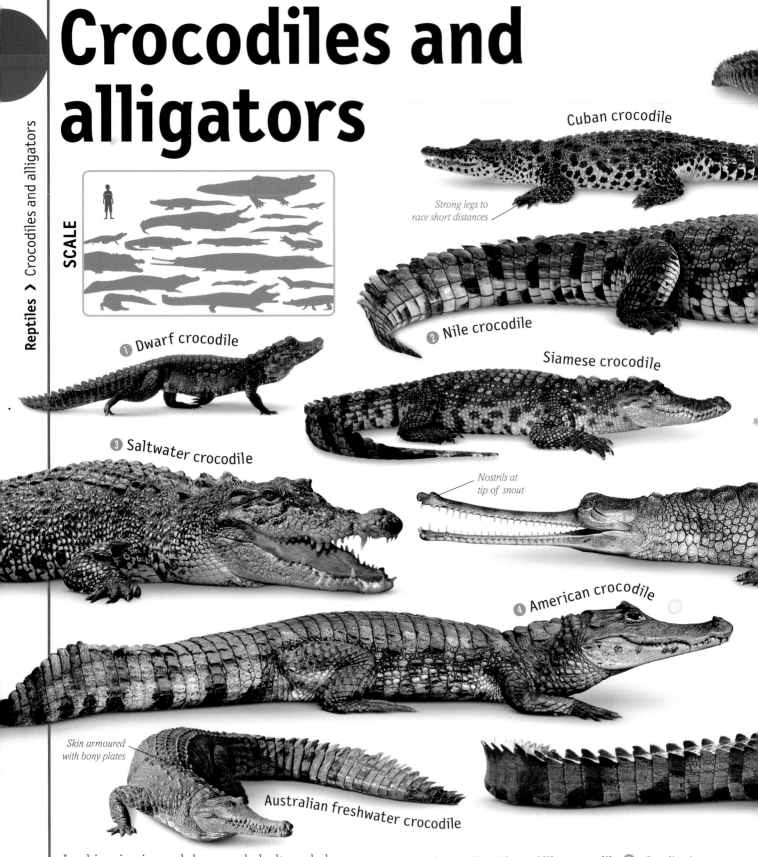

SCALE

Cuban crocodile

Strong legs to race short distances

1 Dwarf crocodile

2 Nile crocodile

Siamese crocodile

3 Saltwater crocodile

Nostrils at tip of snout

4 American crocodile

Skin armoured with bony plates

Australian freshwater crocodile

Lurking in rivers, lakes, and sheltered shores, crocodiles and alligators use stealth and muscle power to ambush and kill their prey. Even the smallest kinds, such as the African **dwarf crocodile 1**, have scales like armour plating, while the largest can smash open boats with their giant jaws. Crocodiles swallow small animals whole. They tear bigger ones apart, after pulling them underwater so they drown. The African **Nile crocodile 2** often lies in wait near the banks of rivers and water holes, where it attacks animals coming to drink. Females are devoted parents, guarding their eggs and carrying their young to water once they have hatched. Found in Australia and Southeast Asia, the **saltwater crocodile 3** is the biggest reptile in the world. Measuring up to 7 m (23 ft) long, it is

American alligator

5

Chinese alligator **6**

Cuvier's dwarf caiman

Broad-snouted caiman **7**

Sharp teeth to tear prey apart

Orinoco crocodile

Spectacled caiman **8**

Gharial **9**

Schneider's dwarf caiman

Eyes high on head to spot prey from underwater

Yacare caiman

Marsh crocodile

Black caiman

a notorious man-eater, often attacking after dark. The **American crocodile 4** feeds mainly on fish, while the **American alligator 5** eats all kinds of animals, from frogs to deer. Like the rare **Chinese alligator 6**, it can be told from true crocodiles by the shape of its head, and by the way its teeth fit together when its mouth is closed. Caimans are relatives of alligators from Central and South America. The **broad-snouted caiman 7** lives in marshes and swamps, while the **spectacled caiman 8** lives on coasts, as well as in inland lakes and rivers. The critically endangered **gharial 9** is a unique fish-eating species from India, with extremely narrow jaws and dozens of sharply pointed teeth. It lives in deep rivers and finds its prey mainly by touch.

Beak ❯ Birds use their beaks as their main tool. This parrot's beak is adapted for cracking open seeds, but other birds use theirs as drills, saws, or even strainers.

Blue-and-yellow macaw

Birds

The masters of the air, birds can fly higher, further, and faster than any other creature. Their front limbs are adapted into wings, and their bodies are covered in feathers for warmth and for a streamlined shape. Their bones are partly hollow, making them light but strong and ideally suited for flying through the air.

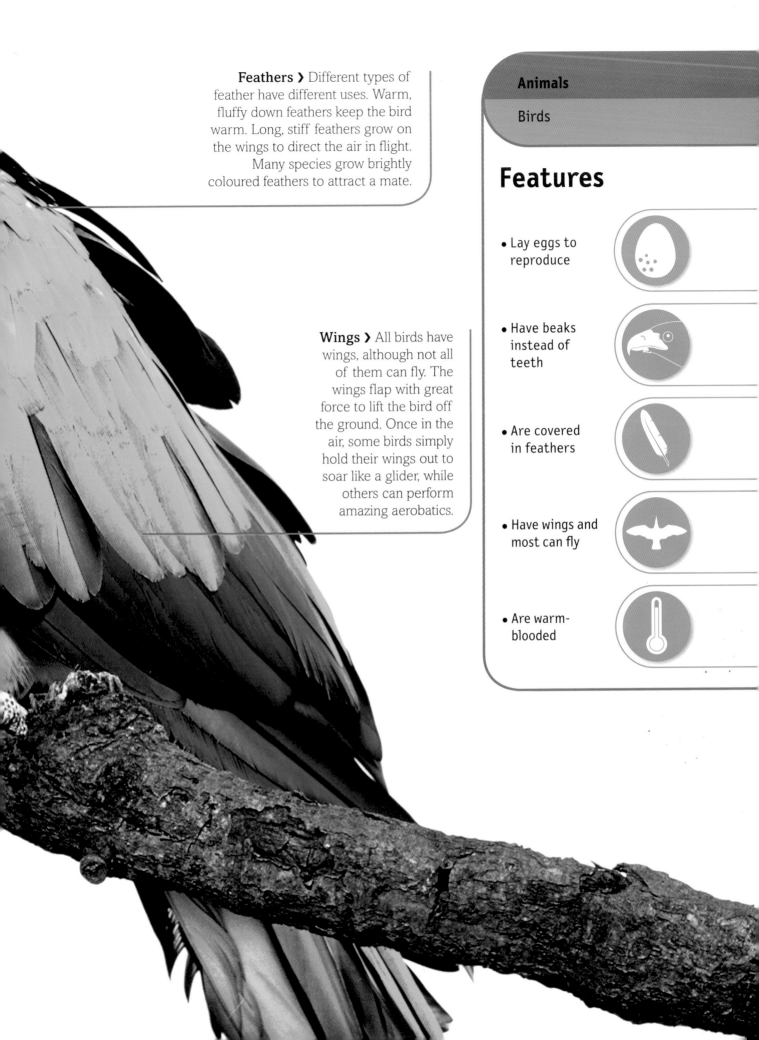

Feathers ❯ Different types of feather have different uses. Warm, fluffy down feathers keep the bird warm. Long, stiff feathers grow on the wings to direct the air in flight. Many species grow brightly coloured feathers to attract a mate.

Wings ❯ All birds have wings, although not all of them can fly. The wings flap with great force to lift the bird off the ground. Once in the air, some birds simply hold their wings out to soar like a glider, while others can perform amazing aerobatics.

Features

- Lay eggs to reproduce

- Have beaks instead of teeth

- Are covered in feathers

- Have wings and most can fly

- Are warm-blooded

Ostriches and relatives

SCALE

Males have pink necks

② Emu

Tokoeka

Long bill to forage for worms

Helmet-like crest or casque

① Ostrich

Wings used for balance while running

Great spotted kiwi

North Island kiwi

Two-toed foot

③ Northern cassowary

Standing more than 2.5 m (8 ft) tall and weighing up to 160 kg (350 lb), twice as much as a man, **ostriches** ① are the world's biggest birds. Ostriches cannot fly but they are the fastest animals on two legs, with a cruising speed of 70 kph (45 mph). They live in Africa and feed on seeds and fruit, swallowing stones as big as golf balls to help them grind up their food. **Emus** ②, from Australia, are almost as big, with feathers that look like shaggy fur. They have tiny wings, and three toes on each foot, where ostriches have two. Thousands of emus sometimes gather together in flocks, crossing deserts and raiding farmland in search of food. The **northern cassowary** ③ and **southern cassowary** ④ are rainforest birds from Australia and New Guinea, with a helmet-like crest on their heads. They live on their own and

Grey neck

⑤ Lesser rhea

Somali ostrich

④ Southern cassowary

⑥ Little spotted kiwi

⑦ Greater rhea

Grey-brown plumage for camouflage

Powerful legs for running and swimming

⑧ Ornate tinamou

⑨ Elegant crested tinamou

can be dangerous if cornered, kicking out with their claws. Rheas come from South America. Males are hard-working parents, sitting on the eggs and taking care of the stripy chicks. **Lesser rheas ⑤** live in flocks of up to 30 birds. During the breeding season, males fight for attention of female partners. Kiwis come from New Zealand and are chicken-sized, flightless birds with long beaks. They live in forests and feed at night, sniffing out insects and worms. Some are very rare. The **little spotted kiwi ⑥** lives on offshore islands, safe from predators. **Greater rheas ⑦** live in flocks of up to 100. Males use impressive wing displays to attract potential mates. The **ornate tinamou ⑧** and **elegant crested tinamou ⑨** also come from South America. They can fly, but prefer to run away from danger instead.

Gamebirds

SCALE

Chukar partridge

1 Red junglefowl

Strong feet kick aside fallen leaves

2 Wild turkey

Inflatable neck sac

3 Greater prairie chicken

Chestnut-bellied hill partridge

Male has red wattles

Palawan peacock-pheasant

Bearded guan

5 Bare-faced curassow

Fan-shaped tail in display

Vulturine guineafowl

4 Satyr tragopan

Spruce grouse

Gamebirds are often good fliers, but the majority of them spend most of their lives on the ground. They peck at seeds and small animals, and scratch up food with their feet. Unlike most other birds, they don't like washing in water, but they love taking a dust bath to keep their feathers clean. The **red junglefowl** **1** from southern Asia looks and sounds just like a farmyard rooster, with its

"cock-a-doodle-do" call. It is the distant grandparent of chickens, which are the most common birds on Earth. Found in North America, the **wild turkey** **2** is another large gamebird that has been tamed. Gamebirds live in a variety of habitats. Some, such as the **greater prairie chicken** **3**, live in open grassland, but others are found in forests, mountains, or wind-swept Arctic tundra. The **satyr**

162

⑥ Lady Amherst's pheasant

① Siamese fireback

Roulroul

Grey francolin

Western capercaillie

Plain chachalaca

Californian quail

Grey-headed chachalaca

⑧ Indian peacock

⑨ Grey partridge

Common quail

Sooty grouse

Rock ptarmigan

Red patches around eyes

Common pheasant

⑩ Malleefowl

Male's extravagant tail used to attract females

Cauca guan

tragopan ④ lives in cool forests high in the Himalayan mountains. Most gamebirds roost, or sleep, in trees, but the **bare-faced curassow** ⑤ feeds above ground, too. Male gamebirds are often much more eye-catching than females. Male **Lady Amherst's pheasants** ⑥ are stunningly coloured, and **Siamese firebacks** ⑦ have red faces and a feathery crest. **Indian peacocks** ⑧ have extraordinary plumes that open like a fan, attracting peahens. Most gamebirds nest on the ground, and some produce incredible numbers of eggs. One **grey partridge** ⑨ laid 25 eggs at one time, which is a world record for any bird. Females usually sit on the eggs to incubate them, but Australian **malleefowl** ⑩ bury their eggs inside a nest that looks like a huge compost heap. The heap warms the eggs until they hatch.

Pigeons and doves

SCALE

Shaggy blue "mane"

Nicobar pigeon

① Mourning dove

European turtle dove

White-tipped dove

Long, tapering tail separates it from similar species

② Woodpigeon

Multicoloured beak

③ African green pigeon

④ Pink pigeon

⑤ Pheasant pigeon

Pied imperial pigeon

Key West quail-dove

Large legs and toes

Pigeons and doves include many common birds, as well as others that are very rare. They have rounded bodies and short legs, and their heads often bob backwards and forwards when they walk. All of them are vegetarians, and many, including the **mourning dove** ❶ and **woodpigeon** ❷, live near fields and farms, which provide a steady supply of food. Pigeons and doves are mostly brown or grey, but some tropical kinds are much more colourful. They include the **African green pigeon** ❸, which clambers about in trees like a parrot, and the very rare **pink pigeon** ❹ from the island of Mauritius in the Indian Ocean. The pink pigeon almost became extinct in the 1990s, but was rescued by conservationists when just 10 birds were left in the wild. The **pheasant pigeon** ❺ from New Guinea

⑥ Wompoo fruit dove

⑦ Spinifex pigeon

Permanently raised spiky crest

Brown cuckoo-dove

Emerald dove

Sulawesi ground dove

Inca dove

Lacy crest bobs backwards and forwards as the bird walks

Speckled pigeon

White-speckled wings

Common bronzewing

Wonga pigeon

Spotted underparts

⑩ Southern crowned pigeon

⑧ Domestic pigeon

Namaqua dove

⑨ Diamond dove

has strong legs and feeds on the ground, while the **wompoo fruit dove** ⑥ lives high up in rainforest trees. It swallows fruit whole and scatters the seeds in its droppings, helping trees to spread. Pigeons and doves are found in dry places, too. The crested **spinifex pigeon** ⑦ lives in the rocky hills of central Australia and feeds on the seeds of desert grasses. The commonest of all, the **domestic pigeon** ⑧ thrives in

urban areas, where it dodges traffic, nests on buildings, and eats scraps of leftover food. The tiny **diamond dove** ⑨ from Australia is often seen in pairs or small groups, feeding on the ground. It is only 20 cm (8 in) long. At the other extreme, the **southern crowned pigeon** ⑩ from New Guinea weighs as much as a chicken. It is one of the biggest pigeons in the world, measuring up to 75 cm (30 in) long.

165

Parrots and cockatoos

Red-fronted macaws

Australian king parrot

Olive-headed lorikeet

❶ Pacific parrotlet

❷ Blue-and-yellow macaw

Powerful beak to crack nuts

Princess parrots

Chattering lory

❸ Grey parrot

Crest can be raised or lowered

❹ Budgerigar

❺ Kakapo

Sharp beak shreds bark and leaves

Eastern rosella

❻ Sulphur-crested cockatoo

Parrots are some of the world's brainiest, noisiest, and most colourful birds. Most of them live in tropical forests, although a few favour open habitats. They use their curved beaks to crack open nuts and seeds. and they vary greatly in size. The tiny **Pacific parrotlet** ❶ is smaller than a sparrow, but the bigger ones, such as the **blue-and-yellow macaw** ❷, can be nearly 1 m (3 ft) from head to tail. Big or small, all parrots have strong feet with fleshy toes. They use them for climbing about and for holding their food. The African **grey parrot** ❸ and the **budgerigar** ❹, from Australian grasslands, are amazingly good at mimicking human speech. One record-breaking budgerigar learned more than 1,700 words, while trained grey parrots can answer questions and even count. Found in New Zealand,

SCALE

Red-fronted parakeet

⑩ Kea

Yellow-collared lovebird

Blue-headed parrot

Female is red, with blue neck band

Male is mainly green

⑨ Eclectus parrots

Red-fan parrot

Scarlet macaw

⑧ Galah

Blue-crowned hanging parrots

Long, sharply pointed crest

Tail as long as body

⑦ Cockatiels

St Vincent parrot

Red-tailed black cockatoo

Distinctive red patch on tail

kakapos ❺ are the world's rarest and heaviest parrots. They cannot fly, and come out only at night. These slow-moving birds are easily caught by predators, and only about 125 kakapos are left in the wild. Cockatoos are parrots with feathery crests. Found in Australia and New Guinea, the **sulphur-crested cockatoo** ❻ sometimes flies into city gardens and parks, while the **cockatiel** ❼, like the budgerigar,

lives in dry scrub and grassland. Most parrots nest in tree-holes, and many, including the **galah** ❽, pair up for life. Male and female parrots often look the same, but **eclectus parrots** ❾ are so unalike that they were once thought to be different kinds of bird. The **kea** ❿ lives in the mountains of New Zealand. Unusually for a parrot, it eats almost anything, including live animals and carrion.

167

MILITARY MACAW

One of the largest and most dazzling members of the parrot family, the military macaw has spectacular plumage, with a bright green body, shimmering sky-blue wingtips, and scarlet patches on its head and tail. Its large beak is adapted for picking fruit and cracking open nuts. Highly intelligent and sociable, it is popular in zoos and is sometimes kept as a pet, although it can be noisy!

Size ❯ Body length up to 75 cm (30 in) **Wingspan ❯** Up to
1.1 m (3 ft 6 in) **Weight ❯** Around 900 g (2 lb) **Habitat ❯**
Lowland tropical forests and semi-arid woodland. Lives in
large flocks, nesting in treetops or on cliff faces. **Distribution ❯**
Central America and northern South America. **Diet ❯** Fruit,
vegetables, berries, nuts, and seeds. In the Amazon rainforest,
they sometimes eat clay from river banks, possibly to remove
toxins they have swallowed in their food. **Breeding ❯** They
perform complex courtship flights and mate for life. **Lifespan ❯**
Up to 60 years in the wild. **Predators ❯** Large mammals, some
reptiles, primates, and birds of prey. **Conservation status ❯**
Threatened by habitat loss and illegal trade in cage birds.

Cuckoos and turacos

1 Common cuckoo

Tail fanned during courtship display

2 Pheasant-cuckoo

3 Jacobin cuckoo

5 Grey go-away bird

4 Giant coua

Common koel

Klaas's cuckoo

6 Great blue turaco

Hartlaub's turaco

Violet turaco

Yellow-billed cuckoo

Raising a family is hard work for birds because they have to build a nest and look after their young. Many cuckoos skip these tasks by laying their eggs in other birds' nests. The nests' owners do not realize that they have been tricked, and raise the young cuckoos themselves. The **common cuckoo** 1 is one of the best-known of these birds, with a loud "cuc-oo" call that gives it its name. It breeds in Europe and Asia and spends the winter in Africa, undertaking a yearly journey of up to 15,000 km (9,300 miles). The **pheasant-cuckoo** 2 from Central and South America and the **jacobin cuckoo** 3 from Africa and Asia also cheat when they breed, but the **giant coua** 4 from Madagascar makes its own nest in trees. Cuckoos feed mainly on small animals such as spiders and caterpillars, but turacos live

Guira cuckoo

SCALE

Fan-tailed cuckoo

Greater coucal

⑦ Greater roadrunner

Wings used for balance when running

Great spotted cuckoo

Permanently raised spiky crest

Dideric cuckoo

⑨ Hoatzin

⑧ Green turaco

Strong toes grip branches tightly

Red-crested turaco

Short, stubby beak

but turacos live mostly on fruit. Found only in Africa, they include the noisy **grey go-away bird** ⑤ and the **great blue turaco** ⑥, which feeds high up in trees. Turacos have strong feet, and they run along branches like squirrels as they look for food. The **greater roadrunner** ⑦, from the USA and Mexico, is an extra-large cuckoo that spends much of its life on the ground. It is a great runner, as its name suggests, with

a top speed of about 30 kph (18 mph). It sprints after lizards and snakes, battering them against rocks before swallowing them whole. The **green turaco** ⑧ lays two eggs in a flimsy nest, and its young clamber out among branches before they learn to fly. The **hoatzin** ⑨ from South America is a strange bird that feeds only on leaves. Its chicks are good climbers thanks to small claws on their wings.

Owls

SCALE

① Ural owl

③ Black-and-white owl

Cuban pygmy owl

② Northern hawk-owl

④ Elf owl

Long tail, like that of a hawk

Wing feathers muffle the sound of flight

Tawny owl

⑤ Great grey owl

Black-capped screech owl

Tropical screech owl

When the sun sets, most birds settle down to sleep. Owls are the opposite, because this is when most of them start to hunt. Guided by their large eyes and super-sensitive ears, they noiselessly swoop on their prey. Owls come in many different sizes, and they live all over the world. The **Ural owl** ① and the **northern hawk-owl** ② are from northern Eurasian forests, while the **black-and-white**

owl ③ lives in the jungles of Central and South America. The tiny **elf owl** ④ is a desert-dweller from the southern USA and Mexico. It weighs only 40 g (1²⁄₅ oz), which is much lighter than a mobile phone. The **great grey owl** ⑤ is nearly 50 times heavier. It has a flat, rounded face and staring yellow eyes. Its face channels sound towards its ears, letting it pinpoint small mammals on the ground,

Eurasian scops owl

❻ Snowy owl

Large ear tufts extend sideways

Buffy fish owl

White plumage flecked with black

Short-eared owl

Spectacled owl

❼ Barn owl

❽ Northern saw-whet owl

Southern white-faced owl

❾ Great horned owl

Ferruginous pygmy owl

Long-eared owl

Desert eagle-owl

Razor-sharp talons can tackle large prey

❿ Eastern screech owl

or even under snow. The **snowy owl** ❻ lives in the high Arctic region, where its white plumage makes good winter camouflage. The sun never sets during the Arctic summer, so the owl has to hunt by day. The ghostly **barn owl** ❼ is one of the world's most widespread birds, and lives on every continent except Antarctica. It can hunt in total darkness, flying with slow wingbeats just a few metres above ground.

Owls are silent when they hunt, but many have strange or spooky calls. When it is alarmed, the **northern saw-whet owl** ❽ makes a sound like a saw being sharpened, while the **great horned owl** ❾ has a deep and echoing hoot. The **eastern screech owl** ❿ is a short, stocky bird, with a large head and almost no neck. Despite its name, this owl doesn't screech, instead it whistles and trills.

173

BARRED OWL
Named for its brown-and-white striped plumage, the barred owl is also known as the hoot owl for its distinctive, repeated call. Barred owls roost in trees during the day and hunt by night, seeking out animals such as rodents and rabbits. The feathers on their wings are specially shaped to allow them to fly almost silently so they can take their prey by surprise, swooping down to grab their victims with razor-sharp talons.

Size ❯ Up to 51 cm (20 in) long **Wingspan ❯** Up to 1.1 m (43 in) **Weight ❯** Males about 630 g (22 oz); females about 800 g (28 oz) **Habitat ❯** Forests, wooded swamps, and suburbs. **Distribution ❯** Originally found in the eastern USA, down to Texas in the south. Now also found in California, Oregon, southwestern Canada, and Mexico. **Diet ❯** Rodents, rabbits, birds, frogs, reptiles, and fish. **Breeding ❯** Females lay a clutch of one to five eggs. The chicks can fly at six weeks and mature at around two years. **Lifespan ❯** Up to 18 years in the wild. **Predators ❯** Great horned owls may occasionally take adult barred owls. Raccoons and weasels may eat eggs and young. **Conservation status ❯** Not threatened.

Hummingbirds and swifts

SCALE

① Racket-tailed puffleg

Brazilian ruby

② Andean hillstar

Broad-billed hummingbird

③ Calliope hummingbird

Buff-bellied hummingbird

Hooded visorbearer

④ Sword-billed hummingbird

Tongue protrudes from beak when feeding

Rufous hummingbird

Collared inca

Blue-throated hummingbird

Ruby-throated hummingbird

⑤ Stripe-breasted starthroat

Allen's hummingbird

Lucifer hummingbird

Scale-throated hermit

In different ways hummingbirds and swifts break all kinds of records as they speed through the air. Beating their wings up to 70 times a second, hummingbirds zip forwards, backwards, or hover on the spot like tiny helicopters. They include species such as the **racket-tailed puffleg** ①, with its eye-catching tail plumes, and the **Andean hillstar** ②, which lives high in the Andes at up to 5,000 m

(16,400 ft). The **calliope hummingbird** ③ spends the winter in Central America but migrates northwards as far north as Canada every spring, an amazing feat for such a little bird. Most hummingbirds have long beaks that work like drinking straws to suck sugary nectar from flowers. The **sword-billed hummingbird** ④ is the only bird with a beak longer than its body. It feeds on large trumpet-shaped flowers, hovering

Violet sabrewing

⑥ Bee hummingbird

① Alpine swift

Anna's hummingbird

White-vented violet-ear

⑧ White-throated swift

Long-tailed sylph

⑨ Common swift

White-necked jacobin

Ruby topaz

white-tipped sicklebill

Curved beak to drink nectar from flowers

Scythe-shaped wings for high-speed flight

Orange-red tail fanned to attract females

underneath them to get at its food. The **stripe-breasted starthroat's** ❺ folded wings are much longer than its tail. The tiny **bee hummingbird** ❻ from Cuba is the smallest bird in the world. Males are 5 cm (2 in) long and weigh less than a sugar cube. Hummingbirds are found only in the Americas, but swifts live all around the world. They feed on insects that they catch on the wing. The **alpine swift** ❼ and

white-throated swift ❽ nest in rocky crevices. Like all swifts they have tiny feet that cling but cannot hop or perch. The **common swift** ❾ from Europe, Africa, and Asia is one of the world's fastest birds. It spends most of its time on the wing, and even eats, drinks, and sleeps in flight. After leaving the nest, a young swift does not land until its second or third birthday, when it starts to breed.

Kingfishers and relatives

Racquet-tipped tail can swing like a pendulum

1 Blue-crowned motmot

2 Red-billed hornbill

Large eyes with feathery eyelashes

Turquoise-browed motmot

3 Northern ground hornbill

Hollow chamber amplifies hornbill's call

5 European bee-eater

4 Malabar pied hornbill

6 White-throated bee-eater

Short claws on strong feet

Tail with central spike seen in adults

Kingfishers often live near water, but most of their relatives are land-based. Many of them hunt small animals, and nearly all dig nest holes in riverbanks or in trees. The biggest of these birds are ground hornbills, which can weigh twice as much as a farmyard hen. At the other extreme, some kingfishers weigh just 10 g (⅓ oz), which is less than a CD. The **blue-crowned motmot** **1** from Central and South America swoops on insects and other animals from a favourite perch. The African **red-billed hornbill** **2** lives on the ground and in trees, while the **northern ground hornbill** **3** patrols Africa's grasslands on its large scaly feet. Hornbills get their name from the helmet, or casque, that many have on top of their beaks. The **Malabar pied hornbill** **4** from South Asia has an

Crest raised on take-off and landing

7 Hoopoe

Racquet-tailed roller

Buff-breasted paradise kingfisher

8 Common kingfisher

Blue-bellied roller

Trumpeter hornbill

Flattened bill for catching insects in flight

Jamaican tody

Slender beak to probe for insects in trees

Green wood hoopoe

Brown plumage camouflages the bird in trees

African pygmy kingfisher

10 Laughing kookaburra

9 Belted kingfisher

Little kingfisher

Pied kingfisher

Yellow-billed kingfisher

SCALE

extra-large casque, and its wings make a distinct whooshing sound as it flies. **European bee-eaters** 5 and **white-throated bee-eaters** 6 are experts at catching bees while flying. After they have caught one, they wipe it against a perch to remove its sting. The **hoopoe** 7 is a migratory bird that breeds in Europe and Asia. It uses its slender beak to probe in the ground for grubs and worms. **Common**

kingfishers 8 live along rivers and streams, where they dive for fish. The North American **belted kingfisher** 9 is another waterside hunter. Like its relatives, it hits its catch against a perch before swallowing it head-first. The Australian **laughing kookaburra** 10 is the world's biggest kingfisher, with a noisy laughing call. It lives in woodland and swoops on anything that it can swallow, including insects, lizards, and snakes.

Toucans and woodpeckers

Great barbet

SCALE

Saffron toucanet

Beak with serrated edges

Collared aracari

Red-breasted toucan

Green-backed honeybird

❶

❸ White-whiskered puffbird

Rusty-breasted nunlet

White-eared puffbird ❹

Beak has honeycomb-like air spaces

❷ Spot-billed toucanet

❻ Chestnut-eared aracari

Black-fronted nunbird

Long, slender tongue

Toucans and woodpeckers look very different but they belong to the same group of birds. They live mainly in woods and forests, and usually nest in holes. All of them have specially shaped feet for clinging to tree trunks, but the most attention-grabbing feature of toucans is a giant multicoloured beak. The **red-breasted toucan** ❶ feeds mainly on fruit. Like many toucans, its beak is filled with air

spaces, saving a lot of weight. The **spot-billed toucanet** ❷ has a smaller beak but it feeds in typical toucan style. After picking a piece of fruit, it tosses it in the air and then swallows it whole. The **white-whiskered puffbird** ❸ and **white-eared puffbird** ❹ feed mainly on insects, and often nest in old termite mounds or in holes in the ground. Like toucans, **collared aracaris** ❺ and **chestnut-eared aracaris** ❻ live

Toucan-barbet

Yellow-fronted tinkerbird

7 Toco toucan

8 Northern flicker

Great spotted woodpecker **9**

Spotted piculet

Red-headed barbet

Beak more than half the bird's body length

D'Arnaud's barbet

Prominent red crest is always raised

Two toes face forwards and two backwards

Northern wryneck

Rufous-tailed jacamar

Long, thin, dagger-like beak

11 Pileated woodpecker

Red-and-yellow barbet

Yellow-fronted woodpecker

10 Heart-spotted woodpecker

Ochraceous piculet

Yellow-bellied sapsucker

Tail braces body against tree-trunk

in the forests in Central and South America. They roam the treetops in small flocks and roost together in hollow trees. The **toco toucan** **7** is one of the largest birds in the toucan family. Its colossal beak allows it to reach fruit growing on the tips of branches. It also eats small animals such as insects and frogs. Some woodpeckers, including the **northern flicker** **8**, feed on the ground, but most cling to tree trunks and hammer into them with their beaks in search of insects to eat. The **great spotted woodpecker** **9** from Europe and Asia eats wood-boring grubs, while the **heart-spotted woodpecker** **10** from Southeast Asia probes for insects under bark. The North American **pileated woodpecker** **11** is one of the largest of these wood-busting birds. Despite its impressive size, it feeds mainly on ants.

Birds of prey

SCALE

① Bateleur

Swainson's hawk

Finger-like flight feathers

Lizard buzzard

Red-tailed hawk

② Harris's hawk

Golden bronze feathers, only present on the head and nape

③ Golden eagle

African hawk eagle

④ Bald eagle

Powerful wings for heavy lifting

With their hooked beaks and piercing claws, birds of prey are natural killers. Most of them use their feet to grab food, and their hooked beaks to tear it apart. Some, such as the African **bateleur** ①, eat carrion as well as live prey. Vultures, on the other hand, are full-time scavengers, gulping down rotting remains. Birds of prey usually hunt alone, but the **Harris's hawk** ② from

North America is one of the few that work in teams. The **golden eagle** ③ hunts over mountains and the Arctic tundra. With its huge wings and powerful legs, it can lift prey as heavy as itself. North American **bald eagles** ④ often gather near water, where they catch live fish or eat dead ones that wash up on the shore. They build massive nests from sticks, and the biggest one on record weighed

⑤ Lanner falcon

⑥ Common kestrel

Eurasian buzzard

Forward-facing eyes for judging distances

⑦ Peregrine falcon

Large, broad wings and a short tail

American kestrel

Long-legged buzzard

Eagle-like head, with a hooked beak

⑨ Secretary bird

Merlin

Snake about to be swallowed whole

⑧ Osprey

Long, partly feathered legs

African pygmy falcon

Reversible outer toe for a better grip of prey

nearly 3 tonnes. Falcons and kestrels are much smaller birds, with slim bodies and slender wings. The **Lanner falcon ⑤** dives down on other birds, while the **common kestrel ⑥** hovers in mid-air before dropping on voles, insects, and even worms. The **peregrine falcon ⑦** is the fastest animal on Earth. Hurtling towards the ground with its wings partly folded, it can hit speeds of more than

300 kph (186 mph), which is almost as fast as a Formula 1 racing car. Found all over the world, the **osprey ⑧** hunts fish, snatching them from the water's surface and then carrying them back to its perch. The African **secretary bird ⑨** has extra-long legs and hunts on the ground. An expert snake-eater, it uses its wings as shields and often stamps on its prey before swallowing it whole.

183

Yellow-headed caracara

Adult has black streak behind the eye

Turkey-vulture ⑪

Striated caracara

⑩ Crested caracara

White collar in adults

⑬ Andean condor

⑫ Black vulture

Hooked beak for tearing food apart

⑭ Red kite

White-tailed kite

⑮ Snail kite

Mississippi kite

SCALE

Many birds of prey won't touch food unless it is alive. Caracaras are less picky, and don't mind if their food is living or dead. The **crested caracara** ⑩ feeds mainly on the ground, but it also behaves like an airborne raider, chasing other birds to make them drop their prey. Most vultures have weak claws and rarely hunt for themselves. Instead they work like a clean-up squad, tracking down and feeding on dead

remains. American **turkey-vultures** ⑪ often feed on animals killed on roads, although **black vultures** ⑫ sometimes push them aside so they can get all the food for themselves. The **Andean condor** ⑬ from South America is the largest vulture, and one of the world's biggest flying birds. With its huge 3.2 m (10½ ft) wingspan, it soars over remote mountains and rocky shores, feeding on all kinds of animal casualties, including

Head and neck almost bald

⑯ Rüppell's vulture

⑰ Egyptian vulture

Bare skin around eyes

⑱ Palm-nut vulture

Streaked chest

Northern goshawk

Northern harrier

⑲ African white-backed vulture

stranded whales. Kites are hunters and scavengers that patrol near the ground. The **red kite** ⑭ often feeds on dead rabbits and birds, but the **snail kite** ⑮ eats freshwater apple snails. Holding them down with one foot, it uses its slender beak to pull the snails out of their shells. Africa and Asia have many vultures of their own. The **Rüppell's vulture** ⑯ is almost bald on its head and neck, as feathers in this area would get

clogged with blood when the bird feeds on animal carcasses. The **Egyptian vulture** ⑰ uses stones to crack open ostrich eggs. The **palm-nut vulture** ⑱ is partly vegetarian. It swallows oil-palm fruit, as well as insects, scorpions, and crabs. The **African white-backed vulture** ⑲ uses its large wings to soar and circle in the air, looking for carrion. Like the Rüppell's vulture, it jostles for food at big carcasses.

KING VULTURE
Found in Central and South America, the king vulture may have got its name from its habit of driving smaller birds away from its food. Like all vultures, this odd-looking, colourful scavenger feeds on carrion. It is one of the largest and most powerful scavenging birds, and its sharp beak and strong muscles can rip open the carcasses of dead animals that other, smaller birds cannot get into.

Size > Body up to 80 cm (32 in) long. **Wingspan >** Up to 2 m (6½ ft) **Weight >** Up to 4.5 kg (10 lb) **Habitat >** Lowland tropical forests and nearby grasslands. **Distribution >** Tropical areas of Central and South America, from Mexico to Argentina. **Diet >** Dead animals **Breeding >** Females lay one creamy white egg, which takes up to 58 days to hatch. Both parents care for the young, feeding it with carrion which they store in a throat pouch called a crop. **Lifespan >** Unknown in the wild. More than 30 years in captivity. **Predators >** Snakes may take the eggs. Jaguars may eat sick or injured adults. **Conservation status >** Not currently in danger, but numbers are declining possibly due to habitat loss.

Ducks, geese, and swans

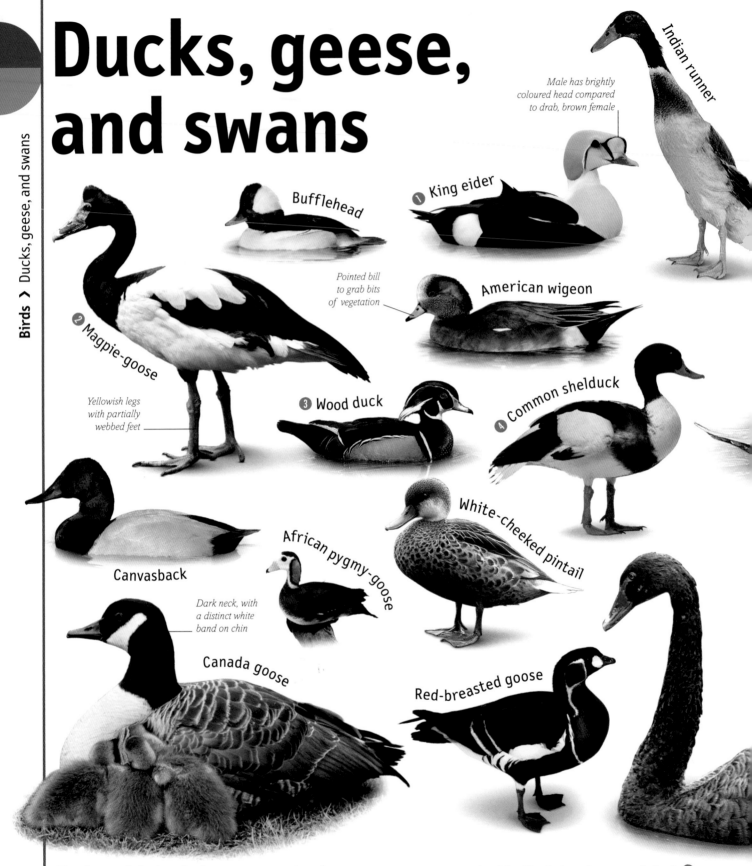

Indian runner

Male has brightly coloured head compared to drab, brown female

① King eider

Bufflehead

Pointed bill to grab bits of vegetation

American wigeon

② Magpie-goose

Yellowish legs with partially webbed feet

③ Wood duck

④ Common shelduck

White-cheeked pintail

Canvasback

African pygmy-goose

Dark neck, with a distinct white band on chin

Canada goose

Red-breasted goose

Ducks and their relatives are expert swimmers, which is why they are also known as waterfowl. Nearly all of them have webbed feet and waterproof feathers. Most live on lakes and rivers, but some ducks, including the **king eider** ①, breed on coasts and spend the winter at sea. **Magpie-geese** ② lay up to 12 eggs a year. Despite having large families, they face lots of predators and only a few of

the young survive. The North American **wood duck** ③ nests high up in tree-holes. Soon after the ducklings hatch, their mother leads them to water, and they have to jump all the way to the ground. The **common shelduck** ④ often breeds in rabbit burrows, but most other waterfowl nest in the open, near the water's edge. Geese feed mainly on grass, but ducks and swans usually eat while afloat. **Northern**

5 Northern shoveler

Large crest can be expanded

Hooded merganser

SCALE

6 Red-breasted merganser

Long-tailed duck

Saw-like red beak for gripping fish

1 Mute swan

Male is black, with white patch on forehead

8 Bar-headed goose

Surf scoter

Grey head with a feathery crest

Plumed whistling duck

Southern screamer

9 Mallard

10 Domestic duck

11 Black swan

Baikal teal

Smew

shovelers **5** use their flat beaks to filter small animals from water, while **red-breasted mergansers 6** have saw-edged beaks for catching slippery fish. **Mute swans 7** tip up on end as they swim, using their long necks to reach for food buried in mud. When threatened, these swans curve their necks and half-raise their wings to scare off attackers. The **bar-headed goose 8** is a long-distance migrant, climbing to over 6,000 m (19,700 ft) as it crosses the Himalayas. Waterfowl include some well-known farmyard birds. The **mallard 9** is the most widespread duck in the world. The **domestic duck 10**, a descendant of the mallard, has been farmed for thousands of years. Found only around wet habitats, the Australian **black swan 11** is a large, nomadic bird, which flies to lakes that fill up after rain.

189

Penguins

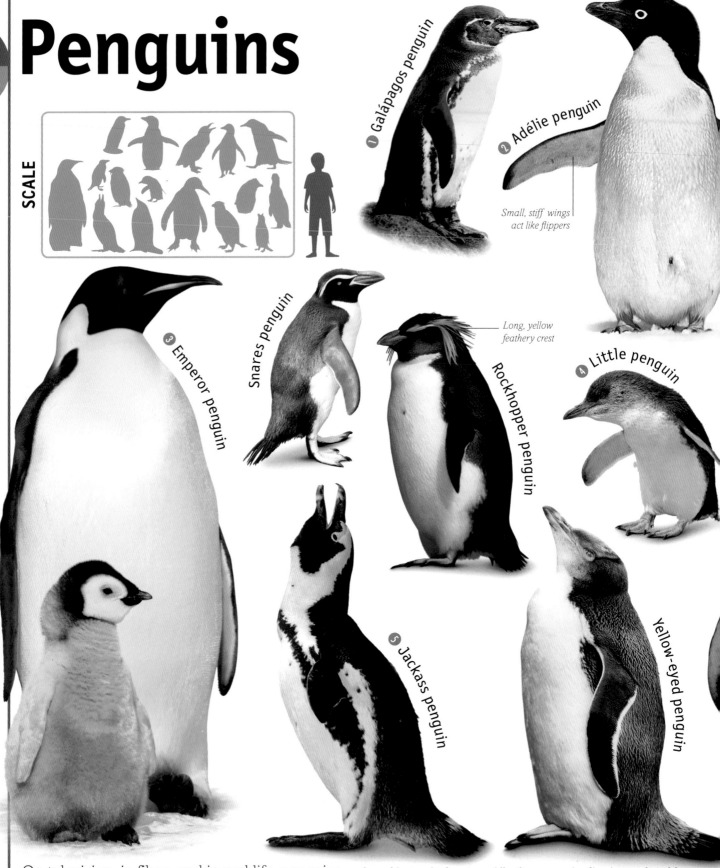

SCALE

① Galápagos penguin

② Adélie penguin

Small, stiff wings act like flippers

③ Emperor penguin

Snares penguin

Long, yellow feathery crest

Rockhopper penguin

④ Little penguin

⑤ Jackass penguin

Yellow-eyed penguin

On television, in films, and in real life, penguins have true star appeal, with their upright bodies and black-and-white plumage. Penguins cannot fly, but they are superb swimmers. They use their wings like flippers to speed after fish and other prey in some of the world's coldest and stormiest seas. **Galápagos penguins** ① live in the Galápagos Islands right on the Equator. They are the only penguins to breed in tropical waters. All other penguins live in much colder waters in the Southern Hemisphere. **Adélie penguins** ② are among the few that breed in Antarctica, building nests out of stones among the rocks in spring. Another Antarctic species, the **Emperor penguin** ③ is the biggest penguin, growing up to 1.2 m (4 ft) in height. It breeds on the ice, and males keep the eggs warm during the long polar winter by balancing

6 Humboldt penguin

Chinstrap penguin

Gentoo penguin

Fiordland penguin

Long beak for catching fish and squid

Magellanic penguin 7

8 King penguin

9 Macaroni penguin

Erect-crested penguin

Short legs and strong feet for swimming

them on their feet. The females, meanwhile, stay out at sea to feed, returning to land when the chicks hatch. The **little penguin** 4, at 40 cm (16 in), is the smallest of all penguins. It nests in burrows on the shores of New Zealand and Australia, coming ashore after dark. The **African** or **jackass penguin** 5 gets its name from its donkey-like call. It is a close relative of the **Humboldt penguin** 6 and Magellanic

penguin 7, both of which nest in the far south of South America. The **king penguin** 8 looks like a smaller version of the emperor penguin. It nests on remote rocky islands in Antarctica, and incubates its eggs in the same way as the emperor penguin. The **macaroni penguin** 9 is one of several kinds of penguin with feathery crests. It comes to land to breed, but spends the rest of the year far out at sea.

EMPEROR PENGUINS
These tall, stately birds are the largest of all penguin species. Emperor penguins live on pack ice and hunt in the freezing waters of the Antarctic Ocean, darting after fish with incredible agility. Their dense feathers and thick layer of fat protect them from the intense cold. On land, adults and chicks huddle together in large colonies, taking turns to enjoy the warmth at the centre of the group.

Size › About 1.15 m (3¾ ft) tall **Weight ›** Up to 37 kg (81.5 lb)
Habitat › Coastal areas, islands, and pack ice. **Distribution ›**
Antarctica **Diet ›** Fish, squid, crustaceans, and krill. **Breeding ›**
Emperor penguins breed once a year during winter. Females
lay a single egg, then leave to find food. Males rest the eggs
on their feet, covering them with a warm layer of skin called a
brood pouch. The females return once the eggs have hatched.
Both parents then care for the chick. **Predators ›** Adults may
be eaten by killer whales, sharks, or leopard seals. The chicks
may be taken by birds such as Antarctic skuas and giant petrels.
Conservation status › Scientists suspect this species will
become threatened as sea ice melts due to climate change.

Storks, ibises, and herons

SCALE

Yellow "saddle" on top of beak

① Great egret

⑥ Saddle-billed stork

Beak turns deep orange during mating season

S-shaped neck straightens to stab prey

② Cattle egret

Reddish egret

④ Eurasian spoonbill

Beak with sensitive spoon-shaped tip

Indian pond heron

③ Eurasian bittern

Little egret

⑤ Roseate spoonbill

Little bittern

With their long beaks and even longer legs, storks and their relatives are built for hunting by stealth. Many of them stride through shallow water in search of food, but some species feed on land. The **great egret** ① waits patiently for fish and frogs and then spears them with a sudden jab of its beak. The **cattle egret** ② hunts in rough grassland, snapping up grasshoppers and other insects stirred up by animal hooves. Bitterns hunt by the water's edge, with their necks hunched and ready to strike. The **Eurasian bittern** ③ is perfectly camouflaged to match dead reeds. If anyone comes nearby, it stands up straight and sways slowly from side to side, just like reeds blowing in the wind. **Eurasian spoonbills** ④ and American **roseate spoonbills** ⑤ catch their prey by wading through water and

Tricoloured heron

Wood stork

7 Black-crowned night heron

Short, thick beak

Boat-billed heron

8 Grey heron

10 Scarlet ibis

Partially webbed toes

Black wingtips

9 European white stork

Large eyes for hunting in dim light

Yellow-crowned night heron

Green heron

Glossy ibis

Long, sturdy legs

Black-faced ibis

sweeping their flattened beaks from side to side. If they feel food with the tip of their beak, the "spoon" instantly snaps shut. African **saddle-billed storks 6** have a wingspan of up to 2.75 m (9 ft). Like other storks, they fly with their necks stretched out and their legs trailing behind. While storks and ibises usually hunt by day, night herons are active after dark. The **black-crowned night heron 7** lives in wetlands all over the world, creeping along the water's edge and ambushing its prey. **Grey herons 8** live year-round in western Europe, but **European white storks 9** migrate northwards every year from Africa and South Asia, soaring high on outstretched wings. The beautiful **scarlet ibis 10** lives in South America and the Caribbean. It gets its amazing scarlet colour from its diet of small crustaceans.

Pelicans and relatives

Sharp eyes can spot prey beneath the water

1 Shoebill

2 White-tailed tropicbird

3 Red-billed tropicbird

Little pied cormorant

4 Great cormorant

5 Flightless cormorant

Flexible neck helps with grabbing fish

Red-legged cormorant

6 Anhinga

Double-crested cormorant

Pygmy cormorant

Pelicans and their relatives nearly all have webbed feet, and most swim or dive to catch their food. The **shoebill** **1** is an odd-one-out. It lives in African swamps, where it scoops up frogs and fish in its enormous beak. The **white-tailed tropicbird** **2** and **red-billed tropicbird** **3** are always on the move. They flutter above tropical oceans, splashing down with their wings partly folded and quickly taking off with their catch. The **great cormorant** **4** chases fish in rivers, lakes, and on coasts. It dives down beneath the surface, using its feet as propellers and steering with its wings. Like other cormorants, its feathers are not waterproof and when it has finished fishing it holds its wings out to dry. The **flightless cormorant** **5**, from the Galapagos Islands, has stumpy wings and is the

SCALE

Hammerkop

Red-faced shag

Masked booby

Black-and-white
colouring develops
in adulthood

❼ American white pelican

Brown booby

Beak has pouch
for catching fish

❽ Brown pelican

Densely streaked
head

❾ Magnificent frigatebird

Blue-footed booby

European shag

❿ Northern gannet

Blue feet impress
potential mates

Spot-billed pelican

only cormorant that cannot fly. The **anhinga** ❻, or snakebird, swims with its body below the waterline, so that only its head and neck can be seen. Pelicans are famous for the huge pouches hanging below their beaks, which they use for catching fish. The **American white pelican** ❼ fishes from the surface, but the **brown pelican** ❽ cruises just above the waves and dive-bombs its prey. The **magnificent**

frigatebird ❾ soars over the ocean on amazingly long and slender wings. It feeds by snatching fish from the surface, or by chasing other birds so that they drop their catch. Boobies and gannets feed by diving into the sea at high speed to grab passing fish. The **northern gannet** ❿ plummets from 30 m (98 ft) up. It folds back its wings as it slams through the water, disappearing with an impressive splash.

197

FLAMINGOS

With their amazingly long necks and legs, and their brilliant pink colouring, flamingos are easy to recognize. These greater flamingos, one of six species in the family, live in huge flocks of up to 250,000 birds, which feed, nest, and breed together. They feed by wading through the shallows with their heads partly underwater. Their specially adapted beaks have a built-in sieve to filter out tiny pieces of food.

Size ❯ Up to 1.5 m (5 ft) tall **Wingspan ❯** 1.7 m (5½ ft) **Weight ❯** Up to 4 kg (8¾ lb) **Habitat ❯** Lagoons, salt lakes, and shallow, muddy coasts. **Distribution ❯** Central and South America, Caribbean, Africa, southwest Europe, and Asia. **Diet ❯** Shrimps, worms, microscopic algae, and small pieces of water plants. Their pink colour is a by-product of the flamingos' diet. **Breeding ❯** Females lay a single egg in a nest that looks like a miniature volcano made out of mud. **Lifespan ❯** 30 years in the wild, longer in captivity. **Predators ❯** Adults have few natural enemies, but chicks may be eaten by hyenas, birds of prey, and marabou storks. **Conservation status ❯** Not threatened.

Cranes and relatives

① Clapper rail

② King rail

③ Common moorhen

Black rail

Red band develops in adulthood

⑤ Brolga

④ Water rail

Ruffled wings can scare off rivals

⑥ Common crane

Buff-banded rail

Sunbittern

Virginia rail

African finfoot

Cranes and rails look very different, but they belong to the same, very varied group of birds. All of them have long legs, and many of them have long, pointed beaks. Cranes live in the open, but rails have slender bodies so they can hide among waterside plants. The **clapper rail** ① likes mangrove swamps, while the **king rail** ② from North and Central America lives in marshes. Although these birds are timid, many of them have noisy calls. The **common moorhen** ③ makes a loud "kurruk", while the **water rail** ④ grunts and squeals. The **brolga** ⑤ is an Australian crane with a red band on its head. It spends its life on the move, travelling to places where it has recently rained. The **common crane** ⑥, from Europe, Asia, and Africa, is a long-distance migrant, travelling thousands of kilometres

SCALE

Red-knobbed coot

Long beak
picks food
out of mud

❾ Red-crowned crane

❿ American coot

Sungrebe

Black crake

Distinctive
feather crown

Corncrake

Red-legged seriema

❼ Great bustard

❽ Grey crowned crane

Black "tail"
is actually
wing feathers

Only breeding
males have
patterned necks

Purple gallinule

Little bustard

Long toes
to walk on
floating plants

each year. Like other cranes, it is legendary for its courtship dances and its amazingly loud trumpeting call. The **great bustard** ❼ is a massive grassland bird from Europe and Asia. Males can weigh up to 21 kg (46 lb), making them some of the heaviest flying birds. **Grey crowned cranes** ❽ live in Africa. Unlike most cranes they can perch, and they spend the night roosting in trees. The beautiful **red-crowned crane** ❾ lives

in Russia, China, and Japan. Standing up to 1.8 m (6 ft) tall, it is one of the largest cranes, and one of the rarest, with fewer than 3,000 left in the wild. The **American coot** ❿ is much more common, and can easily be seen in wetlands across North America. Coots are good swimmers, with paddle-shaped flaps on their toes. They can also be quarrelsome, often kicking and splashing when they fight.

Waders, gulls, and auks

SCALE

Lesser yellowlegs

1 American black oystercatcher

Red-necked avocet

Eurasian golden plover

2 Eurasian oystercatcher

3 Pied avocet

Spur-winged plover

Grey plover

Masked lapwing

4 Black-necked stilt

Northern lapwing

5 Dunlin

6 Red knot

Shortest legs among lapwings

Waders and their relatives live in marshes, on coasts, and in the open sea. Most of them lay their eggs on the ground, and some travel record distances to breed. The **American black oystercatcher** **1** feeds on shrimps and worms, but is also an expert at smashing open shells of oysters and crabs. The **Eurasian oystercatcher** **2** uses the same hunting technique to get at mussels and

other prey. The **pied avocet** **3** feeds by striding through shallow water and sweeping its upturned beak from side to side. The tip of its beak is amazingly sensitive, helping it catch insects, shrimps, and other small animals entirely by touch. **Black-necked stilts** **4** wade through water on pencil-thin, bright-red legs. Relative to their bodies, their legs are gigantic, and they stick out behind when these birds

Eurasian stone curlew

Jack snipe

Hudsonian godwit

Black-tailed godwit

Long, narrow beak digs into mud for food

7 Wattled jacana

American woodcock **8**

Pheasant-tailed jacana

Long toes to spread weight

Curved beak can probe under rocks

Ibisbill

9 Ruff

Breeding males sport brown, black, or white neck ruffs

Long-billed curlew **10**

Spoon-billed sandpiper

Ruddy turnstone

Banded stilt

Common redshank

Cream-coloured courser

sit on their eggs. The **dunlin** **5** and the **red knot** **6** breed in the Arctic tundra and then migrate south in enormous flocks. The red knot travels as far as the tip of South America and New Zealand, an epic round trip of 30,000 km (18,600 miles). The **wattled jacana** **7** from South America has giant toes for walking over lily pads in shallow lakes. The **American woodcock** **8** has 360-degree vision, thanks

to eyes near the top of its head. During their courtship displays, male woodcocks fly at just 8 kph (5 mph), a slow-flying record for a bird, equivalent to a gentle jog. The male **ruff** **9** has bright courtship plumage, with a feathery collar around its neck. The **long-billed curlew** **10** is specially equipped to pull up worms, with a curved beak more than half its body length.

⑪ Little auk

⑫ Razorbill

Beak flattened from side to side

Black skimmer

Marbled murrelet

South polar skua

Great black-headed gull

⑬ Tufted puffin

Black guillemot

⑭ Atlantic puffin

Crested auklet

⑮ Brown noddy

⑯ Arctic tern

Swallow-tailed gull

⑰ Caspian tern

Greater crested tern

Short, sturdy legs

Webbed feet for paddling in water

Gulls and auks are good swimmers, with waterproof feathers and webbed feet. Gulls often wander inland, but auks are true seabirds, using their wings to fly and to swim. The **little auk** ⑪ is the smallest auk, growing up to 19 cm (7 in) long. It has a black-and-white body and a short, stubby beak. It nests among boulders in the high Arctic and feeds in huge flocks that look like swarms of

bees. The **razorbill** ⑫ breeds on rocky ledges, but the **tufted puffin** ⑬ and **Atlantic puffin** ⑭ nest in clifftop burrows. Puffins use their multicoloured beaks to catch sand eels and other fish. Holding them crosswise, they can carry up to a dozen at a time. Terns and noddies are relatives of gulls with long tails and pointed wings. The **brown noddy** ⑮ breeds on tropical islands, while the **Arctic tern** ⑯ migrates

Sooty gull

18 Ross's gull

Dolphin gull

Grey gull

Powerful beak to stab at prey

20 Common gull

19 Great black-backed gull

Breeding adults have white heads

Laughing gull

Heermann's gull

Inca tern

SCALE

Black-legged kittiwake

between the Arctic and the Southern Ocean. In its 30-year lifespan, it can travel up to 2.4 million km (1.5 million miles), six times the distance from Earth to the Moon. The **Caspian tern 17** stays close to coasts, and often breeds near lakes. Like most terns, it is a fiercely protective parent, dive-bombing anyone who comes close to its nest. Auks catch all their food at sea, but gulls often scavenge along the shore and inland.

Ross's gull 18 lives near the edge of the Arctic pack-ice and rarely strays further south. The **great black-backed gull 19** is the biggest gull at 78 cm (31 in) long, and has a fearsome appetite. It often preys on other seabirds, and it can swallow young rabbits in a single gulp. The **common gull 20** often follows tractors ploughing fields, swooping down to snap up worms.

ALBATROSSES
Perhaps the ultimate sea birds, albatrosses spend most of their lives gliding over the oceans. They may fly hundreds of miles in a single day, and they are able to lock their enormous wings open so they can glide with little or no effort. Black-browed albatrosses, like the ones above, are the most common and widespread species, but even they are endangered by human activity.

Size › 83–95 cm (33–37 in) tall **Wingspan ›** Up to 2.4 m (8 ft) **Weight ›** Up to 5 kg (11 lb) **Habitat ›** They spend most of the year at sea but return to land to breed. **Distribution ›** South Atlantic Ocean **Diet ›** Crustaceans, fish, squid, and also dead penguins. They pick food from the ocean surface or dive for it, and sometimes follow trawlers for discarded fish. **Breeding ›** Albatrosses mate for life. The female lays one egg, which both parents care for. **Lifespan ›** Usually about 30 years, but may live as long as 70 years. **Predators ›** Tiger sharks may take adults. Rats or skuas may take the eggs. **Conservation status ›** Endangered, as they often die after becoming tangled in fishing lines.

Perching birds

SCALE

① Scarlet-chested sunbird

Great kiskadee

② Northern cardinal

Conical beak for cracking open seeds

Orange-bellied leafbird

Eastern wood-pewee

Pin-tailed manakin

③ Blue manakin

Vermilion flycatcher

White-bearded antshrike

④ White-throated dipper

Common tody-flycatcher

⑤ Blue-winged pitta

Black-capped vireo

Dunnock

There are thousands of kinds of perching birds, outnumbering all other birds put together. Most are small, with special feet that lock tight when they perch, keeping them in place. During the daytime most perching birds are constantly busy as they search for food, build their nests, and look after their young. The **scarlet-chested sunbird** ① from Africa feeds on sugary nectar from flowers using a curved beak. The **northern cardinal** ② lives in Canada, the USA, and Mexico. In the winter the male's brilliant red plumage stands out against the snow. **Blue manakins** ③ come from the rainforests of Brazil. Males attract females with elaborate dances but play no part in raising a family. The **white-throated dipper** ④ from Europe and Asia is one of the few perching birds that can dive and swim. It

208

Variegated fairy-wren

Rufous hornero **6**

Andean cock-of-the-rock **7**

Males have blue skin around eyes, throat, and neck

Bare-throated bellbird **8**

Scarlet tanager

Males turn bright red in breeding season

Rufous gnateater

Golden bowerbird **9**

Green catbird

Green broadbill

Wide beak almost covered by feathers

Red crossbill **10**

Moustached antpitta

Penduline tit

Chaffinch

Yellow warbler

American redstart

feeds underwater, collecting small animals in rivers and streams. The **blue-winged pitta** **5** lives in Southeast Asia, where it eats insects on the forest floor. **Rufous horneros** **6** from South America make football-shaped nests out of mud. Both parents help in the construction, which includes a slit-shaped entrance and a curved inner corridor. Male **Andean cock-of-the-rocks** **7** put all their energy into

courtship, but the females raise the young. **Bare-throated bellbirds** **8** from South America are some of the world's loudest birds, with piercing metallic calls. Male **golden bowerbirds** **9** attract partners by piling sticks around small trees. These bowers are up to 2 m (6½ ft) high, decorated with fruit and flowers. The **red crossbill** **10** has a cross-tipped beak for extracting seeds from pine cones.

Spotted pardalote

Lapland longspur

11 African paradise flycatcher

Spotted towhee

12 Eastern paradise whydah

Scarlet honeyeater

Long beak for feeding at flowers

13 Black-capped chickadee

Crested drongo

Varied tit

Common waxbill

14 Gouldian finch

Chipping sparrow

16 Lesser bird-of-paradise

15 Eurasian golden oriole

Red-backed shrike

Lark bunting

Yellow plumes along sides

SCALE

Perching birds need lots of high-energy food because they are very active. **African paradise flycatchers** 11 catch insects on the wing, while **eastern paradise whydahs** 12 collect seeds and insects on the ground. During the breeding season male whydahs grow spectacular tail feathers that can be three times their body length. The **black-capped chickadee** 13 from North America often visits bird feeders in the winter months. Like other chickadees it is a natural acrobat, hanging upside down from twigs as it searches for insects and spiders. The multicoloured **Gouldian finch** 14 is a seed-eater from northern Australia. It is rare in the wild but is sometimes kept as a cage bird. The **Eurasian golden oriole** 15 feeds mainly on fruit. Males have striking plumage but they are

Yellow-headed blackbird ⑰

Brown-throated wattle-eye

Crimson-breasted gonolek

Baltimore oriole

Common iora

⑱ Eastern meadowlark

Green jay

⑲ Brown-headed cowbird

Masked woodswallow

Buff-rumped thornbill

Strong perching feet

⑳ Red-billed blue magpie

Eastern yellow robin

hard to see because they feed in treetops. The **lesser bird-of-paradise** ⑯ lives in the forests of New Guinea. Males are much more colourful than females, and they show off their finery in remarkable courtship displays. The **yellow-headed blackbird** ⑰ has a call that sounds like a creaky, rusty gate. It breeds in North America and forms enormous flocks in winter that often feed in fields. The **eastern**

meadowlark ⑱ is another North American bird, with a loud whistling call. It feeds on the ground, probing for insects with its sharply pointed beak. **Brown-headed cowbirds** ⑲ lay their eggs in the nests of other birds. Asian **red-billed blue magpies** ⑳ are nest raiders, stealing and eating other birds' eggs and chicks. They belong to the crow family, which contains the world's biggest perching birds.

211

Apostlebird

Barn swallow

European robin

Adults have orange-red breasts

Yellow wagtail

Subalpine warbler

Eurasian nuthatch

Winter wren

Splendid glossy starling

Bohemian waxwing

Collared sand martin

Common stonechat

Silver-eared mesia

Mistletoebird

Blue-and-white flycatcher

Long-tailed tit

Perching birds include some long-distance travellers as well as some that stay put throughout the year. The **European robin** 21 is one of the stay-at-homes. It often lives in gardens where it feeds on insects and worms. The **barn swallow** 22 catches insects in midair. It breeds in North America, Europe, and Asia but flies south when autumn arrives, a round trip of up to 20,000 km (12,400 miles).

Winter wrens 23 live across the Northern Hemisphere. In cold weather they often roost together, and more than 60 winter wrens have been found in a single nest box. The **Bohemian waxwing** 24 comes from the forests of North America, Europe, and northern Asia but sometimes migrates southwards in winter if insects and berries get hard to find. The **long-tailed tit** 25 forms busy winter flocks that flutter

㉖ Eurasian blackbird

㉗ Song thrush

Broad-ringed white eye

SCALE

㉘ Western bluebird

Eurasian treecreeper

Asian fairy-bluebird

Vinous-throated parrotbill

Red-whiskered bulbul

Wren-tit

㉚ House sparrow

㉙ Northern mockingbird

Chestnut weaver

Short, broad wings

㉛ Eurasian skylark

Blue-grey gnatcatcher

White outer tail feathers

through European woodlands in a single file. The thrush family is famous for its tuneful singers. They include the **Eurasian blackbird** ㉖, **song thrush** ㉗, and the North American **western bluebird** ㉘. Like most perching birds, the male western bluebird sings to attract females and also to warn other males to keep away. The **northern mockingbird** ㉙ sings for hours at a time. It copies the songs of other birds, and even the ringtones of mobile phones. The **house sparrow** ㉚ has followed humans all over the Earth and is now the world's most widespread bird. It often nests under roofs and in holes in walls. House sparrows are a common sight inside supermarkets and warehouses, eating spilled food. The **Eurasian skylark** ㉛ feeds on the ground but sings high up in the air.

213

RED-BACKED SHRIKE
This gruesome display is the larder of the red-backed shrike. A small but efficient hunter, this shrike is sometimes called the butcher bird because of its habit of sticking its prey on thorns. This dries out the bodies, so that they decay slowly and the bird can save them to eat later. The shrike eats larger animals such as lizards by pulling them off the thorns bit by bit.

Size > Up to 18 cm (7 in) long **Wingspan >** 26 cm (10 in)
Weight > 30 g (1 oz) **Habitat >** Heathlands and commons
with thorny bushes in Europe, and dry scrublands in Africa.
Distribution > Continental Europe, western and central Asia.
Winters in central-southern Africa. **Diet >** Bees, beetles, and
other large insects. Also small mammals, birds, and reptiles.

It may chase and catch insects in flight or swoop at prey on
the ground. **Breeding >** From late May to early July. Females
lay up to six eggs. **Lifespan >** Up to eight years. **Predators >**
None known. **Conservation status >** Not threatened.
However, the bird has almost disappeared from the UK
due to habitat loss and possibly pesticide use.

Mammals

All mammals feed their young with milk produced in special glands in the mother's skin. They are warm-blooded, generating heat inside their bodies, and often have fur to protect them from the cold. Most mammals have large brains relative to their body size and are capable of learning, remembering, and forming social relationships.

Ears ❯ Mammals have tiny bones inside their ear canals. Sound waves make these bones vibrate, passing signals to the brain. This system gives mammals exceptionally good hearing.

Fur ❯ Warm-blooded creatures such as mammals need to insulate themselves from outside temperatures. Fur traps air next to their skin, helping them to stay warm.

Tiger

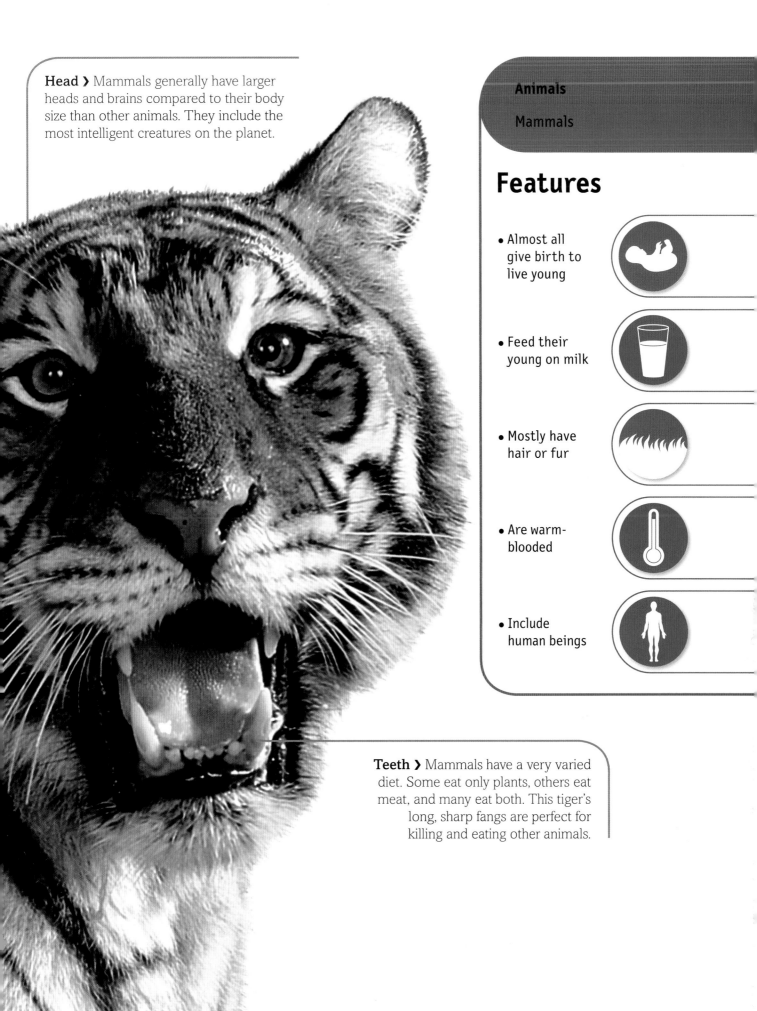

Head > Mammals generally have larger heads and brains compared to their body size than other animals. They include the most intelligent creatures on the planet.

Features

- Almost all give birth to live young

- Feed their young on milk

- Mostly have hair or fur

- Are warm-blooded

- Include human beings

Teeth > Mammals have a very varied diet. Some eat only plants, others eat meat, and many eat both. This tiger's long, sharp fangs are perfect for killing and eating other animals.

Mammals with pouches

Long, stiff whiskers are touch-sensitive

① Virginia opossum

② Parma wallaby

Ears swivel to pinpoint sounds

③ Red-necked wallaby

Brush-tailed bettong

Tail used to carry nesting material

Striped possum

④ Honey possum

Long-nosed potoroo

Bushy, white-tipped tail

⑤ Sugar glider

Tail acts as a prop

Instead of growing inside their mothers, these animals, known as marsupials, develop inside a pouch. They are born very early and find the pouch by crawling through their mother's fur. Some baby marsupials have their mother's pouch to themselves, but young **Virginia opossums** ① share it with up to 12 siblings, and have to hang on tight to survive. They live in the USA, Mexico, and Central America,

often straying into urban areas. Virginia opossums are good climbers and feed at night, sometimes raiding dustbins for leftover food. Marsupials also live in South America, but most of them come from Australia. The **parma wallaby** ② and **red-necked wallaby** ③ have powerful back legs for jumping, but the **honey possum** ④ has tiny paws and a slender wrap-around tail. Weighing just 14 g (½ oz), it is one of the

Eyes placed on sides of head for wider view

Bear-like body with short legs

7 Doria's tree kangaroo

8 Common ringtail

6 Red kangaroo

9 Grey four-eyed opossum

Tail used for balance when climbing

Musky rat-kangaroo

10 Bare-tailed woolly opossum

Pouch tightens while hopping

SCALE

world's smallest marsupials, and feeds on sugary nectar from flowers. The **sugar glider 5** eats insects, fruit, and sap. It can glide up to 50 m (164 ft) between trees, using the stretchy skin between its legs as a parachute. The **red kangaroo 6** is the largest and fastest marsupial, with a top speed of 50 kph (30 mph). Young kangaroos, or joeys, stay in their pouch for up to six months before exploring the world outside. **Doria's**

tree kangaroos 7 from New Guinea spend their lives off the ground. The heaviest tree-climbing marsupials, they feed on leaves, flowers, and fruit. **Common ringtails 8** also eat leaves, but the **grey four-eyed opossum 9** and **bare-tailed woolly opossum 10** have a more varied diet, including earthworms, insects, and birds' eggs. Both live in the Americas and feed mainly at night.

⑪ **Southern hairy-nosed wombat**

Distinctive large ears

⑭ **Greater bilby**

Single young carried in pouch

⑬ **Numbat**

Powerful forefeet rip open termite nests

⑫ **Common wombat**

Australia's marsupials come in many different shapes and sizes. Some live in trees, but they also include burrowers that live and feed on the ground. The **southern hairy-nosed wombat** ⑪ digs a network of tunnels, coming out after dark to feed on grass. The burrows are handed on from one generation to the next and can be more than 50 years old. **Common wombats** ⑫ are bigger and more powerful.

Like other wombats, they have a backward-opening pouch. This stops earth from getting in when they are digging and protects their young from roots and twigs. The **numbat** ⑬ lives in forests and feeds on termites. It can eat 20,000 of these insects a day, lapping them up with its long, sticky tongue. The **greater bilby** ⑭ is one of Australia's strangest-looking marsupials with rabbit-like ears, a pointed snout, and long,

⑮ Tasmanian devil

⑯ Koala

Fingers and toes clamp around branches

⑰ Western quoll

Prominent eyes for night-time hunting

⑱ Mountain brushtail possum

Southern brown bandicoot

⑲ Common spotted cuscus

Male's coat is spotted

Strong, curved claws

Eastern barred bandicoot

silky fur. It lives in dry places, and digs burrows that spiral downwards like a corkscrew, making it harder for predators to get inside. The **Tasmanian devil** ⑮ is the world's biggest meat-eating marsupial with a thick-set body, powerful jaws, and sharp teeth. It is mainly a scavenger, swallowing the skin and even bones of dead animals. Far more appealing and much better known, the **koala** ⑯ lives in gum trees and feeds on

their leaves. It eats for about six hours a day and spends the rest of its time asleep. The **western quoll** ⑰ is active at night and hunts like a cat, while the **mountain brushtail possum** ⑱ lives in thick forests and sleeps in hollow trees. The **common spotted cuscus** ⑲ is another tree-dweller, with a tail adapted for grasping branches. The female carries her young on her back after they have left her pouch.

221

Armadillos, sloths, and anteaters

SCALE

Northern naked-tailed armadillo

Protective plates do not cover the tail

Larger hairy armadillo

Underside covered in dense hairs

2 Pichi

Giant armadillo

1 Three-banded armadillo

3 Nine-banded armadillo

4 Giant anteater

Long, toothless snout

Six-banded armadillo

Armadillos are the only mammals to have a hard, protective shell. They have flexible bands to let their bodies bend and some kinds, including the **three-banded armadillo** 1, can roll themselves up into a ball. The **pichi** 2 has another way of keeping out of trouble. It wedges itself in its burrow, making it hard for predators to drag it out. Most armadillos live in Central and South America but the **nine-banded armadillo** 3 lives as far north as the USA. Its family life is very unusual because it always has identical quadruplets each time it breeds. Armadillos feed mainly on ants and termites, although they do eat other animals such as grubs and worms. The **giant anteater** 4 is one of the biggest insect-eating mammals, swallowing up to 30,000 ants a day. It rips open anthills or

222

Maned sloth

⑤ Southern two-toed sloth

Tough armour of overlapping scales

⑥ Brown-throated sloth

⑧ Ground pangolin

Northern tamandua

① Silky anteater

Prehensile tail used to grip branches

Long-tailed pangolin

Collared anteater

⑨ Indian pangolin

termite mounds with its claws and licks up its food with its sticky 60 cm (2 ft) long tongue. Sloths are distant relatives of anteaters, but they hang from branches, and feed on leaves. The **southern two-toed sloth** ⑤ never moves in a hurry, and the **brown-throated sloth** ⑥ is one of the slowest mammals in the world. Its top speed in trees is about 0.3 kph (⅕ mph) and it eats, sleeps, and even gives

birth upside down. The **silky anteater** ⑦ from Central and tropical South America can climb just as well as a sloth. Large, curved front claws and a prehensile tail help it to live in trees, where it nests in holes. Pangolins are unmistakable animals with their covering of overlapping scales. The African **ground pangolin** ⑧ and **Indian pangolin** ⑨ are so well protected that they can even keep lions and tigers at bay.

Hedgehogs and moles

SCALE

① Desert hedgehog

Long ears help in keeping cool

Long-eared hedgehog

② North African hedgehog

③ European hedgehog

④ Pygmy shrew

Long, furry tail

Southern African hedgehog

Eurasian water shrew

⑤ North American least shrew

When the sun sets, hedgehogs set off to find food. Armed with up to 5,000 sharp spines, they rummage through the undergrowth, rolling up into a spiky ball if they are threatened with attack. They eat small animals, fruit, and carrion. The **desert hedgehog** ① from Africa and the Middle East usually prefers insects and their larvae but can also tackle scorpions and venomous snakes. The **North**

African hedgehog ② gives birth to about six babies, or "hoglets", each time it breeds. At first their spines are soft but they harden within a day. The **European hedgehog** ③ lives in lots of different habitats including farms and gardens. Despite its dumpy shape, it is a great climber, scrambling up fences and walls and dropping unharmed onto the other side. The **pygmy shrew** ④ has a vicious bite. This tiny mammal

Pyrenean desman

6 Hispaniolan solenodon

Front legs have powerful claws for burrowing

7 Moonrat

Small Japanese mole

Alpine shrew

8 European mole

Sensitive tentacles to find food

Common shrew

Bicoloured white-toothed shrew

Reddish-grey musk shrew

Tiny eyes

9 Star-nosed mole

Northern short-tailed shrew

Greater white-toothed shrew

is just 5 cm (2 in) long but can attack earthworms many times its size. The **North American least shrew** **5** is almost as small and has venomous saliva that helps it to overpower its prey. The **Hispaniolan solenodon** **6** looks like a giant shrew. It is only found on Hispaniola, an island in the Caribbean. The **moonrat** **7** from Southeast Asia is related to hedgehogs and eats fruit as well as animal prey. The **European mole** **8**

lives underground and digs tunnels with its spade-like front paws. It feeds on earthworms, storing them in special "larders" and biting off their heads to stop them from getting away. The **star-nosed mole** **9** from North America looks for food with 22 pink tentacles on its nose. A good swimmer, it is amazingly quick on the draw, taking just a quarter of a second to sense and grab its food.

AFRICAN ELEPHANTS
The largest land animals, African elephants are equipped with a long trunk, which they use not only for breathing, smelling, and trumpeting, but also to grip and move objects and to suck up water. Their huge ears allow heat to escape, keeping them cool. Elephants are known for their intelligence, and they form strong family relationships.

Size › Males up to 4 m (13 ft) tall; females up to 2.6 m (8½ ft) tall **Weight ›** Males up to 6 tonnes and females up to 3.2 tonnes **Habitat ›** Savanna **Distribution ›** Sub-Saharan Africa **Diet ›** Leaves and bark from trees, and grass. They can eat up to 160 kg (350 lb) of food a day. **Breeding ›** Females (cows) give birth to one baby every two to four years. Elephant herds consist mainly of females, and other members may help the mother to care for the baby. **Lifespan ›** Around 60 years in the wild. **Predators ›** Adults have no predators. Calves may be killed by lions, leopards, hyenas, or crocodiles. **Conservation status ›** Vulnerable as they are hunted for their ivory tusks.

Rabbits, hares, and pikas

① Lop-eared rabbit

② Angora rabbit

③ European rabbit

Dwarf rabbit

Soft fur can be used to make wool

④ Eastern cottontail

Swamp rabbit

⑤ European hare

⑥ Arctic hare

SCALE

Rabbits and hares have many predators but their keen senses and long legs give them a head start in the race for safety. At the first sign of danger, most rabbits sprint into their burrows. Hares stay above ground, bounding away at up to 80 kph (50 mph). Rabbits and hares have big ears and large front teeth, and they feed entirely on plants. There are more than 50 breeds of rabbit, including the **lop-eared**

rabbit ①, whose dangly ears can measure 70 cm (27 in) long. The **Angora rabbit** ② is valued for its long, soft hair, which is spun into yarn. These two breeds, and many others, are descendants of the **European rabbit** ③, which has been kept in captivity for hundreds of years. In the wild, European rabbits live in big burrow systems called warrens. They breed amazingly quickly, raising up to 40 babies, or "kits", each year.

Marsh rabbit

8 American pika

Short legs and no tail

White-tailed jackrabbit

Large eyes for feeding at night

7 Mountain hare

9 Antelope jackrabbit

Large ears used for hearing and keeping cool

Cape hare

Wide-set eyes provide all-round vision

10 Snowshoe hare

Black-tailed jackrabbit

Coat turns white in winter

The American **eastern cottontail** **4** looks very similar to the European rabbit but breeds above ground. Hares are usually bigger than rabbits and live on their own. The **European hare** **5** stays brown all year round, but many other kinds, including the **Arctic hare** **6** and **mountain hare** **7**, turn white in winter for camouflage against the snow. Pikas are relatives of rabbits and hares, but are much smaller with shorter ears. The **American pika** **8** lives in rocky burrows high up in mountains. To survive the winter, it collects plants and dries them like tiny piles of hay, to eat when other food is scarce. The **antelope jackrabbit** **9** has the biggest ears of all wild hares. The **snowshoe hare's** **10** ears and paws are thickly furred, keeping it warm in the bitterly cold winters of Canada and Alaska.

Rodents

Grey squirrel ❶

Cape ground squirrel

Eurasian red squirrel ❷

Grizzled giant squirrel

Nimble front paws can grip food

❹ Marmot

Black-tailed prairie dog

❸ Southern flying squirrel

Skin "wings" used for gliding

Long tail used for balance

Eastern chipmunk

❺ Capybara

Common vole

Added together rodents easily outnumber all other mammals on Earth. They live almost everywhere on dry land and in fresh water too. Most rodents feed on plants. Their front teeth grow non-stop, enabling them to gnaw through their food and anything in their way. The **grey squirrel** ❶ is an expert climber with nimble front paws. Originally from North America, it has pushed out the **Eurasian red**

squirrel ❷ in many parts of the British Isles. The red squirrel uses its long tail to balance itself while jumping from one tree to another. The North American **southern flying squirrel** ❸ glides between trees on folds of stretchy skin. It can travel almost 30 m (100 ft) in a single flight, landing right on target even in the dark. The **marmot** ❹ lives in mountain burrows and hibernates for up to nine months every year. The world's

Lesser Egyptian jerboa

6 Beaver

Meadow jumping mouse

7 Desert pocket mouse

African dormouse

South African springhare

Merriam's kangaroo rat

8 Azara's agouti

Paddle-shaped tail for swimming and signalling to other beavers

Long legs for high-speed running

Kangaroo-like hind legs

9 Norway lemming

Muskrat

Roborovski's desert hamster

10 Golden hamster

SCALE

largest rodent is the **capybara** 5 from the swamps of South America. It grows to the size of a small pig. To escape its enemies, it dives into water and can hold its breath for up to five minutes. The **beaver** 6 is a good swimmer and is renowned for building dams. The biggest beaver dam on record, in Canada, is 850 m (½ mile) long and was first spotted by satellite. Many other rodents, such as the **desert** **pocket mouse** 7, get all their water from their food. **Azara's agouti** 8 from South America has small families with just two young, but **Norway lemmings** 9 sometimes produce more than 50 babies a year. When their burrows get overcrowded, young lemmings pour across the Arctic tundra in search of food. The **golden hamster** 10 from the Middle East is very rare in the wild but millions are kept as pets.

⓫ Domestic guinea pig

Thick-set body without tail

Long teeth used for digging tunnels

⓬ Naked mole-rat

⓭ Chinchilla

⓮ Mara

Harvest mouse

Pallid gerbil

⓯ Brown rat

Botta's pocket gopher

Wood mouse

⓰ Albino house mouse

Short, thick spines

Brazilian porcupine

Rodents include some rare animals as well as common ones found all over the world. The **domestic guinea pig** ⓫ from South America was once raised for food but is now a popular pet, with many different breeds. The **naked mole-rat** ⓬ from east Africa lives in big families and spends its whole life tunnelling underground. It is one of the world's weirdest-looking mammals with big front teeth, bare

wrinkly skin, and tiny eyes. **Chinchillas** ⓭ have a luxurious fur coat that protects them from the cold. Found in the South American Andes, these rodents are hunted for their fur, and are now endangered in the wild. The **mara** ⓮ looks a lot like a hare. It lives in South America's grasslands and is one of the fastest rodents, bounding along at 45 kph (28 mph). The **brown rat** ⓯ is a worldwide pest. Adaptable and intelligent,

Dense fur for protection against cold

⑰ Mountain viscacha

SCALE

⑱ Coypu

Quills detach and stick in attacker's skin

⑲ Dassie rat

Bare feet give good grip

Degu

⑳ Crested porcupine

it survives in all kinds of habitats, from remote islands to urban drains. An expert climber and a good swimmer, it eats almost anything, including seeds, eggs, leather, and even soap. The **house mouse** ⑯ is another rodent that lives alongside people, although it keeps out of sight. It is found on every continent except Antarctica and has even been discovered aboard planes and deep down in mines. The **mountain**

viscacha ⑰ is a close relative of the chinchilla and lives high up in mountains. The South American **coypu** ⑱ feeds in lakes and swamps. African **dassie rats** ⑲ live in rocky hillsides. They have flat skulls and bendy ribs for squeezing into cracks. The African **crested porcupine** ⑳ is the world's best-armed rodent. When threatened, it charges backwards into its enemy, stabbing it with its sharp, hollow quills.

Bushbabies, lemurs, and tarsiers

① White-footed sportive lemur

Young rides on its mother's back

③ Coquerel's sifaka

② Verreaux's sifaka

④ Senegal bushbaby

⑤ Moholi bushbaby

Strong back legs good for jumping

⑥ Ring-tailed lemur

Long tail used for balancing

Brown greater galago

Mongoose lemur

Bushbabies and their relatives belong to a group of mammals called primates, which includes monkeys, apes, and also humans. Most of these animals live in trees and all of them have forward-facing eyes, allowing them to judge distances in three dimensions. Bushbabies come from Africa, but lemurs are found in Madagascar and nowhere else in the world. There are many different kinds of lemurs and each

has its own way of living. The **white-footed sportive lemur** ① feeds mainly on leaves, but **Verreaux's sifaka** ② also eats fruit, flowers, and bark. **Coquerel's sifaka** ③ is an amazingly acrobatic climber, even with a baby on board. The **Senegal bushbaby** ④ and **moholi bushbaby** ⑤ come out after dark. They can leap 25 times their own body length as they spring from branch to branch. The

⑦ Black-and-white ruffed lemur

Red-bellied lemur

⑧ Slow loris

Forward-facing eyes give good 3D vision

Pygmy slow loris

Spectral tarsier

Red slender loris

Horsfield's tarsier

Head can turn through 180 degrees to keep watch behind

Grey mouse lemur

Potto

Greater dwarf lemur

⑩ Aye-aye

⑨ Philippine tarsier

Tail used to store fat in wet season

SCALE

Slender middle finger for picking grubs out of wood

ring-tailed lemur ⑥ climbs well, but spends much of its time on the ground. It is very sociable and always keeps together in groups. The **black-and-white ruffed lemur ⑦** is the largest lemur at 60 cm (24 in) long, but only weighs about 4 kg (9 lb), about the same as a pet cat. Lorises are plant- and insect-eaters from tropical forests in Asia. The **slow loris ⑧** creeps along branches once the sun has gone

down. The **Philippine tarsier ⑨** is a pocket-sized primate with enormous staring eyes. Like other tarsiers, it leaps on to insects in the dark and crunches them up with its sharp teeth. The nocturnal **aye-aye ⑩** from Madagascar is the world's strangest primate, with skinny hands and scraggy fur. It feeds on fruit, eggs, and insects, and uses its extra-long middle finger to tweak out insect larvae from wood.

Gibbons, apes, and humans

Müller's Bornean gibbon

SCALE

Silvery gibbon

① Hoolock gibbon

③ Lar gibbon

② Siamang

Arms much longer than legs

Buff-cheeked gibbon

Agile gibbon

⑤ Western gorilla

④ Northern white-cheeked gibbon

Cream-coloured young turns darker by two years of age

Black-crested gibbon

Gibbons and apes include our closest relatives in the living world. Not only are they similar to people in appearance, but they are also highly intelligent animals. The **hoolock gibbon** ① lives in South and Southeast Asia, which is where all wild gibbons are found. Like other gibbons, it uses its hands like hooks to swing from branch to branch, speeding through the forest almost as fast as a man can run. The

siamang ② is the biggest gibbon. It eats leaves and fruit, and starts the day with a loud dawn chorus that can be heard from far away. The skin on its throat is elastic and inflates to the size of a grapefruit, amplifying its amazingly loud calls. The **lar gibbon** ③ is black or brown, but **northern white-cheeked gibbons** ④ start life with creamy fur and turn darker as they grow up. Gorillas come from Africa, and spend most

Mature males have "saddle" of silvery fur

⑥ Eastern gorilla

⑦ Chimpanzee

⑧ Sumatran orang-utan

Can grip with hands and feet

⑩ Human male

Human female

⑨ Bornean orang-utan

Bonobo

of their lives on the ground. The **western gorilla** ⑤ can weigh three times as much as an adult man, but the **eastern gorilla** ⑥ is even bigger, weighing a massive 220 kg (485 lb). Despite their size, gorillas are peaceful plant-eaters and rarely attack people unless their young are threatened. Also from Africa, the **chimpanzee** ⑦ is the primate most similar to us. It lives in large groups and eats all kinds of food, from termites to monkeys, which it ambushes in trees. The **Sumatran orang-utan** ⑧ and **Bornean orang-utan** ⑨ are two fruit-eaters from Southeast Asia. Like chimps, they are highly intelligent and are good at problem-solving and making simple tools. **Humans** ⑩ are the only living primates that walk upright on two legs. Today there are more than 7 billion of us, spread over every land habitat on Earth.

ORANG-UTANS
These apes are some of humans' closest relatives. In fact, their name means "person of the forest" in Malay. These shy treetop dwellers are very intelligent animals. Long arms and flexible hands and feet help them to move around in trees, looking for fruit and other food. Young orang-utans stay with their mothers for up to seven years, learning the skills they need to survive as adults.

Size > Males up to 1.5 m (5 ft); females up to 1.3 m (4¼ ft) tall **Weight >** Males 50–80 kg (110–176 lb); females 30–45 kg (66–99 lb) **Habitat >** Rainforest. Orang-utans are solitary animals, but females and their offspring may be seen together. **Distribution >** Tropical forest in Borneo and in northern Sumatra, Indonesia. **Diet >** Mainly figs and other fruit, leaves, occasionally insects, honey, and birds' eggs. **Breeding >** Orang-utans start breeding in their teens. Females give birth once every eight years and infants stay with them for six to seven years. **Lifespan >** Up to 50 years in the wild and 60 years in captivity. **Predators >** Tigers **Conservation status >** Critically endangered due to habitat loss.

New World monkeys

Black-capped squirrel monkey

Long tail used for balance

Common squirrel monkey

Goeldi's monkey

① Black-capped squirrel monkey

② White-faced saki

Colombian spider monkey

⑤ Pygmy marmoset

Long, white crest

③ Red bald-headed uakari

④ Northern night monkey

Collared titi monkey

Cotton-top marmoset

Black-bearded saki

Common marmoset

Long waterproof fur

New World monkeys come from Central and South America. Many of them have flat noses and tails that wrap around branches like an extra hand. **Black-capped squirrel monkeys** ① live in large groups in the treetops, feeding on fruit and insects. They have more than two dozen separate calls, including special alarm sounds if they spot a predator such as an eagle or a snake. The **white-faced**

saki ② has shaggy fur and feeds closer to the ground. The **red bald-headed uakari** ③ looks as if its head has been shaved. Its red face is thought to attract potential mates. Most New World monkeys feed during the day, but the **northern night monkey** ④ wakes up after dark and is most active on moonlit nights. The tiny **pygmy marmoset** ⑤ is the world's smallest monkey, weighing just five times as much

240

⑥ Southern muriqui

⑦ Venezuelan red howler

Throat works like an amplifier

Emperor tamarin

Thick, prehensile tail can grip tree branches

⑧ Golden lion tamarin

Weeper capuchin

Long, silky mane

⑨ Grey woolly monkey

⑩ White-headed capuchin

Golden-headed lion tamarin

SCALE

as a mouse. Like other marmosets it scampers along branches, and has hands with sharp claws. It gnaws holes in the bark of trees and licks up the sap that oozes out. The **southern muriqui** ⑥, also known as the woolly spider monkey, is the largest New World monkey. The **Venezuelan red howler** ⑦ is the noisiest land animal with a roar that can be heard up to 5 km (3 miles) away. Howlers live in trees and eat leaves.

They call at dawn to claim their feeding territory high above the ground. The beautiful **golden lion tamarin** ⑧ is one of the most endangered monkeys in the world. It was rescued from extinction in the 1980s when fewer than 100 were left. The **grey woolly monkey** ⑨ stays high up in trees, but the **white-headed capuchin** ⑩ sometimes feeds on the ground, and is good at walking on all fours.

Old World monkeys

SCALE

① L'Hoest's monkey

② Rhesus macaque

③ De Brazza's monkey

④ Proboscis monkey

Nose is largest in males

Blue monkey

⑤ Patas monkey

Old World monkeys live in Africa and Asia, as far north as Japan. Most of them are tree-dwellers, although baboons spend much of their time on the ground. Unlike New World monkeys, they cannot grip with their tails but they include some amazingly good climbers as well as the fastest monkey on all fours. **L'Hoest's monkey** ① from Central Africa lives in mountain forests. It mainly eats fruit and leaves and has cheek pouches for storing food. The **rhesus macaque** ② is found in South Asia, Thailand, and China. It lives in all kinds of habitats, from forests to the outskirts of towns. **De Brazza's monkey** ③ from Africa has a long, white beard, while the **proboscis monkey** ④ from Borneo has a huge, fleshy nose. Proboscis monkeys live in mangrove swamps and are great swimmers and divers.

Toque macaque

Southern pig-tailed macaque

7 Hamadryas baboon

6 Olive baboon

8 Grivet

Tufted grey langur

Muscular limbs for fast movement

Long tail for balance

9 Yellow baboon

10 Mandrill

Females are smaller than males

They leap from a height of 15 m (50 ft), hitting the water in a noisy belly-flop. The African **patas monkey** ❺ is a ground-dweller and a great runner, with a record-breaking top speed of 55 kph (34 mph). Baboons also come from Africa but they have big teeth and a much heavier build. The **olive baboon** ❻ forages in open grassland, while the **hamadryas baboon** ❼ lives in rocky places. If baboons

are threatened, the biggest males face up to the enemy, giving the rest of the troop time to escape. The **grivet** ❽ eats insects and plant food. Its predators include the **yellow baboon** ❾, which hunts smaller monkeys for food. The multicoloured **mandrill** ❿ from West Africa has a vivid blue and red face. It lives in giant troops called hordes, which can contain 800 animals, a record for any primate.

Bats

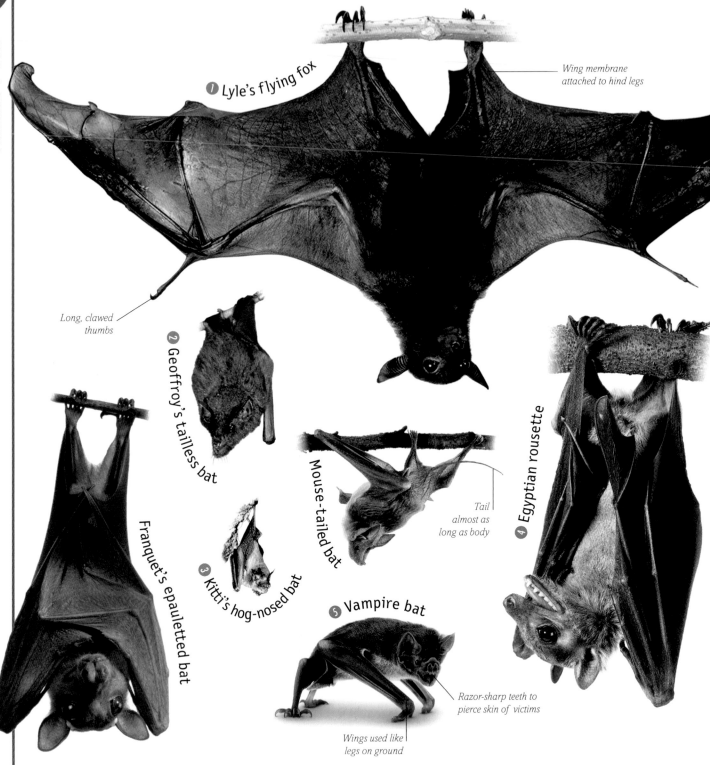

① Lyle's flying fox

Wing membrane attached to hind legs

Long, clawed thumbs

② Geoffroy's tailless bat

Franquet's epauletted bat

③ Kitti's hog-nosed bat

Mouse-tailed bat

Tail almost as long as body

④ Egyptian rousette

⑤ Vampire bat

Razor-sharp teeth to pierce skin of victims

Wings used like legs on ground

Lots of small mammals can glide, but bats are the only ones that can really fly, using muscle power to flap their wings. Their wings are made of skin stretched between amazingly slender finger bones, which can be as thin as a human hair. Small bats usually feed on flying insects but most big ones eat fruit, which they find using keen eyesight and a superb sense of smell. **Lyle's flying fox** ① is a fruit-eater from the forests of Southeast Asia. Named after its fox-like face, it spends the daytime roosting upside down in trees, using its large clawed thumbs to move along branches. **Geoffroy's tailless bat** ② comes from Central and South America and feeds on sugary nectar with its brush-tipped tongue, but **Kitti's hog-nosed bat** ③ from Thailand and Myanmar hunts insects, snatching them out

SCALE

Proboscis bat

❻ Large flying fox

Large eyes for seeing after dark

❼ Spectacled flying fox

Body wrapped in wings when roosting

❽ Wahlberg's epauletted fruit bat

❾ Lesser horseshoe bat

Seba's short-tailed bat

Nose leaf helps in echolocation

of the air or picking them off plants. It is the world's tiniest mammal with large ears but a body as small as a bumblebee's. The **Egyptian rousette** ❹ eats fruit, but the legendary **vampire bat** ❺ from Central and South America drinks blood from mammals and birds. Silent and stealthy, it scuttles up to its victims on all fours, slicing through their skin with its sharp teeth and lapping up a meal of blood. The **large**

flying fox ❻ is one of the world's biggest bats, with a wingspan of 1.5 m (5 ft). Like the **spectacled flying fox** ❼ from Australia and New Guinea, it sets off to feed at sunset, flying up to 50 km (31 miles) in search of food. **Wahlberg's epauletted fruit bat** ❽ is a fruit-eater from Africa, but the **lesser horseshoe bat** ❾ is an insect-eater, with a small body and surprisingly big wings.

SCALE

⑩ Common noctule bat

⑪ Grey long-eared bat

Skin between legs and tail aids in flight

⑫ Natterer's bat

⑬ Broad-eared free-tailed bat

Greater mouse-eared bat

Slender finger bones

⑭ Daubenton's bat

Davy's naked-backed bat

Most of the world's micro-bats feed on flying insects, which they catch after dark. They have small eyes and find their prey by echolocation, using bursts of high-frequency sound to form an "image" of their surroundings. The **common noctule** ⑩ from Europe and Asia catches most of its food in the air. It also snatches insects off leaves and swoops on them on the ground. The European **grey**

long-eared bat ⑪ has enormous ears that are almost as long as its body. During the winter when it hibernates, it carefully tucks them away under its wings. **Natterer's bat** ⑫ from Europe hibernates in caves and mines. During its long winter sleep, its body temperature can drop to just 2°C (35°F) and it may breathe just once an hour. The **broad-eared free-tailed bat** ⑬ lives in Central and South America where it is warm all

15 European free-tailed bat

16 Common pipistrelle

Kuhl's pipistrelle

Big brown bat

17 Ghost bat

Long-fingered bat

18 Spix's disc-winged bat

Suction disc for gripping leaves

Nathusius' pipistrelle

year round. It roosts in small groups, but some of its relatives sleep and breed in huge colonies, numbering a million bats or more. **Daubenton's bat** **14** scoops up insects from the surface of lakes and ponds, hunting mainly at dawn and dusk. The **European free-tailed bat** **15** spends the whole night on the wing. Like other free-tailed bats, it has a distinctive mouse-like tail. The **common pipistrelle** **16** is the smallest bat in Europe. It often roosts in old buildings and hunts around streetlamps, catching insects that are attracted by the light. The **ghost bat** **17** is the biggest predatory species in Australia. As well as catching insects, it eats frogs, lizards, birds, and even other bats. **Spix's disc-winged bat** **18** lives in Central and South American forests. It has suction cups on its wrists and ankles for roosting underneath leaves.

247

HONDURAN WHITE BATS
These tiny Central American bats have fluffy white fur, making them look like puffs of cotton wool. They also have eye-catching, golden-yellow ears, black wings, and a snout with a pointed top. They are often found huddled in a colony of four to eight bats roosting under a *Heliconia* leaf, which they adapt to make a tent for themselves.

Size > 3.5–4.5 cm (1½–1¾ in) **Weight >** About 6 g (⅕ oz)
Habitat > Tropical rainforest. The bats chew through the
veins of *Heliconia* leaves, so that the two sides of the leaf
hang down to form a tent. They roost inside this tent, which
protects them from sun, rain, and predators. **Distribution >**
Lowlands of Central America. **Diet >** Fruit **Breeding >**

Females produce one baby in the rainy season. Males and
females roost together until the young are born, then the
males leave. The young suckle for 20–21 days. **Predators >**
Snakes and small mammals such as opossums.
Conservation status > Numbers have declined sharply
in recent years due to destruction of their habitat.

Dogs, foxes, and relatives

① Chihuahua

Dalmatian

③ African wild dog

Large, rounded ears

② Husky

Bush dog

④ Coyote

Dhole

Black-backed jackal

Raccoon dog

Black face "mask" with a white muzzle

⑤ Dingo

Dogs and foxes are expert hunters, although most of them also eat plants and carrion. Dogs originally developed from wolves, which people gradually learned to tame. There are now hundreds of different breeds of dog, from the tiny **chihuahua** ①, the smallest of domestic dog breeds, to the hardy **husky** ②, which is used for pulling sledges. Huskies can work in temperatures as low as -50°C (-58°F).

They are the only mammals, apart from humans, that have walked to both the North and South Pole. **African wild dogs** ③ live in highly organized packs, rearing young co-operatively and hunting together to kill animals much bigger than themselves. Each wild dog has its own coat pattern, which is as unique as a fingerprint. **Coyotes** ④ come from North and Central America. They hunt alone, in pairs, or in packs, and

Blanford's fox

Arctic fox ⑥
White winter coat turns brown or blue in summer

① **Red fox**

Bat-eared fox

Crab-eating fox

Large ears help to lose heat

Maned wolf

Fennec fox ⑧

Golden jackal

Ethiopian wolf

Thick fur traps heat to keep body warm

Very long, black-haired legs

Arctic wolf

Grey wolf ⑨

SCALE

can run at up to 65 kph (40 mph). **Dingoes** ⑤ were introduced into Australia from Asia by humans about 4,000 years ago. They hunt small animals on their own but band together to attack kangaroos. **Arctic foxes** ⑥ are specially suited to life in the far north. In winter their coat turns pure white, and they can hunt on drifting ice hundreds of kilometres out at sea. The **red fox** ❼ is one of the world's most widespread predators,

occuring throughout the Northern Hemisphere. It often lives in cities, where it scavenges leftover food from bins and rubbish dumps. The North African **fennec fox** ⑧ is smaller than a cat. It pounces on rodents and insects, pinpointing them with its giant ears. The **grey wolf** ⑨ is the biggest member of the dog family. It lives in packs and communicates with an eerie howl that can be heard from far away.

Bears

SCALE

Pale patch gives this species alternate name "moon bear"

1 Asiatic black bear

2 American black bear

Strong legs allow bear to walk upright

4 Grizzly bear

"Grizzled" hairs lighter at tip than at base

3 Brown bear

Legendary for their size and strength, bears are some of the world's biggest land mammals, with stocky bodies and flat paws. Most of them stay well away from people but some can be highly dangerous, particularly when they are hungry or protecting their cubs. The **Asiatic black bear 1** lives in forests from India to Japan. It spends more than half its life in trees and feeds on fruit, nuts, and small

animals. The **American black bear 2** is slightly bigger but also good at climbing. Like all bears, it has a superb sense of smell, and sometimes breaks into cars or campsites to get at stored food. The **brown bear 3** is the most widespread, with several forms found in different parts of the world. Most famous is the **grizzly bear 4**, which lives in western North America. Standing up to 3 m (10 ft) tall on

⑥ Polar bear

White fur provides camouflage in snow and ice

⑤ Kodiak brown bear

Large front paws used as paddles while swimming

⑦ Sun bear

Furry soles provide good grip on ice

⑩ Giant panda

⑧ Sloth bear

⑨ Spectacled bear

Long claws for breaking open termite mounds

its back legs, it is strong enough to drag away a moose or a horse. It eats almost anything that it can catch or collect, including deer, fish, berries, and even moths. The **Kodiak brown bear** ⑤ from Alaska is even bigger, but the **polar bear** ⑥ is the largest of all. It is the only bear that actively hunts people, although seals are its usual prey. The **sun bear** ⑦ and **sloth bear** ⑧ live in southern Asia. The sun

bear's tongue can protrude up to 25 cm (10 in) to extract food such as honey and grubs from holes and crevices. The **spectacled bear** ⑨ comes from forests high up in the South American Andes. It feeds on fruit, plant shoots, and meat. The **giant panda** ⑩ lives in central China, where it feeds entirely on bamboo. Like all bears, it has tiny cubs. They weigh only about 120 g (4 oz) when they are newly born.

POLAR BEAR
This powerful Arctic predator is the largest land-based meat-eater. Instantly recognizable by its thick white fur, the polar bear is a strong swimmer and a lethally effective hunter. Its usual prey is seals, which it ambushes as they surface through holes in the ice to breathe. The polar bear is often curious about people and can be dangerous if it comes too close to human settlements.

Size ❯ Males up to 3 m (10 ft); females up to 2.2 m (7 ft) tall, standing on their hind legs **Weight ❯** Males weigh 300–800 kg (660–1,760 lb); females about 150–300 kg (330–660 lb) **Habitat ❯** Arctic tundra and sea ice. Spends a lot of its time hunting on sea ice. **Distribution ❯** Arctic Circle; Canada and northern Alaska; Greenland; northern Scandinavia, Russia, and Siberia. **Diet ❯** Seals, narwhals, walruses, and seabirds. They may go without food for months, living off their body fat. **Breeding ❯** They mate from March to May. Cubs are born from November to January. **Lifespan ❯** Up to 30 years. **Predators ❯** None. **Conservation status ❯** Vulnerable. Melting of ice due to climate change is reducing their habitat.

Seals and walrus

Male can inflate muzzle to look ferocious

Galapagos fur seal

① Antarctic fur seal

③ California sea lion

Body propped up by front flippers

② Brown fur seal

⑤ Steller's sea lion

④ Walrus

Southern sea lion

Seals are awkward on land but fast and graceful in the sea. All of them have streamlined bodies, and flippers instead of legs. The smallest seals are just over 1 m (3 ft) long but the biggest measure more than 4 m (13 ft) around their blubbery waists and weigh more than 3 tonnes. The **Antarctic fur seal** ① breeds on islands in the Southern Ocean, while the **brown fur seal** ② lives along the coasts of Australia and South Africa. The **California sea lion** ③ is an expert at catching fish, and is a star performer at wildlife parks and zoos. At full speed it can swim at 40 kph (25 mph). **Walruses** ④ have huge wrinkly bodies, bristly moustaches, and white tusks up to 1 m (3 ft) long. They live in the Arctic and feed on clams and other seabed animals, sucking them out of their shells. **Steller's sea lion** ⑤ from the North

Hooded seal

Trunk-like nose in males

6 Southern elephant seal

Thick layer of blubber keeps body warm

7 Weddell seal

Front flippers used for steering

Common seal

Streamlined body for speedy swimming

8 Grey seal

Harp seal

Baikal seal

9 Leopard seal

Large eyes for good vision in deep water

Flippers have short claws

Bearded seal

Pacific is the biggest of its kind. Like all sea lions and fur seals it can walk on its flippers, while other seals crawl on their stomachs when they come ashore. The **southern elephant seal 6** is the largest seal and a record-breaking diver. It can plunge more than 2 km (1¼ miles) deep to catch fish and squid, holding its breath for an hour and a half. **Weddell seals 7** live around Antarctica. These expert divers specialize in long, deep dives under Antarctic ice shelves. In the winter season, they gnaw holes in the sea ice so that they can come to the surface to breathe. **Grey seals 8** are fish-eaters from the North Atlantic, but the Antarctic **leopard seal 9** is a ferocious killer of warm-blooded animals, including penguins and other seals. Unusually for a true seal, it uses its front flippers to swim and steer.

Cats

Geoffroy's cat ①

Black leopard ②

Retractable front claws

Clouded leopard ③

Snow leopard ④

Extra-long tail can wrap around the body

Ocelot ⑤

Agile body adapted for climbing

Margay

Jaguar ⑦

Leopard ⑥

Sleek, stealthy, and patient, cats are natural killers. Apart from lions, most of them hunt on their own, using their claws and teeth to catch their prey. They include the fastest animals on four legs as well as some of the world's laziest predators, which snooze up to 20 hours each day. **Geoffroy's cat** ① from South America is a typical small cat. It hunts at night, catching mammals, birds, and fish. The

black leopard ② is a variety of the regular leopard, with unusually dark fur. The **clouded leopard** ③ gets its name from its cloud-shaped markings. It comes from the forests of South and Southeast Asia, and often hunts in treetops. The **snow leopard** ④ lives in the mountains of Central Asia, where its thick coat and wrap-around tail protect it from the cold. **Ocelots** ⑤ are forest cats from Central and

Dark fur with black spots

SCALE

Fishing cat

⑩ Tiger

⑧ Lion

⑨ Rusty-spotted cat

Males have thick mane

Vertical stripes for camouflage

Long legs and large feet to knock down big prey

South America. Night hunters, they prey on rodents but can climb trees to stalk monkeys and birds. **Leopards** ⑥ live in Africa and Asia. To safeguard their food from scavengers, they sometimes haul prey high into trees. The **jaguar** ⑦ is the biggest cat in the Americas. It is a good swimmer and often feeds on turtles, crushing their shells with its powerful bite. The **lion** ⑧ is the only wild cat that lives in groups,

known as prides. Although males are bigger than females, or lionesses, the females do most of the hunting and take sole charge of raising the young. The **rusty-spotted cat** ⑨ from India and Sri Lanka is the smallest wild cat, while **tigers** ⑩ are the biggest and the most dangerous. Tigers are found from Asia's tropical rainforests to eastern Siberia, but fewer than 5,000 are left in the wild.

Sphynx cat

Thin, very short fur

⑪ Cheetah

⑫ Persian cat

⑬ Siamese cat

Sand cat

Jungle cat

Tail balances legs when sprinting

Tabby cat

Long ear tufts

⑭ Cornish Rex

⑮ Manx cat

Pallas's cat

⑯ Caracal

SCALE

Most cats hunt after dark, creeping up on their prey and pouncing. The **cheetah** ⑪ is different because it hunts by day, relying on speed to make a kill. This lean African cat is the world's fastest sprinter. It speeds after antelope at up to 100 kph (62 mph), tripping up its victims with a swipe of its front paws. Domestic or pet cats are found all over the world, and have lived alongside people for about 10,000 years. There are many different breeds, including the fluffy **Persian cat** ⑫, with its long hair and short muzzle, and the elegant **Siamese** ⑬. The **Cornish Rex** ⑭ has ultra-soft fur, while the **Manx cat** ⑮ does not have a tail. Most pet cats are good hunters and they sometimes go back to living in the wild. Both domestic and wild cats are renowned for their agility. The **caracal** ⑯ is a long-legged

⑰ European wild cat

Black-footed cat

Eurasian lynx

Short, bobbed tail

⑱ Canadian lynx

Large paws for running over snow

Iberian lynx

Asian golden cat

Indian desert cat

⑲ Bobcat

⑳ Puma

Powerful jaw for attacking large prey

Marbled cat

Serval

Tail used for balance while climbing

wild cat from Africa and western Asia. A stunning acrobat, it leaps up to 3.1 m (10 ft) off the ground to knock birds out of the air. The **European wild cat** ⑰ feeds mainly on rodents, but it also attacks ground-nesting birds, swallowing everything including their feathers and bones. Lynxes and bobcats have stubby tails and tufted ears. The **Canadian lynx** ⑱ is found mostly across Alaska, Canada, and in a few areas of the

northern USA. Its main prey is the snowshoe hare, while the North American **bobcat** ⑲ stalks and pounces on all kinds of animals, from insects to young deer. The **puma** ⑳, also known as the cougar or mountain lion, is one of the most widespread cats in the world, found all the way from western Canada to the tip of South America. It is normally shy but it sometimes attacks humans and can kill.

LIONS

Perhaps the most famous of all wild animals, lions are instantly recognizable by their size, brownish-orange coat, and the male's bushy mane. They are renowned for their strength and ferocity. These African lion cubs are practising hunting skills, play-fighting with each other and their mother. These games may look like fun, but they teach the cubs how to stalk, ambush, and kill prey. These will be essential skills when they reach adulthood.

Size ❯ Males up to 2.5 m (8 ft 2 in) long; females up to 1.7 m (5½ ft) long. **Weight ❯** Males weigh 190 kg (418 lb), females 126 kg (278 lb) **Habitat ❯** Hot, dry grassland, scrubland, and occasionally forests. Lions live in groups called prides. Males defend the pride's territory, which can be up to 260 km² (100 sq miles). **Distribution ❯** Asian lions live in the Gir Forest in western India. African lions are found in sub-Saharan Africa. **Diet ❯** Antelope, zebra, and wildebeest, hunted by the females. **Predators ❯** None, but may be killed by rival males, hyenas, and humans. **Breeding ❯** Lions breed all year round. Females give birth to up to six cubs per litter. **Conservation status ❯** Lions are in danger due to hunting and habitat loss.

Otters, raccoons, and weasels

Dense, warm coat can contain one billion hairs

① Sea otter

Tail has dark rings

② Giant otter

Asian small-clawed otter

Markings warn off attackers

③ Striped skunk

Eastern spotted skunk

Large webbed paws

④ Wolverine

Stocky, bear-like body

Greater grison

Otters and their relatives include many expert hunters as well as the smelliest mammals on Earth. They have slender bodies and short legs, with small ears and thick fur. Most of these animals catch their food on land or in fresh water. The **sea otter** ① is the only one that lives offshore. It feeds on shellfish, breaking them open with a stone using its stomach as a worktop. The rare **giant otter** ② from South America's rivers is longer but lighter and has a paddle-shaped tail. North American **striped skunks** ③ have an overpowering method of self-defence. If anything or anyone comes too close, they squirt a foul-smelling liquid from glands beneath their tails. The liquid smells like a mixture of burning rubber and rotting eggs and takes days to fade away. **Wolverines** ④ live in northern parts of Canada, USA,

⑤ Raccoon

⑥ Least weasel

Skunk-like stripes extend from head to tail

African zorilla

SCALE

South American coati

① Kinkajou

Large eyes for good night vision

European polecat

Black-footed ferret

⑧ Honey badger

North American river otter

Paddle-like tail for swimming

⑨ Eurasian badger

American mink

Beech marten

Stoat

Europe, and Asia. Up to 1 m (3 ft 5 in) long, they are the world's strongest mammals for their size, capable of killing a reindeer or a moose. In North America the **raccoon** ⑤ is a common nocturnal visitor to gardens and backyards. Intelligent and curious, it often raids dustbins for leftover food, and catches fish and frogs in ponds. The **least weasel** ⑥ is the smallest meat-eating mammal. As thin as a finger, it

hunts mice in their burrows underground. **Kinkajous** ⑦ from South America feed mainly on fruit, while the **honey badger** ⑧ from Africa breaks into bees' nests. It has very thick fur, which protects it from angry bees' stings. The **Eurasian badger** ⑨ eats plants and animals, and lives in burrow systems called setts. Some setts contain more than 300 m (984 ft) of tunnels, and can be 100 years old.

265

Mongooses, civets, and genets

SCALE

① Banded mongoose

Yellow mongoose

Bushy white-tipped tail

② Meerkat

Tail with brush-like tip

③ Egyptian mongoose

Ruddy mongoose

Cape genet

Common dwarf mongoose

White-tailed mongoose

④ Indian grey mongoose

Mongooses are famous for fighting snakes, although they eat lots of other animals, including insects, lizards, birds, frogs, and even scorpions. Alert and watchful, their quick movements protect them from getting bitten or stung by their prey. They often live in groups and are generally active during the day. The African **banded mongoose** ① makes its home in old termite mounds, while **meerkats** ② use their long front claws to burrow underground. The **Egyptian mongoose** ③ hunts in thick undergrowth and sometimes catches fish and crabs at the edge of streams and ponds. The **Indian grey mongoose** ④ often lives near towns and villages where it helps out by killing rats, snakes, and scorpions for food. Civets and genets are different to mongooses in that they usually feed at night

Asian palm civet 5

Oriental civet

Small Indian civet

Sharp claws
for climbing

6 Binturong

7 Masked palm civet

African palm civet

African civet

8 Small-spotted genet

Large eyes to
see in the dark

9 Banded linsang

and live on their own. The **Asian palm civet** 5 eats fruit and flowers as well as small animals, and stays mainly in trees. The **binturong** 6 from Southeast Asia has shaggy black fur, tufted ears, and a prehensile tail. **Masked palm civets** 7 live in forests in Southeast Asia and China. Like other civets they can squirt attackers with a powerful-smelling fluid, produced by glands at the base of their tails.

The **small-spotted genet** 8 looks like an extra-long cat with a slender tail. Found in southern Europe and Africa, it is an expert climber and often catches birds roosting in trees. In some areas it raids farms and is considered a pest. The **banded linsang** 9 from Southeast Asia has a beautifully striped and spotted coat. It nests in trees and spends most of its life off the ground.

MEERKATS

These cheeky, sociable animals are related to mongooses. Meerkats live in groups called mobs. They dig burrows to protect them from the hot African sun and from predators. Mobs feed and hunt together, with some meerkats acting as lookouts, standing on their hind legs to watch for danger. If a predator approaches, the lookout gives a warning cry and the whole mob dives for cover.

Size ❯ Up to 60 cm (24 in) long. Males are slightly larger than females. **Weight** ❯ Up to 1 kg (35 oz) **Habitat** ❯ Open plains, dry, hot grasslands, and savanna. **Distribution** ❯ Southern and southwestern Africa **Diet** ❯ Insects, birds and birds' eggs, lizards, rodents, and fruit. **Lifespan** ❯ 5–15 years in the wild. **Breeding** ❯ Meerkats breed all year round, but more so in warmer months between August and March. Usually only the dominant female breeds. She may have up to four litters a year, with two to four young per litter. Males and siblings help raise the young, teaching them hunting and survival skills. **Predators** ❯ Hawks, eagles, and jackals. **Conservation status** ❯ Not currently in danger.

Rhinos and tapirs

1 African black rhinoceros

2 Javan rhinoceros

Long front horn

4 Indian rhinoceros

3 Sumatran rhinoceros

Three-toed feet

5 Mountain tapir

After elephants, rhinos are the world's largest land animals, with barrel-shaped bodies and thick, folded skin. They have few natural enemies but most rhinos are threatened by illegal hunting for their horns. The **African black rhino** 1 weighs up to 1.5 tonnes. Notorious for its poor eyesight and bad temper, it feeds on leaves and twigs using its flexible upper lip, and does not like being disturbed. They eat twigs and leaves,

which they grasp with their flexible upper lips. The **Javan rhino** 2 and **Sumatran rhino** 3 are found in the forests of Indonesia. Javan rhinos have a single horn, and are some of the rarest mammals in the world, with fewer than 50 left in the wild. Sumatran rhinos are also critically endangered. They have two horns and are born with a wiry coat of brown fur. Smallest of all rhinos, they can still grow to a height of 1.5 m (5 ft). The

⑥ Baird's tapir

SCALE

⑧ Malayan tapir

⑦ South American tapir

Long, flexible snout to grasp leaves overhead

⑨ White rhinoceros

Thick, grey protective skin

Square mouth for grazing

Indian rhino ④ is the biggest Asian species, with a single horn and armour-plated skin. It lives in tall grasslands, and almost became extinct in the early 1900s, when fewer than 200 were left. About 3,000 live in India today, protected by armed guards. Tapirs are distant relatives of rhinos, with long noses like miniature trunks. They eat fruit and leaves and find their food mainly by smell. The **mountain tapir** ⑤, **Baird's**

tapir ⑥, and **South American tapir** ⑦ come from Central and South America. The largest of all, the **Malayan tapir** ⑧ is the only Asian species, and the only one that is black and white when fully grown. The African **white rhino** ⑨ is the giant of its family. It has two horns and can weigh almost 3 tonnes. Despite its colossal size, it is astonishingly quick and agile, galloping at nearly 50 kph (31 mph).

271

Horses and relatives

1 Grévy's zebra

Stripe pattern is unique to each animal

2 Grant's zebra

Upright mane

3 Somali wild ass

4 Donkey

Striped legs

6 Przewalski's horse

5 Persian onager

Kiang

Khur

The horse family contains some of the fastest and best-known mammals in the world. They live in herds and have very good eyesight and hearing. At the first sign of danger they quickly gallop away. Zebras are wild animals and so are most asses, but donkeys and horses were tamed thousands of years ago. **Grévy's zebra** 1 is the biggest wild member of the horse family, with narrow stripes and a white underside. It lives in East Africa, and is in danger of dying out, with fewer than 5,000 alive in the wild. **Grant's zebra** 2 also comes from East Africa. It is the smallest zebra, growing up to 1.4 m (4½ ft), and has thick stripes and a black upright mane. The **Somali wild ass** 3 lives in the rocky deserts of northeast Africa. It is the ancestor of the **donkey** 4, a sure-footed animal used by humans to

Hinny

8 Shire horse

Furry or "feathered" legs

7 Mule

Paint horse

Exmoor pony

9 Arab horse

Trailing mane

SCALE

carry burdens in many parts of the world. The **Persian onager** ❺ is a wild ass from Asia and is now found only in Iran. **Przewalski's horse** ❻ from Mongolia is the last true wild horse in the world. It almost died out in the 20th century, but is slowly recovering thanks to the work of conservationists. The **mule** ❼ is a hybrid, or mixture, between a male donkey and a female horse. However, there are also more than

1,000 pure horse and pony breeds. The **Shire horse** ❽, bred in Britain, is one of the biggest and the best at pulling loads. The heaviest Shire horse on record, born in 1848, weighed more than 1.5 tonnes. Today, Shire horses are quite rare, but some are still used in forestry. **Arab horses** ❾ are the fastest breed, and are used in horse racing. The most valuable can fetch a price of more than $10 million.

PLAINS ZEBRAS
They may look like peaceful creatures, but zebras can be vicious when it comes to defending themselves or their territory. Males sometimes fight for a chance to breed with females, kicking out and biting at each other. Even predators such as lions and cheetahs have to be careful around zebra herds, as they can be injured or even killed in battles with large males.

Size ❯ Up to 1.4 m (4½ ft) tall **Weight ❯** Males weigh around 360 kg (794 lb); females around 320 kg (705 lb) **Habitat ❯** Grasslands and open savannas. They usually keep close to water holes. In the dry season, they move in huge herds to find food and water. **Distribution ❯** Southern Africa **Diet ❯** Grass, occasionally shrubs. **Breeding ❯** Plains zebras breed all year round. Foals are often born in the rainy season, and can walk within an hour of being born. **Lifespan ❯** 15–20 years in the wild. **Predators ❯** Lions, cheetahs, leopards, and hyenas. Zebras may team up with each other or even with other species such as wildebeest, for protection against predators.

Cows, antelope, and sheep

SCALE

❶ Gaur

❷ Texan longhorn

Horns are hollow, with a bony base

❸ Yak

Lowland anoa

Long hair for keeping warm

Thick winter coat falls off in summer

❹ American bison

Jersey cow

Cattle and their relatives all have hooves, and special stomachs for digesting leaves and grass. Some of them live on their own, but most keep together in herds. The **gaur** ❶ is the largest kind of wild cattle, weighing up to 20 times as much as an adult man. It comes from the forests of tropical Asia and has few natural enemies apart from tigers and crocodiles. Domesticated cattle such as the **Texan**

longhorn ❷ can be almost as big. This breed has some of the world's biggest horns, measuring an incredible 3 m (10 ft) from tip to tip. The **yak** ❸ comes from the mountain pastures of Central Asia, while the **American bison** ❹, or buffalo, is a grassland animal from the Great Plains in Canada and the USA. At one time there were more than 50 million of these massive grazers, but after years of hunting only about 500,000

Sitatunga

5 Common eland

Nilgai

*Feet have two
main hooves*

Greater kudu

Addax

6 Gemsbok

*Horns have
knobbly rings*

Sable antelope

Bohor reedbuck

7 Common waterbuck

*Stripes provide
camouflage*

Zebra duiker

8 African buffalo

9 Wildebeest

Hartebeest

10 Klipspringer

are left. Antelope live in Africa and Asia. The African **common eland 5** is one of the biggest kinds. It is a gentle animal and is sometimes farmed. **Gemsboks 6** live in the deserts of southern Africa. Like most antelope, both males and females have horns. The **common waterbuck 7** lives in grassland and woods but runs into lakes and swamps when threatened. The **African buffalo 8** is one of the biggest and most

dangerous grassland animals. Adult males can even kill lions and demolish cars. **Wildebeest 9** are some of the commonest African antelope, migrating in huge herds that follow the yearly rains. Each migration involves up to 1.5 million wildebeest and thousands of other animals including zebras. The **klipspringer 10** lives on rocky outcrops in eastern and southern Africa. Its rubbery hooves give it a good grip.

277

SCALE

① Thomson's gazelle

⑫ Springbok

Ridge of hair along back

Impala

Steenbok

⑬ Günther's dik dik

Grant's gazelle

Goitered gazelle

Extra-long neck

⑮ Blackbuck

Alpine chamois

⑭ Gerenuk

There are more antelope in Africa than anywhere else in the world. **Thomson's gazelle** ⑪ lives in East Africa's grasslands, where it often mixes with herds of zebras and wildebeest. It keeps a constant lookout for predators, sleeping in five-minute bursts for just an hour every day. The **springbok** ⑫ from southern Africa can leap more than six times its own length. Males lock horns during

the breeding season, when they fight for the right to mate. **Günther's dik dik** ⑬ is a miniature antelope that lives in shrubby places, while the **gerenuk** ⑭ stands on its back legs to feed in shrubs and trees, helped by its long, slender neck. The **blackbuck** ⑮ lives in India and Nepal. Females are mainly brown, but males are black and white with spirally-twisted horns. The **muskox** ⑯ is named after the strong

⑰ Mountain goat

⑯ Muskox

Markhor

Sharp hooves have soft inner pads for better grip

Thick, curved horns longer in males

Angora goat

Wool is used to make mohair, a costly fabric

⑱ Alpine ibex

Takin

Cotswold sheep

Curved horns

⑲ Mouflon

Barbary sheep

⑳ Bighorn sheep

smell emitted by males during the breeding season. It looks like a buffalo, but is actually a relative of wild goats and sheep. It lives in the high Arctic and has a thick, shaggy coat to protect it from the intense winter cold. The North American **mountain goat** ⑰ is a fearless and agile climber. It can leap along narrow ledges just a few hours after being born. The **Alpine ibex** ⑱ is just as sure-footed. It lives high

above the treeline in the European Alps, and is famous for its horns, which can be up to 1 m (3 ft) long. The **mouflon** ⑲ from Europe and Asia is the wild ancestor of sheep that live on farms. Male **bighorn sheep** ⑳ from North America use their horns to fight with their rivals. They crash head-on with enormous force and their fights can last several hours until one of the contestants walks away.

HIPPOPOTAMUSES
Hippopotamus means "river horse", and these animals love water. They spend the day submerged to stay cool and keep their skin moist, coming ashore to graze at night. Hippos can close their nostrils to hold their breath, and sometimes even fall asleep underwater, coming up to breathe without waking up. With their long tusks, hippos can be dangerous, especially if their young are threatened.

Size ❯ Up to 1.7 m (5½ ft) tall **Weight ❯** Males up to
4.5 tonnes; females up to 1.5 tonnes **Habitat ❯** Shallow
lakes, rivers, swamps, and grassland around these areas.
Distribution ❯ Sub-Saharan, Eastern, and Central Africa.
Diet ❯ Grass, reeds, and small shoots of plants. **Breeding ❯**
Hippos breed about once every two years and have just one
calf each time. The calves suckle for nearly a year and can do
so even underwater. **Lifespan ❯** About 50 years. **Predators ❯**
Adults have no predators apart for humans. Young hippos
may be eaten by crocodiles, lions, and hyenas. **Conservation
status ❯** Numbers have fallen sharply in recent years due to
habitat loss and because they are hunted for their teeth.

Pigs, peccaries, and deer

SCALE

② Wild boar

① Piétrain pig

Long snout for rooting up food

④ Buru babirusa

③ Collared peccary

Pale white neck collar

Bearded pig

Red river hog

White-lipped peccary

Developing antlers covered in velvety skin

⑤ Warthog

Two pairs of tusks

Sambar

Roe deer

Red-brown summer coat turns dense and grey in winter

Pigs come in many shapes and colours. Domestic varieties are raised for their meat in farms across the world. The spotty **Piétrain** ① pig, originally from Belgium, is one popular variety. Domestic pigs have descended from the **wild boar** ②. With its bristly fur and bulldozer-like snout, this formidable creature digs up roots, burrowing animals, and also crops in fields. It originally comes from Europe, North Africa, and Asia, but has been released in many other places where it is sometimes a serious pest. The **collared peccary** ③ is found from southern USA to South America and is similar to a wild boar. The **Buru babirusa** ④ from Indonesia has some of the strangest tusks of any pig. It has two growing out of its mouth and two more growing upwards through its snout. The **warthog** ⑤ lives in Africa's grasslands.

Pampas deer

Fallow deer **6**

Antlers fall off when winter ends

7 Wapiti

Axis deer

Musk deer

Southern pudu

8 Java mouse deer

Moose **9**

Sika deer

Both males and females grow antlers

White-tailed deer

10 Reindeer

Like other wild pigs it can be dangerous if cornered, particularly if it has piglets to protect. Pigs eat almost anything, but deer are vegetarians, feeding on leaves, lichens, and bark. Most male deer have antlers, which they shed and regrow each year. The **fallow deer's 6** antlers are flat like the palm of a hand, but the **wapiti 7** has branching antlers that end in sharp points. Every autumn, male wapiti or stags clash head-on in a trial of strength that decides who gets a chance to breed. The tiny **Java mouse deer 8** is the world's smallest hoofed mammal, no bigger than a rabbit, while the **moose 9** is by far the largest deer, with a record weight of more than 800 kg (1,760 lb). Moose live on their own, but **reindeer 10** are much more sociable. In the Canadian Arctic, half a million of them can travel in a single herd.

Camels, llamas, and giraffes

SCALE

❶ Dromedary

Round feet with two toes

❷ Bactrian camel

Shaggy beard on throat

❸ Masai giraffe

❹ Okapi

Striped upper legs

For thousands of years, the one-humped camel or **dromedary** ❶ has been used as a working animal in North Africa and the Middle East. Nicknamed the "ship of the desert", it can go for two weeks without drinking, and when it does find water it can swallow enough to fill four kitchen sinks. Its hump stores an emergency reserve of fat, and it has cushioned feet that stop it from sinking in the desert sand. The **Bactrian camel** ❷ from Central Asia is even tougher because it has to cope with extreme winter cold. It has two humps instead of one and a thick winter coat that falls off when spring arrives. Giraffes are the world's tallest animals. They live in Africa's tree-studded grasslands, feeding on leaves and twigs that other mammals cannot reach. The **Masai giraffe** ❸ is the largest, with a record height of

⑤ Guanaco

⑥ Alpaca

Long, woolly coat

⑦ Suri alpaca

⑧ Vicuña

⑨ Llama

Bony horns covered in skin

Thornicroft's giraffe

Reticulated giraffe

Large ears for keeping cool

⑩ Rothschild's giraffe

6 m (20 ft). The **okapi** ❹ from Central Africa is a forest-dwelling relative of giraffes, while the **guanaco** ❺ belongs to the camel family. It lives high in the Andes like the South American **alpaca** ❻. Alpacas are raised for their silky fleece. Some breeds have short coats but **suri alpacas** ❼ can have a fleece so long that it trails along the ground. All alpacas are descendants of the **vicuña** ❽. This wild grazer, also from the Andes, can survive at 5,000 m (16,400 ft), a height that would leave many people gasping for breath. The **llama** ❾, a tame relative of the guanaco, is used for carrying burdens on narrow mountain paths. Back in Africa, **Rothschild's giraffe** ❿ is easily recognizable with its big spots and long white "socks" on its lower legs. Loss of habitat has threatened its existence, with fewer than 670 left in the wild.

GIRAFFES
With their amazingly long necks reaching into the treetops, giraffes are the tallest living animals. They have only seven bones in their necks, the same number as humans. Their long, slender legs allow them to gallop as fast as a horse, but become a problem when they have to bend down to drink. Giraffes also have long, bluish-purple tongues, and horn-like growths on their heads. Each giraffe can be recognized by its unique pattern of blotches.

Size > Males up to 6 m (20 ft); females up to 4.7 m (15½ ft) tall **Weight >** Males weigh up to 1.6 tonnes; females up to 1.1 tonnes **Habitat >** Grassland, savanna, and open woodland. **Distribution >** Sub-Saharan Africa **Diet >** Giraffes mainly feed on acacia trees. They have tough mouths and tongues to cope with the thorns. **Breeding >** Giraffes breed in the rainy season, and calves are born in the dry season. Females give birth standing up, and a calf can walk within an hour of being born. **Lifespan >** About 25 years in the wild. **Predators >** Lions, but young giraffes may also be killed by leopards, hyenas, wild dogs, and crocodiles. **Conservation status >** Numbers of some giraffe species are reducing due to habitat loss.

Dolphins and porpoises

① Striped dolphin

Pygmy killer whale

Atlantic white-sided dolphin

② Risso's dolphin

Distinctive blunt, rounded head

Mostly grey body becomes lighter with age

Southern right whale dolphin

Burmeister's porpoise

③ Vaquita

④ Dall's porpoise

Steeply sloping head

Franciscana

⑤ Amazon river dolphin

⑥ Indus river dolphin

Finless porpoise

Dolphins and porpoises are related to whales, but they are smaller and faster, with sharply pointed teeth. Some live alone but most travel in groups called pods or schools. Intelligent and playful, they communicate with clicks and whistles. Like some whales, dolphins use sound waves to find their food. The **striped dolphin** ① lives worldwide, mainly where the sea is warm. It feeds on fish and squid, and often surfs the bow-waves in front of fast-moving boats. **Risso's dolphin** ② has a flattened head instead of a beak. As it gets older, its body often becomes scarred from fighting with other dolphins and grappling with squid. Porpoises are usually shorter than dolphins, with barrel-shaped bodies and blunt jaws. The tiny **vaquita** ③ is one of the rarest and smallest species, measuring just 1.2 m (4 ft) long, while **Dall's**

⑦ Bottlenose dolphin

Peale's dolphin

⑧ Commerson's dolphin

Hector's dolphin

⑨ Killer whale

Atlantic spotted dolphin

*Powerful body
suited for hunting*

Hourglass dolphin

Short-beaked common dolphin

SCALE

porpoise ④ is the fastest with a top speed of about 55 kph (34 mph). The **Amazon river dolphin** ⑤ has small eyes and the **Indus river dolphin** ⑥ is almost blind. Both these dolphins live in fresh water and rely on sound waves to hunt. The **bottlenose dolphin** ⑦ is smart and agile, making it a popular performer at aquariums. It frequently interacts with humans in the wild, too. **Commerson's dolphin** ⑧, on the other hand, is a much rarer species from icy southern seas. The **killer whale** ⑨, or orca, is by far the biggest member of the dolphin family, weighing up to 7 tonnes. A cunning and quick-witted predator, it attacks other dolphins and whales, and sometimes tips up ice floes to make seals slide into the sea. It is even known to attack seals on beaches, using large waves to wash itself back out to sea after grabbing its prey.

Whales

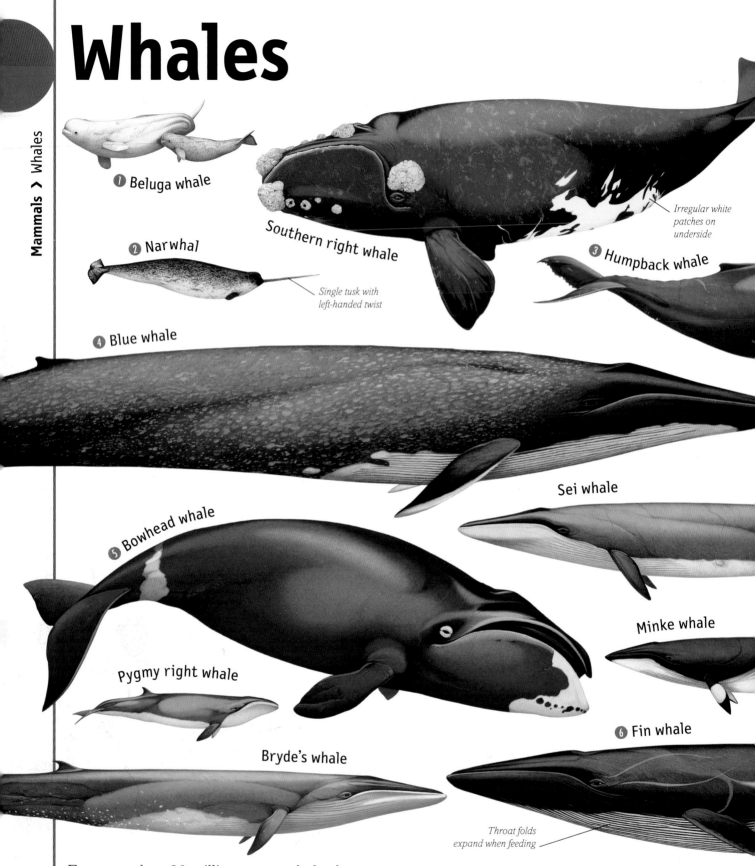

① Beluga whale

② Narwhal

Single tusk with left-handed twist

Southern right whale

Irregular white patches on underside

③ Humpback whale

④ Blue whale

⑤ Bowhead whale

Sei whale

Minke whale

Pygmy right whale

⑥ Fin whale

Bryde's whale

Throat folds expand when feeding

For more than 30 million years, whales have roamed the open seas. They include some of the biggest animals that have ever lived. They breathe air through blowholes on top of their heads and swim by beating their flukes, or horizontal tails. The **beluga** ① and **narwhal** ② are two small whales from the Arctic. Belugas have white skin that blends with Arctic ice floes. Narwhals have a long twisted tusk, which they were hunted for in the past. The tusks were sold as "unicorn horns" and were thought to have magical powers. The **humpback whale** ③ is a fish-eater and an incredible acrobat. It sometimes bursts right out of the water, crashing back onto the surface with a massive splash. The humpback is much longer than a bus, but it is only half the size of the **blue whale** ④, the largest animal on Earth. This mega-

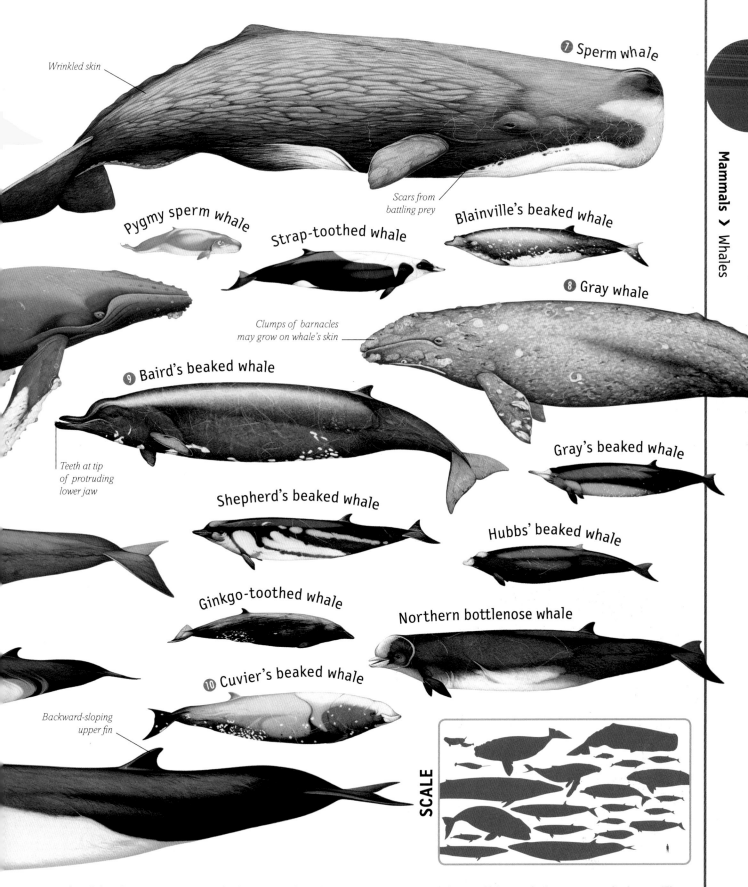

7 Sperm whale

Wrinkled skin

Scars from battling prey

Pygmy sperm whale

Strap-toothed whale

Blainville's beaked whale

8 Gray whale

Clumps of barnacles may grow on whale's skin

9 Baird's beaked whale

Teeth at tip of protruding lower jaw

Gray's beaked whale

Shepherd's beaked whale

Hubbs' beaked whale

Ginkgo-toothed whale

Northern bottlenose whale

10 Cuvier's beaked whale

Backward-sloping upper fin

SCALE

mammal weighs about 150 tonnes, which is more than the heaviest dinosaur, and grows up to 27 m (89 ft) long. It feeds on tiny animals called krill, filtering them out of the water, swallowing up to 8 billion every day. The **bowhead whale** **5** and **fin whale** **6** are also filter-feeders, but the **sperm whale** **7** is the world's biggest hunter-killer with a huge head and about 50 enormous teeth. It feeds on giant squid, diving up to 3,000 m (9,840 ft) beneath the waves to find prey. The **gray whale** **8** makes the longest migrations of any mammal, a round trip of 20,000 km (12,430 miles) from Alaskan waters to warmer waters off Mexico. Beaked whales feed in seabed canyons, sucking up squid and fish. **Baird's beaked whale** **9** is the biggest of these mysterious animals while **Cuvier's beaked whale** **10** is the most widespread.

291

HUMPBACK WHALE
These whales are famous for the males' complex, haunting songs, which carry for thousands of kilometres through the ocean. Humpback whales are remarkably agile for their size. They can push themselves right out of the water, twisting in the air to land on their backs with an enormous splash. This movement is known as breaching. Many whales do it, but scientists do not know why.

Size ❯ Males up to 14 m (46 ft) long; females up to 16 m (52½ ft) long **Weight ❯** Up to 40 tonnes **Habitat ❯** Ocean; humpback whales breed in warm tropical and subtropical waters but migrate to cooler waters to feed. **Distribution ❯** Oceans and coastal areas across the world. **Diet ❯** Plankton, krill, and small fish, which they filter out of the water.

Breeding ❯ Females breed once every two to three years and nurse their calves for about 12 months. Humpback whales become adult at about five years. **Lifespan ❯** Up to 95 years. **Predators ❯** Killer whales may hunt young humpbacks. **Conservation status ❯** No longer threatened since hunting by humans was banned in 1966.

INDEX

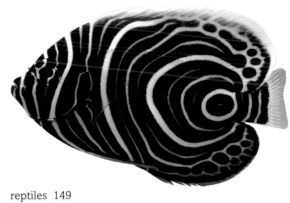

ACKNOWLEDGMENTS

THE SMITHSONIAN INSTITUTION:

Reviewers for the National Zoo: Donald Moore III, Director, Animal Care Sciences, Scott R. Derrickson, Deputy Director, Smithsonian Conservation Biology Institute, Ed Bronikowski, Senior Curator, Tony Barthel, Curator, Elephant Trails, Asia Trail, and Cheetah Conservation Station, Alan Peters, Curator, Invertebrate Exhibit & Pollinarium, Bob King, Curator, Primates, Steven Sarro, Curator, Small Mammal House, Jim Murphy, Curator, Reptile Discovery Center, Craig Saffoe, Curator, Great Cats, Kids' Farm and Andean Bears, Frank Clements, Park Manager, Horticulture, Stacey Tabellario, Animal Keeper, Asia Trail, Juan Rodriguez, Animal Keeper, Asia Trail, Gil Myers, Animal Keeper, Cheetah Conservation Station, Kate Volz, Animal Keeper, Cheetah Conservation Station, Mike Henley, Biologist, Invertebrate Exhibit & Pollinarium, Donna Stockton, Biologist, Invertebrate Exhibit & Pollinarium, Michael Miller, Animal Keeper, Invertebrate Exhibit & Pollinarium, Erin Stromberg, Animal Keeper, Primates, Kenton Kerns, Animal Keeper, Small Mammal House, David Kessler, Animal Keeper, Small Mammal House, Rebecca Smithson, Animal Keeper, Small Mammal House, Sara Hallager, Animal Keeper, Bird House, Hillary Colton, Animal Keeper, Bird House, Lori Smith, Animal Keeper, Bird House, Debi Talbott, Animal Keeper, Bird House, Kathleen Brader, Animal Keeper, Bird House, Gwendolyn Cooper, Animal Keeper, Bird House, Warren Lynch, Animal Keeper, Smithsonian Conservation Biology Institute, Budhan Pukazhenthi, Reproductive Physiologist, Smithsonian Conservation Biology Institute, Peter Marra, Research Ecologist, Smithsonian Migratory Bird Center, Pamela Baker-Masson, Director, Communications, Jennifer Zoon, Communications Assistant, and special thanks to Susie Ellis.

Reviewers for the National Museum of Natural History: Dr Don W Wilson, Curator Emeritus, Department of Vertebrate Zoology, Dr Carole C Baldwin, Curator of Fishes, Lynne R Parenti, Curator of Fishes and Research Scientist, G David Johnson, Ichthyologist/Curator, Division of Fishes, Carla J Dove, PhD, Feather Identification Lab.

DK would like to thank:
Katie John for text assistance, Alison Gardner, Sunita Gahir, Konica Juneja, Kanika Mittal, Divya PR, and Upasana Sharma for design assistance, Hedi Hunter for design styling, Lili Bryant, Neha Chaudhary, Megha Gupta, Nandini Gupta, Suefa Lee, Vineetha Mokkil, Yamuna Matheswaran, and Rupa Rao for editorial assistance, Kealy Wilson and Ellen Nanney from the Smithsonian Institution, Angela Baynham for proofreading, Elizabeth Wise for the index.

The publisher would like to thank the following for their kind permission to reproduce their photographs:

(Key: a-above; b-below/bottom; c-centre; f-far; l-left; r-right; t-top)

1 **Fotolia:** He2 (ca). 3 **Fotolia:** He2 (ca). 5 **Science Photo Library:** Pasieka (tc). 6 **Dorling Kindersley:** Jeremy Hunt - modelmaker (cra). **Getty Images:** Joel Sartore (br). 8 **Science Photo Library:** CNRI (tl). 9 **Dorling Kindersley:** Natural History Museum, London (tr); Weymouth Sealife Centre (tl). **Getty Images:** Mint Images / Frans Lanting (bc). 10 **Dreamstime.com:** Isselee (cr). Science Photo Library: Pasieka (br). 11 **Alamy Images:** cbimages (bc). **Dorling Kindersley:** Jerry Young (cla). **FLPA:** Minden Pictures (clb). 12-13 **Science Photo Library:** 3d4medical.com (c). 14 **Alamy Images:** BSIP SA (c). CDC: (cl). **Corbis:** Visuals Unlimited (fcl). **Getty Images:** J. L. Carson (cla). **Science Photo Library:** CNRI (tc); Pasieka (tr); Professor N. Russell (fcr); A.B. Dowsett (br); Dr Kari Lounatmaa (bc, cra). 15 **CDC:** (cla, cra). **Corbis:** Dennis Kunkel Microscopy, Inc. / Visuals Unlimited (cb). **Dorling Kindersley:** Uniformed Services University, Bethesda, MD (tl). **Science Photo Library:** Eye Of Science (c); SCIMAT (cl); Dr Kari Lounatmaa (br). **USDA Agricultural Research Service:** Courtesy of USDA_ARS / Eric Erbe (tr). 17 **Photo Biopix.dk:** Jens Schou (cr). 20-21 **Science Photo Library:** Laguna Design. 26-27 **Getty Images:** Michael & Patricia Fogden. 27 **Dorling Kindersley:** Stephen Hayward (cr). 32 **Photo Biopix.dk:** Jens Schou (ca). 33 **Photo Biopix.dk:** Jens Schou (br). 34 **Photo Biopix.dk:** Niels Sloth (bl). **Corbis:** Visuals Unlimited / William Ormerod (ca). **Dorling Kindersley:** Natural History Museum, London (cla). 35 **Photo Biopix.dk:** Jens schou (bc, cb, cl, cra, tr). **Getty Images:** Ed Reschke (br). **Science Photo Library:** Scott Camazine (bl). 38 **Dreamstime.com:** Gabriela Insuratelu (clb). 39 **Dorling Kindersley:** Neil Fletcher (clb). **Dreamstime.com:** Markit (c); Voltan1 (crb). 41 **Dreamstime.com:** Liumangtiger (cl). 42-43 **Dreamstime.com:** Marcouliana. 44 **Alamy Images:** WoodyStock (crb). 45 **Dreamstime.com:** Pehttt (tl). 46 **Dorling Kindersley:** Natural History Museum, London (ca). 47 **Dorling Kindersley:** Courtesy of Harry Tomlinson (c). **Getty Images:** (bc). 50-51 **Photoshot:** Laurie Campbell (c). 50 **Alamy Images:** VWpics / Ricardo Fernandez (clb). **FLPA:** (fclb). **Getty Images:** Age Fotostock / Marevision (cb, cl); Wolfgang Poelzer (tr); De Agostini Picture Library / DEA / P. Donnini (crb). **naturepl.com:** Jose B. Ruiz (ca). 51 **Alaska Fisheries Science Center, NOAA Fisheries Service:** (ftr). **Corbis:** Minden Pictures / Norbert Wu (tl); Visuals Unlimited / David Wrobel (c). **Getty Images:** Age Fotostock / Marevision (tr); Fotosearch Value (cr). 52 FLPA: Panda Photo (c). **Getty Images:** Fotosearch (br); Axel Rosenberg (cr); Nature / UIG (fcrb). **naturepl.com:** Solvin Zankl (cl). 53 **Dorling Kindersley:** Natural History Museum, London (cra, tl). imagequestmarine.com: (tc). 54 **Ardea:** Steve Hopkin (c). **Corbis:** Minden Pictures / Fred Bavendam (cl); Visuals Unlimited / Dr. Robert Calentine (cb). naturepl.com: Sinclair Stammers (bl). **Photoshot:** ANT (tc). **Science Photo Library:** James H. Robinson (cla). 54-55 **Corbis:** Kerrick James. **FLPA:** D P Wilson (c). 55 **Alamy Images:** blickwinkel (cl). **FLPA:** Nigel Cattlin (cla). **Science Photo Library:** Dr Morley Read (ca, tc). 59 **Getty Images:** Age Fotostock / Marevision (c). 60 **Getty Images:** Age Fotostock / Mary Jonilonis (br). **Science Photo Library:** Alexander Semenov (crb). 61 **FLPA:** Minden Pictures / Kevin Schafer (tc); Walter Rohdich (tr). 62-63 **Corbis:** Science Faction / Norbert Wu. 64 **Corbis:** Visuals Unlimited (clb). **Dorling Kindersley:** Weymouth Sealife Centre (cb). **naturepl.com:** Sue Daly (c). **Science Photo Library:** Dante Fenolio (tr). 65 **Alamy Images:** Mike Veitch (clb). **Getty Images:** Photographer's Choice / Steven Hunt (tr); WaterFrame / Reinhard Dirscherl (ca). **Richard Ling:** (cl). **naturepl.com:** David Shale (tc). 66 **Corbis:** Minden Pictures / Fred Bavendam (bl). **Getty Images:** Botanica / James Baigrie (cl). 67 **Corbis:** Brandon D. Cole (tl); Minden Pictures / Fred Bavendam (tr). **Getty Images:** Oxford Scientific / Karen Gowlett-Holmes (cra); Workbook Stock / Frederic Pacorel (cr). 68 **FLPA:** David Hosking (clb). **Getty Images:** Flickr Open / Alan Cressler (crb); Visuals Unlimited, Inc. / Gerry Bishop (cl); Peter Arnold / James Gerholdt (bl). **naturepl.com:** Kim Taylor (tr). 69 **Alamy Images:** Leslie Garland Picture Library / Doug McCutcheon (ca). **Ardea:** Steve Hopkin (cla). **Corbis:** Minden Pictures / Thomas Marent (crb). **Dreamstime.com:** Milosluz (b). **Getty Images:** Flickr Open / Shailesh Makwana (cb). 70 **Dreamstime.com:** Scott Harms (tr). **FLPA:** Olivier Digoit (cl). **Getty Images:** James H Robinson (cra). 71 **Corbis:** Steve Parish Publishing / Patrick Honan (clb). **Dorling Kindersley:** Geoff Brightling / Chris Reynolds and the BBC Team - modelmakers (bc). **FLPA:** Minden Pictures / Pete Oxford (cr). **Science Photo Library:** Simon D. Pollard (br). 72 **Corbis:** Science Faction / Stefan Sollfors (ca). **FLPA:** Photo Researchers (tc). **Getty Images:** Kallista Images (clb); Visuals Unlimited, Inc. / Robert Pickett (br). 73 **Corbis:** Minden Pictures / Albert Lleal (bl). 74-75 OceanwideImages.com. 76 **Corbis:** Foto Natura / Minden Pictures / Stephen Belcher (bl); Minden Pictures / Fred Bavendam (cl). **Getty Images:** Visuals Unlimited, Inc. / Fabio Pupin (cb). **imagequestmarine.com:** (crb). 77 **Corbis:** Ocean (c). **Getty Images:** Age Fotostock / Marevision (tc); (tr). 78 **Corbis:** Gary Bell (cl); Photocuisine / J.Garcia (tl); Design Pics / Dave Fleetham (bl). **Getty Images:** Visuals Unlimited / Gerald & Buff Corsi (bc). 79 **Dreamstime.com:** Olga Demchishina (cla). FLPA: Gerard Lacz (bc). **imagequestmarine.com:** (crb, tl). 83 Fotolia: Roque141 (tr). 84-85 **Dorling Kindersley:** Thomas Marent. 86-87 **FLPA:** Ingrid Visser (tc). 86 **FLPA:** Dave Pressland (c). **Getty Images:** AWL Images / William Gray (cla). **naturepl.com:** MYN / John Tiddy (bl); Ann & Steve Toon (br). 87 **Corbis:** Ocean (b); Damon Wilder (cra). **Dorling Kindersley:** Natural History Museum, London (cr). 88 **Corbis:** Minden Pictures / Ingo Arndt (cl); Visuals Unlimited / Alex Wild (br). **Dorling Kindersley:** Natural History Museum, London (b). 90-91 **Getty Images:** Adegsm. 92 **Dorling Kindersley:** Natural History Museum, London (cl, br); Jerry Young (ca). 93 **Dorling Kindersley:** Natural History Museum, London (cr). 94 **Dorling Kindersley:** Andrew Mackay (fcrb); Natural History Museum, London (ftr, tc, tl, ftl, ca, cl, c, cr, fcr, clb, cb, crb, fbl, bl, bc, br). 95 **Dorling Kindersley:** Natural History Museum, London (tl, tc, tr, fcla, cla, ca, cra, fcra, cl, c, crb, cr, clb, fbl, bc, br, fbr). 96 **Dorling Kindersley:** Natural History Museum, London (t, tl, tc, cla, ca, cra, cl, c, cr, fcr, clb, cb, crb, fbl, bl, br, fbr). 97 **Dorling Kindersley:** Natural History Museum, London (tl, tc, cla, cr, cl, fclb, clb, crb, fcrb, cb, fbl, bl, br, fbr). 98-99 **Dorling Kindersley:** Thomas Marent. 99 **Dorling Kindersley:** Booth Museum of Natural History, Brighton (br). 100 **Alamy Images:** Premaphotos (fbr). **Dorling Kindersley:** Natural History Museum, London (bc); Jerry Young (tl). **Getty Images:** First Light / Grambo Grambo (cl). 101 **Corbis:** Minden Pictures / Stephen Dalton (bl). **Dorling Kindersley:** Natural History Museum, London (cl, br). **The Natural History Museum, London:** (tr). 102 **Dreamstime.com:** Dbmz (bc); Ryszard Laskowski (c); Meoita (cr). 103 **Dreamstime.com:** Amskad (tr). 106 **Corbis:** Minden Pictures / Pete Oxford (bl). **FLPA:** Norbert Wu (clb). **Getty Images:** Visuals Unlimited, Inc. / Andy Murch (cla). **Photoshot:** (ca, cl). 106-107 **Ardea:** Kenneth W Fink (tl). 107 **Alamy Images:** Stephen Frink Collection (ca). **Corbis:** Visuals Unlimited / Patrice Ceisel (crb). **Getty Images:** Dr Peter M Forster (b). 108 **Alamy Images:** Roberto Nistri (cr). **Getty Images:** Visuals Unlimited, Inc. / Andy Murch (tl, cl). 108-109 **Corbis:** Science Faction / Norbert Wu (bc). **Dorling Kindersley:** Jeremy Hunt - modelmaker (ca). 109 **Corbis:** Dave Fleetham / Design Pics (tl). **Getty Images:** De Agostini Picture Library (cb). 110-111 **Corbis:** National Geographic Society / Colin Parker. 112 **Dorling Kindersley:** Weymouth Sea Life Centre (bc). **Dreamstime.com:** Isselee (tr). 112-113 **Dreamstime.com:** Asther Lau Choon Siew (c). 113 **Alamy Images:** cbimages (cra). **Dorling Kindersley:** Weymouth Sea Life Centre (cb, c). **Dreamstime.com:** Peter Leahy (bl). **Getty Images:** Marevision (crb). **imagequestmarine.com:** (bc). 114-115 **Alamy Images:** Emilio Ereza (bc). 115 **Dreamstime.com:** Lunamarina (br, cra). 116 **Dreamstime.com:** Andylid (bl); Serg_dibrova (tc). 117 **Corbis:** Dpa / Hinrich Baesemann (cr). **Dreamstime.com:** Yordan Rusev (crb). 118-119 **FLPA:** Imagebroker / Norbert Probst. 120-121 **Alamy Images:** Diarmuid Toman (c). 120 **Jón Baldur Hlíðberg (www.fauna.is):** (crb). **Corbis:** Visuals Unlimited / David Wrobel (cla). **naturepl.com:** David Shale (br); Doc White (bl). 121 **Alamy Images:** Roberto Nistri (cb). **FLPA:** Norbert Wu (c). **Getty Images:** Dan Kitwood (ca). **naturepl.com:** David Shale (cla, cra). 122 **Alamy Images:** Blickwinkel (bl). **Dorling Kindersley:** Jerry Young (c, fbl). **Getty Images:** DEA / A. Calegari (cb). 122-123 **Alamy Images:** Stocktrek Images / Michael Wood (bc). **Corbis:** Minden Pictures / Norbert Wu (tc). 123 **Alamy Images:** Blickwinkel (cra). **Dorling Kindersley:** Natural History Museum, London (tc); Linda Pitkin (tr). **Fotolia:** poco_bw (c). 124 **Dreamstime.com:** Stephan Pietzko (clb). **FLPA:** (cr). **Getty Images:** Ken Lucas (cl). 124-125 **FLPA:** OceanPhoto (bc). **Science Photo Library:** Tom Mchugh (c). 126-127 **SuperStock:** Chris Mattison / age fotostock. 128 **Photoshot:** James Carmichael Jr (ca, bl). **Science Photo Library:** Dr.Morley Read (cla). 130 **Getty Images:** Photodisc / Life On White (cl); Purestock (clb). 131 **Corbis:** All Canada Photos / Jared Hobbs (crb). 132 **Corbis:** Minden Pictures / Piotr Naskrecki (tc). **Dreamstime.com:** Mgkuijpers (cr). **FLPA:** Imagebroker / Winfried Schäfer (clb); Photo Researchers (cra). **naturepl.com:** Michael D. Kern (bc). 133 **Corbis:** Minden Pictures / Stephen Dalton (c); Reuters / Jose Luis Saavedra (tc). **FLPA:** Minden Pictures / Michael & Patricia Fogden (tr); Minden Pictures / Piotr Naskrecki (cra). 134-135 **Getty Images:** Gail Shumway. 136 **FLPA:** Photo Researchers (tr). **naturepl.com:** Nature Production (bl). **Science Photo Library:** Dante Fenolio (cb). 137 **Alamy Images:** Ladi Kirn (tr); Vibe Images / Jack Goldfarb (cr). **Corbis:** Minden Pictures / Pete Oxford (tl). **Dreamstime.com:** Jason P Ross (br). **Getty Images:** Visuals Unlimited, Inc. / Michael Redmer (crb). **naturepl.com:** Barry Mansell (cra). **Science Photo Library:** E.R.Degginger (bc). 140-141 **Dreamstime.com:** Lloyd Luecke (tc). 140 **Corbis:** Minden Pictures / SA Team / Foto Natura (bl); David A. Northcott (crb). **Dorling Kindersley:** Jerry Young (br). **Dreamstime.com:** Amwu (tc). 141 **Corbis:** Visuals Unlimited / Michael Redmer (cb). **Dreamstime.com:** Peter Leahy (crb). **Getty Images:** Visuals Unlimited, Inc. / Michael Redmer (ca). 142 **Dreamstime.com:** Checco (crb). 143 **Corbis:** Imagemore Co., Ltd (cb). **Dorling Kindersley:** Jerry Young (cr, cl, br). **Dreamstime.com:** Amwu (cra). 145 **Alamy Images:** Searagen (br). **Dorling Kindersley:** Jerry Young (crb). 146 **Getty Images:** Mint Images / Frans Lanting (c). **Photoshot:** A.N.T. Photo Library (tc); Ken Griffiths (ca). 148-149 **Getty Images:** Cordier Sylvain. 150 **Alamy Images:** Michal Cerny (crb). **Corbis:** Auscape / Minden Pictures / Jean-Paul Ferrero (cr); David Northcott (cla). **Dorling Kindersley:** Diego Reggianti (cra). 151 **FLPA:** Minden Pictures / Mitsuhiko Imamori (clb); Minden Pictures / Michael & Patricia Fogden (crb). **Getty Images:** Joel Sartore (tl). 154-155 **Getty Images:** Mark Kostich. 156

Acknowledgments

Alamy Images: Jan Csernoch (cb). **Dorling Kindersley:** Jerry Young (ca). **Dreamstime.com:** Nico Smit (bl). **Getty Images:** Minden Pictures / Mike Parry (cl). 156-157 **Photoshot:** Andrea & Antonella Ferrari (bc). 157 **Alamy Images:** Prisma Bildagentur AG/ Dani Carlo (cla). **Corbis:** Minden Pictures / Pete Oxford (clb); Minden Pictures / Luciano Candisani (crb). **Dreamstime.com:** Lukas Blazek (c). **Getty Images:** Age Fotostock / Morales (br). 160 **Alamy Images:** Holger Ehlers (br). **Corbis:** Eurasia Press / Steven Vidler (cr). **FLPA:** Minden Pictures / Tui De Roy (cra, bl). 161 **Alamy Images:** Images of Africa Photobank / David Keith Jones (c). **Dreamstime.com:** Tomas Pavelka (tr). **Getty Images:** Nigel Pavitt (tl). 162 **Corbis:** (ca); Kevin Schafer (cra). 163 **Dorling Kindersley:** Mike Lane (cr); Ian Montgomery (bc); Markus Varesvuo (clb); Jari Peltomaki (cl); Judd Patterson (cb); Brian E. Small (ca). **FLPA:** John Hawkins. 164 **Dorling Kindersley:** Tom Grey (tl); Brian E. Small (ftr). 165 **Alamy Images:** Genevieve Vallee (cla). **Corbis:** Martin Harvey (ca). **Dorling Kindersley:** Bob Steele (cra). **FLPA:** Martin B Withers (cb). **Science Photo Library:** Michael Mccoy (tl). 168-169 **Corbis:** Minden Pictures / Pete Oxford. 169 **Alamy Images:** paul abbitt rml (bc). 170 **Alamy Images:** Regis Martin (cla). **Dorling Kindersley:** Brian E. Small (bc). **FLPA:** John Watkins (tl); Ignacio Yufera (clb). **Getty Images:** Nigel Pavitt (crb). 171 **Alamy Images:** Peter Fakler (tc). **Dorling Kindersley:** Brian E. Small (c). **Getty Images:** Jared Hobbs (br); J & C Sohns (tl). 172 **Dorling Kindersley:** Brian E. Small (cra, ca). 173 **Dorling Kindersley:** E. J. Peiker (crb); Bob Steele (cla, cl); Brian E. Small (fbr). **FLPA:** Ignacio Yufera (bl). 174-175 **Corbis:** All Canada Photos / Glenn Bartley. 176 **Dorling Kindersley:** Mike Danzenbaker (br); Robert Royse (fcr); Garth McElroy (fcl); Bob Steele (cb); Brian E. Small (fcra, cl); Brian E Small (fcrb). **Getty Images:** Visuals Unlimited, Inc. / Glenn Bartley (clb). 177 **Alamy Images:** George Reszeter (cl). **Corbis:** Kevin Schafer (br). **Dorling Kindersley:** Mike Danzenbaker (c). **Getty Images:** Jay B. Adlersberg (cla). 178 **Corbis:** Winfried Wisniewski (crb). **FLPA:** Rolf Nussbaumer (tr). **Getty Images:** Matti Suopajärvi (cla). 179 **Corbis:** Minden Pictures / Foto Natura / Grzegorz Lesniewski (tl). **Dorling Kindersley:** Alan Murphy (crb). **FLPA:** Mark Sisson (tr). 180 **Fotolia:** Eduardo Rivero (cr). **Getty Images:** Kevin Schafer (cl). 181 **Dorling Kindersley:** Brian E. Small (crb). **Fotolia:** Impala (clb). **Getty Images:** CR Courson (tr). 184 **Dorling Kindersley:** The National Birds of Prey Centre, Gloucestershire (cl). 185 **Dorling Kindersley:** Chris Gomersall Photography (bl); The National Birds of Prey Centre, Gloucestershire (ca, cr). 186 **Dorling Kindersley:** The National Birds of Prey Centre, Gloucestershire (tl, cra, bc); Pert S. Weber (c). 186-187 **Corbis:** Minden Pictures / Gerry Ellis. 188 **Dorling Kindersley:** E. J. Peiker (cl); South of England Rare Breeds Centre, Ashford, Kent (tr); Markus Varesvuo (tc); Brian E. Small (tl, cra). 189 **Corbis:** All Canada Photos / Glenn Bartley (tc, tl). **Dorling Kindersley:** Garth McElroy (cra); Steve Young (ca). 190 **Corbis:** Nick Rains (c). **Dreamstime.com:** Lukas Blazek (cr); Inaras (fcr); Nico Smit (bc); Olga Khoroshunova (br). **Getty Images:** Photographer's Choice RF / Frank Krahmer (cl). 191 **Corbis:** Galen Rowell (bc). **Dreamstime.com:** Gentoomultimedia (crb); Pu Sulan (tl). **FLPA:** Minden Pictures / Tui De Roy (br). **Getty Images:** Darrell Gulin (tr); Nigel Pavitt (tc). **Photoshot:** John Shaw (cr). 192-193 **Getty Images:** Mint Images / Frans Lanting. 194 **Corbis:** Joe McDonald (tr); Robert Harding World Imagery / Peter Barritt (cr). **Dorling Kindersley:** Chris Gomersall Photography (bc); Roger Tidman (br); David Cottridge (bl). 195 **Dorling Kindersley:** Brian E. Small (tc); Roger Tidman (bl). **Getty Images:** Josh Manring - JourneymanGallery.com - Travel Photographer (bc). 196 **Dorling Kindersley:** Brian E. Small (bl). FLPA: Minden Pictures / Tui De Roy (bc); Tui De Roy (tr). **Fotolia:** Imagevixen (cra); Petergyure (br). 197 **Dorling Kindersley:** Judd Patterson (cb); Brian E. Small (crb, cl). **Dreamstime.com:** Worakit Sirijinda (br). **FLPA:** John Holmes (tr). **Fotolia:** CPJ Photography (cr); Impala (fcrb). **Getty Images:** Mint Images / Frans Lanting (ca). 198-199 **Corbis:** Theo Allofs (c). 200 **Corbis:** Eric and David Hosking (fcra); Minden Pictures / Foto Natura / Jasper Doest (c). **Dorling Kindersley:** Mike Lane (cra); Brian E. Small (tr, fcla); Bob Steele (tc). **Dreamstime.com:** Mirceax (bc). 201 **Corbis:** Frank Lukasseck (cr). **Dorling Kindersley:** Melvin Grey (bl). **naturepl.com:** Jose B. Ruiz (tr). 202 **Alamy Images:** Craig Ingram (cra). **Dorling Kindersley:** Robert Royse (ca); Bob Steele (crb). **Getty Images:** Glenn Bartley (tr). 203 **Alamy Images:** Keith J Smith (bc). **Dorling Kindersley:** Chris Gomersall Photography (ftl); Kevin T. Karlson (tl); Garth McElroy (cra); George McCarthy (cb). **FLPA:** Steve Young (bl). **Getty Images:** Dieter Schaefer (br). 204 **Dorling Kindersley:** Mike Danzenbaker (tr); Hanne and Jens Erikson (ftl); Melvin Grey (tl); Brian E. Small (ftr); E. J. Peiker (fcl); Mike Lane (c); Bob Steele (fcr, clb); Tomi Muukonen; Robert Royse (bl). **Dreamstime.com:** David Steele (bc). **FLPA:** IMAGEBROKER / INGO SCHULZ (br). 204-205 **FLPA:** Yossi Eshbol (ca). 205 **Dorling Kindersley:** E. J. Peiker (bc); Brian E. Small (crb); Bob Steele (cr). **Dreamstime.com:** Edurivero (tr). **FLPA:** Mike Lane (tl); James Lowen. 206-207 Corbis: Naturbild / Lars-Olof Johansson. 208 **Dorling Kindersley:** Brian E. Small (cra, fcr). **Dreamstime.com:** Foxyjoshi (tr); Susan Robinson (bc). **FLPA:** Imagebroker / Rolf Nussbaumer (clb). 209 **Corbis:** Frans Lemmens (ca). **Dorling Kindersley:** Robert Royse (cla); Brian E. Small (br, fbr). **FLPA:** David Hosking (cb); (cr). 210 **Dorling Kindersley:** Alan Murphy (ca); Jari Peltomaki (tc); Brian E. Small (ftr). **Dreamstime.com:** Rossco (tl). **FLPA:** Hugh Lansdown (fcra). **Getty Images:** Nacivet (fcrb); Roberta Olenick (crb). 211 **Dorling Kindersley:** Brian E. Small (ca). **Getty Images:** Vishdesh photography (cra). **Photoshot:** Marie Read (tl). 212 **Alamy Images:** Greg C Grace (fbl). **Dorling Kindersley:** Garth McElroy (cb); Brian E. Small (tr, fcrb). **FLPA:** David Tipling (tc). 213 **Corbis:** Joe McDonald (cra). **Dorling Kindersley:** Chris Gomersall Photography (fclb); Brian E. Small (clb, bc). **FLPA:** Imagebroker / Rolf Nussbaumer (cb). 214-215 **Photoshot:** Dave Watts (c). 218 **Corbis:** Steve Parish Publishing (c). **Dreamstime.com:** Brian Lasenby (tr). **FLPA:** Jurgen & Christine Sohns (crb); Martin B Withers (cr, cb). 219 **Dorling Kindersley:** Ian Montgomery (crb). **Dreamstime.com:** Eastmanphoto (c). **FLPA:** Photo Researchers (cb); Eric Woods (tr). 220 **Corbis:** EPA / Julian Smith (tl); Minden Pictures / Auscape / Glen Threlfo (cra). **Dreamstime.com:** Marco Tomasini (b). FLPA: Martin B Withers (c). 221 **Alamy Images:** Gerry Pearce (tl). **Corbis:** Steve Kaufman (br). **FLPA:** Gerry Ellis (bl); Martin B Withers (c, cl). 222 **Dorling Kindersley:** Jerry Young (cl). **Dreamstime.com:** Eastmanphoto (c). **FLPA:** Imagebroker / Nico Stengert (cr). **Fotolia:** Eric Isselée (b). **Getty Images:** Tom Brakefield (crb). **naturepl.com:** Luiz Claudio Marigo (clb). 223 **Dorling Kindersley:** Greg and Yvonne Dean (tr). **Dreamstime.com:** Isselee (clb). **FLPA:** ImageBroker (cl); Minden Pictures / Kevin Schafer (tc); Frans Lanting (crb). **Getty Images:** Nigel Dennis (c). **Photoshot:** Gerald Cubitt (br); Jany Sauvanet (cb). 224 **Dorling Kindersley:** Rollin Verlinde (cb); Jerry Young (bl). **Dreamstime.com:** Martinsevcik (c); Naasrautenbach (crb). **FLPA:** David Hosking (bc); Konrad Wothe (tr); Minden Pictures / ZSSD (cl); S & D & K Maslowski (br). 224-225 **Photoshot:** Photo Researchers (cb). 225 **Dorling Kindersley:** Rollin Verlinde (clb, bl, br). **Dreamstime.com:** Melinda Fawver (bc). **FLPA:** Biosphoto / Daniel Heuclin / B (tl); Biosphoto / Gregory Guida (tr); Panda Photo (c); S & D & K Maslowski (crb); Chris & Tilde Stuart (cb). **naturepl.com:** Nature Production (cra). 226-227 **stevebloom.com.** 228 **Dreamstime.com:** Samfoto (br). **naturepl.com:** Barry Mansell (c). 229 **Corbis:** Minden Pictures / Donald M. Jones (cra). **Dreamstime.com:** Rafael Angel Irusta Machin (tc); Peter.wey (c); Derrick Neill (br). **FLPA:** Martin B Withers (tl). **Getty Images:** Purestock (bc). **Science Photo Library:** C.K. Lorenz (crb). 230 **Corbis:** Joe McDonald (c); Minden Pictures / Ch'ien Lee (tr). **Dorling Kindersley:** Rollin Verlinde (crb). **Dreamstime.com:** Isselee (cl, fcr). 231 **Dorling Kindersley:** Josef Hlasek (clb). **Dreamstime.com:** Docbombay (tr); Sergey Uryadnikov (bl). **FLPA:** Frank W Lane (cb); Minden Pictures / Michael & Patricia Fogden (cra); S & D & K Maslowski (cla). Fotolia: Mgkuijpers (tl). **Getty Images:** David Campbell (ca); Peter Schoen (crb). 232 **Corbis:** Ocean (fbr). **Dreamstime.com:** Erllre (bc); Isselee (cr). **Getty Images:** Steve Allen (fbl). 233 **Dreamstime.com:** Jarous (tl). **FLPA:** ImageBroker (cra). 234 **FLPA:** Bernd Rohrschneider (cla). **naturepl.com:** Pete Oxford (ca). 235 **Dorling Kindersley:** Thomas Marent (fcr). **Dreamstime.com:** Davthy (cb). **FLPA:** ImageBroker (bl); Minden Pictures / Chien Lee (tr); R & M Van Nostrand (c); Minden Pictures / Pete Oxford (crb); Minden Pictures / Konrad Wothe (clb); Chien Lee (ca). **Getty Images:** Mint Images (cr). **naturepl.com:** Jabruson (cl). 236 **Dorling Kindersley:** Courtesy of Twycross Zoo, Atherstone, Leicestershire (bc); Ian Montgomery (tr); Jerry Young (fcr). **Dreamstime.com:** Eric Gevaert (bl). **FLPA:** Minden Pictures / Thomas Marent (clb); Jurgen & Christine Sohns (fcl). **naturepl.com:** Eric Baccega (cr); Bernard Castelein (cra). 237 **Dorling Kindersley:** Courtesy of Twycross Zoo, Atherstone, Leicestershire (bl). **FLPA:** Minden Pictures / Thomas Marent (tc). **Getty Images:** Tom Brakefield (cl). 238-239 **Dorling Kindersley:** Thomas Marent. 240 **Alamy Images:** Amazon-Images (cb). **Corbis:** Minden Pictures / Thomas Marent (clb). **Dorling Kindersley:** Jerry Young (fcrb, bc). **Dreamstime.com:** Laurent Renault (fcr); Wojphoto (crb). **FLPA:** Jurgen & Christine Sohns (cra). 241 **Dorling Kindersley:** Exmoor Zoo, Devon (c); Jerry Young (crb). **FLPA:** Frans Lanting (t). Fotolia: Eric Isselée (br). 242-243 **Dreamstime.com:** Benjamin Schalkwijk (c). 242 **Corbis:** Minden Pictures / Thomas Marent (bl); Visuals Unlimited / Thomas Marent, (tr). **Dorling Kindersley:** Jerry Young (cl, br). **naturepl.com:** Suzi Eszterhas (bc). 243 **Alamy Images:** The Africa Image Library (bc). **Getty Images:** Comstock (ca). 244 **Dorling Kindersley:** Jerry Young (cr, cb, bc). **Science Photo Library:** Merlin Tuttle (clb). 245 **Dorling Kindersley:** Greg and Yvonne Dean (cl); Natural History Museum, London (cr). 246-247 **Dorling Kindersley:** Rollin Verlinde (c). 246 **FLPA:** Minden Pictures / Michael Durham (bl). 247 **Dorling Kindersley:** Rollin Verlinde (tl, c, bl); Jerry Young (tc). **Dreamstime.com:** Stevenrussellsmithphotos (cra). **Getty Images:** Kelley Miller (bc). **Science Photo Library:** B. G Thomson (cb). 248-249 **Corbis:** Minden Pictures / Konrad Wothe. 250 **Dorling Kindersley:** Jerry Young (cl, crb, bc). **FLPA:** David Hosking (br); ImageBroker (bl). **Getty Images:** Tom Brakefield (cr). 251 **Dorling Kindersley:** Jerry Young (tc, cla, ca, cb, br, bl). 252-253 **Dreamstime.com:** Jens Klingebiel (c). 252 **Corbis:** Design Pics / Deb Garside (br). 253 **Dreamstime.com:** Mikhail Blajenov (bl); Petr Mašek (t). Fotolia: Wusuowei (br). 254-255 **Dreamstime.com:** Mirage3. 256 **Dreamstime.com:** Perseomedusa (c); Vladimir Seliverstov (bl). **FLPA:** Pete Oxford (tc). 256-257 **FLPA:** Gerard Lacz (tc). 257 **Dreamstime.com:** Africapics (bc); Brendan Van Son (br); Pablo Caridad (tr); Vladimir Melnik (clb); Ongm (cb). 258 **Corbis:** Tom Brakefield (cla); Daniel J. Cox (c). **Dorling Kindersley:** Philip Dowell (bl). **Dreamstime.com:** Jeff Grabert (crb). 259 **Corbis:** Frank Lane Picture Agency / Terry Whittaker (c). **Dreamstime.com:** Lukas Blazek (ca); Isselee (bc). 260 **Dorling Kindersley:** Berlin Zoo (cr). **Dreamstime.com:** Lukas Blazek (bl). **Fotolia:** Sarah Cheriton-Jones (ca). 261 **Alamy Images:** Terry Whittaker (br). **Corbis:** Ocean (cl); Kevin Schafer (tc). **Dreamstime.com:** Rafael Angel Irusta Machin (cra); Outdoorsman (ca). 262-263 **FLPA:** Bernd Zoller / Imagebroker. 264-265 **Dreamstime.com:** Lukas Blazek (c). 264 **Dorling Kindersley:** Rollin Verlinde (clb). **Dreamstime.com:** Jeanninebryan (ca). **FLPA:** Mike Lane (br); L Lee Rue (c). 265 **Dreamstime.com:** Meoita (cb). **FLPA:** Silvestris Fotoservice (br); Minden Pictures (cra); W T Miller (ca). 266-267 **Getty Images:** Peter Chadwick (cb). 266 **Dorling Kindersley:** Marwell Zoological Park, Winchester (clb). **FLPA:** Biosphoto / Patrice Correia (bl); Minden Pictures / Suzi Eszterhas (c); Martin B Withers (cb); Philip Perry (bc). 267 **Alamy Images:** Arco Images GmbH (tl). Corbis: Reuters / China Photo (cb). Dorling Kindersley: Berlin Zoo (bc). **Dreamstime.com:** Lukas Blazek (tr); Smellme (bl). **FLPA:** Cyril Ruoso (cla). **naturepl.com:** Jabruson (cr). **Photoshot:** Gerald Cubitt (br); Nick Garbutt (ca). 268-269 **Getty Images:** Thomas Dressler. 270-271 **Alamy Images:** Jeremy Cozannet (tc). **Dreamstime.com:** Susan Pettitt (bc). 270 **Dreamstime.com:** Pavel Cheiko (br); Judy Whitton (bl). 271 **Dreamstime.com:** Lukas Blazek (tc). 272 **Corbis:** Minden Pictures / Theo Allofs (bl). **Dreamstime.com:** Bahadir Yeniceri (br). 273 **Dorling Kindersley:** Persimmon(Horse) belongs to Pat and Joanne Maxwell, Lodge Farm Arabian Stud, Oxon (br). **Dreamstime.com:** Tracie Grant (cr). 274-275 **Getty Images:** Ingram Publishing. 276 **Dreamstime.com:** F9photos (tr); Michael Flippo (cl); Isselee (c). 277 **Dreamstime.com:** Anankkml (tr); Isselee (bc); Efesan (fbr). **FLPA:** Michael Gore (crb); Martin B Withers (clb); Ariadne Van Zandbergen (tc). 278 **Alamy Images:** Bill Gozansky (bl). **Corbis:** Visuals Unlimited / Adam Jones (c). **FLPA:** David Hosking (br). **Getty Images:** Digital Vision (cla). **Photoshot:** Paul Brough (fcl). 279 **Dreamstime.com:** Mikhail Blajenov (tc); Frameangel (bc); Prillfoto (c); Robin Winkelman (fcl); Dragoneye (tr); Lukas Blazek (br). **FLPA:** ImageBroker (bl). 280-281 **Corbis:** Reuters / HO / San Diego Zoo / Ken Bohn. 282 **Dorling Kindersley:** Rough Guides (cl). **Dreamstime.com:** Scattoselvaggio (bc). **Fotolia:** Anankkml (bl). 282-283 **Dreamstime.com:** Stephenmeese (ca). 283 **Corbis:** Minden Pictures / Claus Meyer (tl); Minden Pictures / Thomas Marent (cr). **Dorling Kindersley:** Marwell Zoological Park, Winchester (c). **Dreamstime.com:** Handsomepictures (tc); Tony Northrup (bc); Helen Panphilova (br); Smellme (cb); Paul Schneider (tr). 284 **Corbis:** DLILLC (br). **Getty Images:** Fotosearch (bc). 285 **Alamy Images:** Paul Springett C (tc). **Dreamstime.com:** Hasanugurlu (cra). **Fotolia:** StarJumper (bl). **Getty Images:** LatitudeStock / Patrick Ford (bc). 286-287 **FLPA:** Frans Lanting. 292-293 **Getty Images:** Watt Jim. 294-294 **Dorling Kindersley:** Philip Dowell (bc). 296 **Corbis:** Dennis Kunkel Microscopy, Inc. / Visuals Unlimited (tr). 300 **Dorling Kindersley:** Natural History Museum, London (tl). 302 **Dorling Kindersley:** Staab Studios / Geoff Brightling - modelmakers (tl)

Jacket images: *Front:* **Alamy Images:** Robert Eastman (fcra); **Corbis:** The Food Passionates (crb); **Dorling Kindersley:** Natural History Museum, London (fclb), Staab Studios / Geoff Brightling - modelmakers (tl); **Dreamstime.com:** Amwu (fcl), Isselee (cla, cra); *Back:* **Alamy Images:** Juniors Bildarchiv GmbH (bl); **Corbis:** Visuals Unlimited / Alex Wild (tc); **Dorling Kindersley:** Natural History Museum, London (ftl), Markus Varesvuo (ca), Weymouth Sealife Centre (tl); **Dreamstime.com:** Isselee (tr, br); **Getty Images:** Tom Brakefield (cr), Mint Images / Frans Lanting (cra); *Spine:* **Dorling Kindersley:** Natural History Museum, London (c); **Dreamstime.com:** Isselee (cb)

All other images © Dorling Kindersley
For further information see: www.dkimages.com